MILTON STUDIES

XLV

M I L T O N
S T U D I E S

XLV ❧ *Edited by*

Albert C. Labriola

UNIVERSITY OF PITTSBURGH PRESS

MILTON STUDIES

is published annually by the University of Pittsburgh Press as a forum for Milton scholarship and criticism. Articles submitted for publication may be biographical; they may interpret some aspect of Milton's writings; or they may define literary, intellectual, or historical contexts—by studying the work of his contemporaries, the traditions which affected his thought and art, contemporary political and religious movements, his influence on other writers, or the history of critical response to his work.

Manuscripts should be upwards of 3,000 words in length and should conform to *The Chicago Manual of Style*. Manuscripts and editorial correspondence should be addressed to Albert C. Labriola, Department of English, Duquesne University, Pittsburgh, Pa., 15282–1703. Manuscripts should be accompanied by a self-addressed envelope and sufficient unattached postage.

Milton Studies does not review books.

Within the United States, *Milton Studies* may be ordered from the University of Pittsburgh Press, c/o Chicago Distribution Center, 11030 South Langley Avenue, Chicago, Ill., 60628, 1-800-621-2736.

Published by the University of Pittsburgh Press, Pittsburgh, Pa. 15260

Copyright © 2006, University of Pittsburgh Press

Manufactured in the United States of America

Printed on acid-free paper

10 9 8 7 6 5 4 3 2 1

ISBN 0-8229-4267-4

CONTENTS

FROM ORTHODOXY TO HERESY: A THEOLOGICAL ANALYSIS OF *SONNETS XIV* AND *XVIII*

Timothy J. Burbery

THE COMMENTARY ON Milton's eighteenth sonnet ("On the Late Massacre in Piedmont") is rich and extensive. Kester Svendsen's often-cited 1945 essay, the first close reading of the poem, ushered in many other interpretations of its biblical imagery, as well as speech-act analyses, reader-response discussions, and at least one Foucaldian study. Yet even though a religious conflict inspired the sonnet, and although numerous interpreters have paid close attention to the work's biblical texture, no sustained theological account of the poem has been offered.[1] The present essay seeks to fill that gap by examining the work in light of two heresies that Milton was probably thinking through when he wrote the poem, namely, Mortalism and Traducianism. Mortalism holds that, at death, the soul dies (or, in some versions, sleeps) with the body, and that both are resurrected at the end of the age.[2] Traducianism (from Latin *tradux,* a shoot or sprout) is Mortalism's correlative. Like Mortalism, it assumes that the soul is corporeal, but while Mortalism draws out the logical consequences of that assumption for the end of life, Traducianism does so for its beginning, claiming that the soul is passed from one generation to the next in the act of intercourse. Milton considers each idea at length in *De Doctrina Christiana,* and John Shawcross surmises that the poet's thinking about the two concepts solidified between 1647 and 1655. The sonnet was probably composed in May or June 1655.[3]

Prior to that period, Milton believed in the standard doctrine, held by Roman Catholics and Calvinists alike, that at death the soul immediately ascends to God. Lycidas's apotheosis fits this pattern, as do the souls of the Fair Infant and the Marchioness of Winchester. By the time he composed *Paradise Lost,* however, Mortalism had become a salient influence. Most notably, a central Mortalist tenet appears in Adam's soliloquy in Book Ten of the epic, where he intuits that at death "all of me then shall die" (792).[4] Moreover, William Kerrigan, Mary Ann Radzinowicz, and Anthony Low have each argued that *Samson Agonistes* may reflect Mortalism in certain speeches by the protagonist and Manoa. I would add that when Samson declares that the soul is "in every part" of the body (93), he echoes a central Scholastic precept that Milton relies on in *De Doctrina Christiana* when arguing in favor of Traducianism and against its opposite, Creationism, which holds that God creates a new soul every time someone is conceived.[5]

The poet's Mortalism and Traducianism matter because they comprise critical facets of his evolving heretical and radical views. Both doctrines appear to have developed concurrently with his most serious heresy, Arianism. Perhaps most importantly, the two heresies may be the only ones to have had any discernible influence on Milton's poetry prior to *Paradise Lost*. As such, they could provide a key missing link in his evolution from orthodoxy to heterodoxy. Our present knowledge of that process can be outlined as follows: The poet was orthodox in the 1630s and 1640s, became heterodox when he composed *De Doctrina Christiana* in the 1650s, and in the next decade incorporated certain heresies into *Paradise Lost* and, perhaps, *Samson Agonistes*. Yet this bare summary does not take into account the sense of many critics that, in fact, Milton was moving away from orthodoxy before the 1650s. Regarding his Arianism, for example, Barbara Lewalski notes that "we cannot be sure when Milton abandoned [his Trinitarian] position: he wrote the Nativity ode as an orthodox Trinitarian, though his inability to complete a poem on Christ's passion or to produce a very effective poem on the circumcision suggests that even in the 1630s the redemptive sacrifice of the incarnate Son was not at the center of his religious imagination."[6] Still, no one has found specific Arian elements in the early poetry, nor have they done so with his Mortalism. Virginia Mollenkott was, apparently, the first to declare that no traces of the latter can be found in any work prior to *Paradise Lost,* and her judgment has been iterated by Norman Burns, Kerrigan, and Raymond Waddington.[7]

Even so, the consensus about the lack of Mortalism in the earlier poetry has not been monolithic. Kerrigan, for instance, concedes that his own assessment is a "limiting half-truth" since it omits consideration of implicit, unstated influences the doctrine could have exercised on the poet. He then proceeds to make a compelling case for the indirect impact of Mortalism on *Paradise Lost, Paradise Regained,* and *Samson Agonistes*. Similarly, Christopher Hill, in *Milton and the English Revolution* (1979), initially concurs with the received view when he states that "we do not know when Milton became a Mortalist." However, he follows this up with a helpful caveat:

We should not attach too much importance to the fact that the dead Edward King was described in "Lycidas" as sleeping. The "Epitaphium Damonis" (line 123), the dedication to Parliament of *The Judgment of Martin Bucer* and the sonnet which Milton

wrote to the memory of Mrs. Thomason in 1646 seem to express non-mortalist sentiments; but Milton published the poems in 1673, when his mortalism is hardly in
doubt.[8]

Hill also notes in passing that the Piedmont sonnet "finds no consolation in
immortality: its hope is that the suffering of the Vaudois will help to bring
other Italians to abandon Catholicism on earth."[9] He thus anticipates my own
reading of the poem. It is also worth noting that Hill's intuition about potential Mortalist intimations in the pre–*Paradise Lost* poetry has already been
confirmed in a 1994 study by A. E. B. Coldiron, which argues that *Sonnet XIV*
(the tribute to Mrs. Thomason) accommodates both Mortalist and non-
Mortalist interpretations.[10] Because *Sonnet XIV* provides our first glimpse of
Milton's emerging Mortalism, I shall begin by reviewing and extending Coldiron's findings, then proceed to the Piedmont sonnet, which, like the earlier
poem, can be read as both non-Mortalist and Mortalist.

I

Milton's interest in Mortalism seems to have begun in the early 1640s during
the Toleration controversy, when *The Doctrine and Discipline of Divorce* was
consistently linked by its detractors with Richard Overton's Mortalist treatise,
Man's Mortalitie, first published (under the initials R. O.) in 1643. That Milton
read *Man's Mortalitie,* met Overton, and perhaps even helped to revise the
pamphlet for the new edition of 1655 are possibilities raised by Denis Saurat.
While subsequent critics have attacked this supposition, Norman Burns
points out that "if our caution is too great we shall fall into the error of making
Milton impossibly independent, a figure who stood aloof from the intellectual
and social ideas of his time and unassisted developed his own ideas of man and
God." Burns proceeds to strengthen Saurat's conjecture by documenting the
numerous similarities between Overton's and Milton's discussions of Mortalism, such as their privileging of 1 Corinthians 15:17–19 as a key Mortalist text,
and by citing their mutual belief in Traducianism.[11]

Throughout the 1640s, Milton maintained a lively friendship with
George and Catharine Thomason; the husband, a bookseller and pamphlet
collector of both licensed and unlicensed works, purchased one of the first
editions of *Man's Mortalitie* on 19 January 1644.[12] It is possible that he lent
Milton this copy of Overton's treatise, perhaps in return for four of Milton's
pamphlets that the poet had donated to Thomason's collection. Mrs. Thomason was an avid reader and book collector in her own right, and Milton refers
to her as his "Christian friend" in the manuscript title of *Sonnet XIV.* Moreover, his donations to the main collection ceased at her death. Anna Nardo

surmises that Milton's "own pamphlet gifts stopped with Catharine's death, which suggests that they may have been intended for her rather than George."[13] While we cannot know if Mrs. Thomason and the poet ever discussed Mortalism, it may be significant that Milton's first possible allusions to the belief occur in *Sonnet XIV*, composed shortly after her death in December 1646. The poem, originally titled "On the Christian memory of my friend Mrs. Thomason," can be seen as an orthodox eulogy, and indeed E. A. J. Honigmann, Barbara Lewalski, and John Leonard regard it as such.[14] However, certain elements of the sonnet seem reminiscent of *De Doctrina* and its exploration of Mortalism.

For one thing, Honigmann observes that the work's principal personifications, Faith and Love, constitute the two main divisions of *De Doctrina:* at the beginning of the seventh paragraph of the treatise's first chapter Milton writes, "The PARTS of CHRISTIAN DOCTRINE are two: FAITH, or KNOWLEDGE OF GOD, and LOVE, or the WORSHIP OF GOD" (YP 6:128).[15] In the sestet of the sonnet's first draft, the lady is escorted into the heavenly realm by Faith, the only named personification, who is seconded by Mrs. Thomason's other personified virtues. In the final version, however, Love has joined Faith as one of the leaders: "Love led them [the virtues] on, and Faith who knew them best" (8). This elevation of Love may reflect the treatise's statement that love is worship of God, since the lady will soon be one of heaven's votaries.

Coldiron has identified another similarity between Milton's discussion of Mortalism and the poem. Lines 3 and 4, "Meekly thou didst resign this earthy load / Of Death, call'd Life; which us from Life doth sever," utilize the same terms set forth in the title of chapter 13 of *De Doctrina,* "Of the Death Which is called the Death of the Body." She also points out that lines 3–4, which initially read, "Meekly thou didst resigne this earthy clod / Of Flesh & sin, which man from heav'n doth sever," and then were changed to "Meekly thou didst resign this earthy load / Of Death, call'd Life; which us from Life doth sever," reflect *De Doctrina*'s understanding that the body does not necessarily denote the physical flesh, but, rather, earthly life:

Milton took care to detach the old signifiers from the medieval body-soul debate . . . and [in the revised version] stress[es] their reattachment to another, slightly shifted, set of signifiers. Separation [in the revised version] is not at death—death is in fact the moment of reunion following a long prior separation of God and man by fleshly life. Milton opposes our common mistake of calling the body "life." . . . Such a reinterpretation of "death" and "life" is, in fact, precisely consistent with *De Doctrina*'s redefinition of the same terms. . . . [Milton claims that] "Strictly speaking, the body cannot be killed . . . since it in itself is lifeless" (408), and "the word 'body' here must be taken to mean this frail worldly life." (413)[16]

Milton's revision of lines 5–8 may also indicate an interest in Mortalism. Here are the two versions:

> Thy Works, & Almes, and all thy good Endeavor
> > Strait follow'd thee the path that Saints have trod
> > Still as they journey'd up from this dark abode
> > Up to the Realm of peace & Joy for ever.   (Draft)

> Thy Works and Almes and all thy good Endeavour
> > Staid not behind, nor in the grave were trod;
> > But as Faith pointed with her golden rod,
> > Follow'd thee up to joy and bliss for ever.   (Final)

The drafted lines furnish an explicit statement about translated saints who have preceded Mrs. Thomason. The final version, however, omits those saints and their journey and focuses solely on the flight of the deceased lady. This alteration could be explained if Milton was becoming more sympathetic to Mortalism, as follows: The initial draft echoes the traditional view that throughout the ages all the saints have journeyed from earth to heaven immediately following their death; like them, Mrs. Thomason is traveling that familiar road. When Milton removed from the final version any mention of that ongoing collective narrative, he might have simply been rewording the poem to emphasize her individual apotheosis, yet he may have done so because he was starting to question the traditional claim. He might not have been a Mortalist yet, but the alteration could represent a step toward *De Doctrina*'s flat dismissal of the non-Mortalist view. In the treatise he states that "[t]here is no reward of good or evil *after* death until the day of judgment" (YP 6:414; my emphasis).[17]

If the poet were leaning toward Mortalism when he composed these lines, Mrs. Thomason's apotheosis would not take place right after her death, but rather at the end of the age. The sestet's imagery, I believe, reinforces that inference. For instance, the poem alludes to the Judge weighing the works of the deceased, an action that seems inspired by Revelation 20:12b: "And the dead were judged out of those things which were written in the books, according to their works." Also, the final version's representation of Faith pointing with her golden rod may be indebted to Revelation 21:15: "And he [that is, an angel, similar to the angelic Faith] that talked with me had a golden reed to measure the city, and the gates thereof, and the wall thereof." Similarly, the reference to drinking from "immortal" streams seems to be based on Revelation 21:6: "I am the Alpha and the Omega, the beginning and the end. I will give unto him that is athirst of the fountain of the water of life freely." If these images do point to the Last Day, it would appear that Milton narrowed his focus, not to keep from attenuating the eulogy, but rather, to present Mrs. Thomason as typical of what will happen to every good soul at Judgment.

Even so, one could argue that the sonnet's past tense narrative undercuts the notion that her glorification is deferred until the Trump of Doom. I would agree with such an objection to some extent: The poem can be, and has been, interpreted as a straightforward account of what happens to her promptly after death. Nevertheless, *De Doctrina* provides a way to have it both ways, to read her apotheosis as immediate yet deferred. In his account of Mortalism, Milton attempts to explain one verse that would seem to refute the doctrine, namely, Saint Paul's claim in Philippians 1:23, in which the apostle voices the hope of departing from earthly life and joining Christ in heaven immediately. To do so, Milton adduces the Aristotelian notion that there is no time without motion, and applies it to those who have died: "for those who have died, all intervening time will be as nothing, so that to them it will seem that they die and are with Christ at the same moment" (YP 6:410). Coldiron applies this passage to "When Faith and Love": "This [Aristotelian concept] is one way to unite the sonnet's immediate apotheosis with *De Doctrina*'s indefinite deferral: for Mrs. Thomason, the time passing between December 1646 and the Last Judgment will be as nothing, and it will seem to her (and to the reader of the sonnet) that her ascent is immediate." However, she rejects this reading in favor of an Augustinian understanding in which God exists outside of time, in eternity, so that the elegy "represents both the human-time, narrative, sequential future and the heavenly, non-narrative, eternal present."[18]

Coldiron may be right to privilege the Augustinian interpretation, yet it strikes me as significant that Milton quotes Aristotle's theory, not only in *De Doctrina,* but also in his second poem on Hobson, the university carrier (line 7), whereas he never cites Augustine's theory in his poetry or prose. In any case, whichever thinker one adduces to reinforce a Mortalist interpretation is less important than Coldiron's more fundamental claim, which I agree with, that the sonnet lends itself to Mortalist and non-Mortalist analyses. Such indeterminacy could reflect the poet's ongoing progress toward the heresy.

Still, while Milton appears to have used this sonnet to explore such notions, subsequent events might have made him reluctant to publish these or related ideas. (The Thomason tribute, as we saw, did not appear in print until 1673.) In 1647, the year following the composition of *Sonnet XIV,* the Westminster Confession censured both *The Doctrine and Discipline of Divorce* and Mortalism. Chapter 22 states, in part, that "The bodies of men, after death, return to dust, and see corruption, but their souls (which neither die nor sleep) having an immortal subsistence, immediately return to God who gave them." And in 1648 Parliament prescribed imprisonment for those who maintain that "the soul of man dieth or sleepeth when the body is dead."[19]

The closest Milton came to going public was in 1650, when, as Latin secretary, he approved the publication of a translation of a Latin document that came to be known as the Racovian Catechism. The catechism was the main text of the Socinian movement, which denied Christ's divinity. While the catechism was not a Mortalist text, it held, among other things, that soul and body are so closely joined that man is neither. Milton came under questioning for allowing this translation to see print, though he was not punished for doing so.[20] Nevertheless, the experience probably made him reluctant to discuss Mortalism publicly. It would be another seventeen years before *Paradise Lost* was published, with Adam's references to the belief, and even in the long poem this passage does not occur until the tenth book.[21] If Milton was trying to foil the busy Restoration censor, Thomas Tomkyns, he seems to have succeeded, since Tomkyns did not flag Adam's Mortalist reflections.

He may have been equally shrewd when composing the Piedmont sonnet. Although it was not published until 1673, David Masson speculates that it circulated at the Protector's court, and of course it reacts to a very public event.[22] Moreover, it praises the Waldensians for their theological purity, so any overt references to heterodox beliefs would have been inappropriate. Nonetheless, I believe that the sonnet is compatible with Mortalism, as well as with Traducianism. As we saw, *Sonnet XIV* proves that Milton could write a poem that lends itself to both orthodox and heterodox interpretations; such an experience may have enabled him to do so again, though in different ways, with "Avenge O Lord."

II

To understand how he might have done so, we first need to consider the extent of Milton's theological debt to the Waldensian sect. As I noted at the outset, *Sonnet XVIII* appears to have been composed in May or June 1655; the slaughter of the Waldensians took place on April 24 of that year, and the sonnet's title indicates that the event was recent. Like many early modern Protestants, Milton believed that the Waldensians, or Vaudois, dated back at least to patristic times, or even the apostolic era. His own view, in fact, may be evident in the poem's ninth line, which possibly puns on vales/Vaudois, based on the belief that the Waldensians derived their name from the Alpine valleys where they first sought refuge, starting in the early fourth century. Today, most historians regard the group as less ancient, arguing that they started as followers of Peter Waldo (1140–1218), a wealthy merchant of Lyons who donated most of his estate to the poor, and, upon acquiring disciples, began sending them out into villages to preach. In or around 1184, the Vaudois were excommunicated for heresy.

There is no evidence that Milton knew any Waldensians personally, nor did his Italian journey take him through any of their valleys. However, in addition to the nine letters of state written for the Commonwealth to protest the massacre, Milton alludes to the Waldensians ten times in his prose. The references are all favorable and indicate that his interest in, and approbation of, the Vaudois predates the sonnet by a decade. In or around 1645, for example, he cites their official history in his commonplace book; that history first appeared in 1644. Milton was impressed by the sect's willingness to translate the Bible into the vernacular, by their refusal to support their clergy with tithes, and by their readiness to take up arms against tyrants. In *Considerations Touching the Likeliest Means to Remove Hirelings* (1659), he deems them "our first reformers" and the "ancient stock of our reformation," and in *Tenure of Kings and Magistrates* (1649) Milton refers to them as one of the first "Protestant churches" (YP 7:306, 312; 3:227).

His knowledge about the sect came primarily from Pierre Gilles's *Histoire Ecclesiastique des Eglises Reformees . . . en Quelques Valees de Piedmont* (Geneva, 1644), and from a collection of writings on the Vaudois included in John DuBrau's *Historia Bohemica ab Origine Gentis* (Hanover, 1602). William Hunter cites the parallels between Milton's beliefs and theirs, including an animus toward the Roman Catholic church, repudiation of genuflection, the notion that clergy should have no possessions or special attire and should be self-supporting, and contempt for church councils. Like Milton, the Vaudois also rejected all sacraments, reserved baptism for adults, denied transubstantiation, allowed ministers to marry, and did not believe in Purgatory.[23]

Hunter concedes that Milton differs from them on certain points, such as support for polygamy. Even so, he concludes, "Milton found in [the Waldensians] . . . an authority for or primitive analogy to beliefs which he came to adopt as his own. How many of them were first suggested to him in [the histories of the sect] is problematical. The similarities, nevertheless, between his mature conclusions [in *De Doctrina*] and [the Vaudois] are remarkable. Milton may indeed be closer to Waldensian practice . . . than to those of any other established church of his day."[24]

Did they influence the poet's thinking on Mortalism? Their rejection of Purgatory accords with the doctrine, which condemns any notion of an intermediate state after death. However, the Vaudois did hold that deceased believers unite with God immediately after death. In 1655, shortly following the massacre, the sect published a confession to offset what had become a smear campaign. Jean Leger, moderator of the Piedmont churches at this time, was probably the author of the confession. The introduction reads: "Having understood that our adversaries, not contented to have most cruelly persecuted us, and robbed us of all our goods and estates, have yet an intention to render us odious to the world by spreading abroad many false reports, and so not only to defame our persons, but likewise to asperse with most shameful calumnies that holy and wholesome doctrine which we progress, we feel obliged . . . to make a short declaration of our faith."[25]

This confession was brought back to England by Samuel Morland, Cromwell's special envoy, who was sent to protest the massacre to Carlo Emmanuel II, who had ordered it. We do not know if Milton read the document, but if he did, he would have seen Article 23: "Those who are already in possession of eternal life in consequence of their faith and good works ought to be considered as saints and glorified persons, and to be praised for their virtue and imitated in all good actions of their life, but neither worshiped nor invoked, for God only is to be prayed unto, and that through Jesus Christ."

Nevertheless, although the Vaudois cannot be called proto-Mortalists, it is significant that Milton commends them for the fact that their clergy learned trades to support themselves. Such a custom, he felt, enabled them to "cure both soul and bodie, through industry joining that to their ministry" (YP 7:307). A unified view of soul and body is, as noted earlier, a basic presupposition of Mortalism.

III

That view may also be implicit in *Sonnet XVIII,* and if Milton believed that the victims had physically perished, he would also have held that their souls were dead as well. As we have seen, he certainly believed this doctrine by 1655, but are there traces of it in the poem? Its opening phrase, "Avenge O Lord," might seem to refute Mortalism. Beginning with Warton's 1781 text, nearly all editors have adduced Revelation 6:9–10 as a source for the phrase.[26] In this passage John, the traditional author/secretary of the Apocalypse, witnesses the Lamb of God opening seven sealed scrolls. Some of the events presaged by the opening of each seal include famine, warfare, and death. At the unraveling of the fifth seal, John writes, "I saw under the altar the souls of them that were slain for the word of God, and for the testimony which they held. And they cried with a loud voice, saying, 'How long, O Lord, holy and true, dost thou not judge and avenge our blood on them that dwell on the earth?' " Hence, this text indicates that while the bodies of the martyrs are dead, their souls are alive in heaven, petitioning God to revenge their deaths on earth.

Such an interpretation became standard during the seventeenth century, and in fact the passage was sometimes quoted to contest Mortalism. For example, in his explication of the Apostles' Creed, William Perkins argues: "Divers have thought, that the soules then, though they doe not die, yet are still kept within the body (being as it were asleep) till the last day. But Gods word saith to the contrary. For the soules of the godly lie under the altar, and crie, how long Lord Jesus." His marginal notes cite Revelation 6:9. Similarly, Calvin interprets the passage by concluding that "[the] soules of the dead do crye, and white garments are geven unto them" (YP 6:411 n. 29).

When editors cite the passage in connection with Milton's opening phrase, they imply that he echoes it in a relatively straightforward way. That is, the Vaudois are now before the throne, protesting their cause, and Milton is poetically adding his voice to the chorus. However, such an understanding is complicated by the fact that *De Doctrina* denies the orthodox reading of the passage and argues that it does not contradict Mortalism:

The sixth passage quoted [by anti-Mortalists] is Rev. vi. 9: *I saw the souls beneath the altar.* My answer is that in biblical idiom the word *soul* is regularly used to mean the whole animate body, and that here the reference is to souls not yet born, unless, that is, the fifth seal had already been opened in John's day. Similarly, Christ makes no distinction whatsoever, in the parable about Dives and Lazarus in Luke xvi, between the soul and body. He does, however, for purposes of instruction, speak of things which will not happen until after the day of judgment as if they had already happened, and represents the dead as existing in two different states. (YP 6:411)

Hence, by interpreting John's vision as a future scenario of the Last Judgment, Milton disputes the claim that Revelation 6 indicates that souls precede their bodies to heaven. Still, even if he held this view privately, the question remains: Did that opinion affect the poem? By appearing to echo Revelation 6, it would seem that Milton was aligning himself with the common view of the massacre. For these verses were central to the Protestant understanding of the crisis. After returning from the Continent, Morland published an official account of the event that included eyewitness accounts of the atrocities, vivid illustrations of the catastrophe, and other related documents. This collection included the eight state letters composed by Milton to various heads of state regarding the tragedy, as well as Morland's protest speech to the Duke of Savoy. Barbara Lewalski notes that the speech, though anonymous, has been correctly attributed to Milton, partly because its imagery resembles that of *Sonnet XVIII,* and partly because Morland, "who had but three days to prepare for his mission, would likely not have been entrusted to draft a speech in the Protector's own name, and he does not claim credit for it in his *History [of the Evangelical Churches of Piemont* (1658)]."[27] The *History* became the chief source of the massacre to most Englishmen; its title page quotes Revelation 6:9. Hence, given the centrality of that citation to Protestant reflection on the atrocities, Milton may have felt compelled to allude to the verses; indeed, not doing so might have raised questions.

The deeper issue, however, is not whether but how he appropriates the passage. Does he simply echo the martyrs—or does he stand in for them? After all, it is Milton's persona who utters the lines. This change need not indicate Mortalism, of course; he protests the injustice of the tragedy, so it makes sense for him to voice what many Protestants felt the Vaudois themselves were presently saying to God. And yet the change could be in line with the heresy, which obliged him to dispute the common notion that, at death, the soul "wings its way, or is conducted by angels, directly to its appointed place of reward or punishment."[28] Because he would have assumed that the souls as well as the bodies of the victims perished in the massacre, Milton may have felt that they needed someone to plead their case. Since he was still alive, he could, in a sense, stand before God and make that case; the Waldensians, in their present state, could not. Indeed, it is possible that Milton felt compelled to write the sonnet precisely because vengeance for the victims seemed slow in coming. Even though his letters of state had been sent to various leaders on the Continent, and these potentates had been given ample time to respond, most apparently dragged their feet. Masson notes that after six weeks had passed with little action, "Cromwell [grew] dissatisfied with the coolness of the French King and [Cardinal] Mazarin, and also with the shuffling and timidity of the Swiss Cantons."[29] The sonnet might reflect both the Protector's frustration and Milton's own, and that frustration could have been compounded for the poet by his Mortalism.

Other biblical passages alluded to in the octave might have been similarly appropriated by Milton. For instance, as Charles Goldstein points out, lines 1 and 2 may be based on Psalm 141, in which David petitions God for deliverance from his enemies:[30]

Lord, I cry unto thee; make haste unto me; give ear unto my voice, when I cry unto thee. . . . Let my prayer be set forth before thee as incense; and the lifting up of my hands as the evening sacrifice. . . . Let the righteous smite me; it shall be a kindness. And let him reprove me; it shall be an excellent oil, which shall not break my head; for yet my prayer also shall be in their calamities. When their judges are overthrown in stony places, they shall hear my words; for they are sweet. *Our bones are scattered* at the mouth of Sheol, as when one cutteth and cleaveth wood on the earth. (1–2, 5–7; my emphasis).

Similarly, lines 6 and 7 are informed by Romans 8:36, which quotes the Septuagint version of Psalm 44:2: "for thy sake we are killed all the day long; we are accounted as sheep for the slaughter." Echoes here include not only "slaughter" and "sheep" but the situation as well: that is, the Waldensians are treated like sheep, killed "in their ancient fold" (6). Throughout the octave Milton makes these protests his own, like a priest interceding for victims whom he might have regarded as inert, and therefore incapable of prayer on their own behalf.

The imperative of line 5, "Forget not: in thy book record their groans," is also consonant with the Mortalist assumption that the dead will not be able to press their suit before the heavenly throne. The exhortation of the opening two words could be motivated by the fear that God may somehow overlook the sufferings of his people, a concern that would seem more plausible if the souls of the dead were not present before Him. And the demand that God record their death-cries in his book may also reflect a statement in the conclusion of *De Doctrina*'s discussion of Mortalism: "there is no rewarding of good or evil after death until [the] day of judgment" (YP 6:414). (One of the main charges leveled against the Mortalists was that the belief encouraged sinful living, since it removed the fear of immediate judgment after death.) On the other hand, if the Vaudois had gone promptly to heaven, there would be less need for God to record their sufferings in a document to be consulted later.[31]

Perhaps the most important section for a Mortalist interpretation of the sonnet is at lines 8b–10a, which depict the death throes of the victims: "Their moans / The vales redoubled to the hills, and they / To Heav'n." Honigmann has demonstrated that these and other phrases in the sonnet are based on descriptions from contemporary newsletters of the event. He quotes one that probably provided the source for these lines: "But amongst so many furious assaults . . . did resound nothing else but the Cries, Lamentations, and fearful Scriechings, made yet more pitiful by the multitude of those Eccho's, which are in those Mountains and Rocks [*sic*]."[32]

The lines are especially significant for what they say or imply about any potential apotheosis of the victims. Were the Waldensians somehow translated to heaven through their screams? Anna Nardo raises this possibility by highlighting the ambiguity of the passage. A straightforward explication of the lines would hold that the moans of the victims were echoed by the valleys to the hills, which then sent the moans heavenward. However, Nardo argues that "they / To Heav'n" can also be taken to refer to the Vaudois, resulting in alternate readings: "(1) the valleys reechoed the Waldensians' moans to the hills, and the Waldensians repeated . . . their moans to heaven, and (2) through the valleys' echoes of their dying moans, the Waldensians themselves were translated to heaven."[33]

While Nardo's first point does not present any problems for a Mortalist analysis of the poem, her second point does. I find the second untenable, however, for several reasons. First, it is ungrammatical, as Nardo admits ("'they' cannot be the object of 'redoubl'd'").[34] Also, as we saw, the poet asks God to record groans that, apparently, have remained groans even when they reach him, and there is no reason to believe that the moans should undergo a change on their way to the heavenly throne room. Furthermore, according to a strict non-Mortalist, the souls of the Vaudois would go to heaven the instant they died; there would be no need for nature to assist the process of translation, nor would any time elapse, not even the few seconds involved as they echoed off the hills and valleys. Hence, there would be little point in urging God to pay attention to the cries of the dying if their souls had already arrived ahead of them.

The closest Milton may come here to suggesting translation is in the possible implication that the moans and groans of the slain constitute their *ruach,* or life-breath. He insists that the *ruach* is not the same thing as the soul, in *De Doctrina* 1.7, where he remarks that "the breath of life mentioned in Genesis was not a part of the divine essence, nor was it the soul, but *a kind of air or breath* of divine virtue, fit for the maintenance of life and reason and infused into the organic body" (YP 6:318; my emphasis). Might the groans and moans of the dying constitute this "air or breath" returning to God? Perhaps. If so, however, their souls remain behind. Indeed, it is possible that Milton intended here to depict a purely "naturalistic" ascent of air and breath emanating from the slain, to contrast with "immortalist" poetry—which of course includes some of his own works—in which souls fly to God.

IV

Editors often point out probable sources for the sestet's image of a new crop of faithful Waldensians springing forth from their sown remains. These include the comments of Milton's friend and correspondent J. B. Stouppe, who remarked on the atrocity that "the children of God are not lost when being massacred . . . we may find in their blood and ashes the seed of the church."[35] There also seems to be an echo of Saint Cyprian's commentary on the parable of the sower (Matt. 13); in *De Habitu virginum,* Cyprian argues that the hundredfold mentioned in the parable figure the martyrs. Furthermore, the myth of Cadmus may be referenced. (After killing a dragon on the way to founding Thebes, Cadmus was advised by a god to sow dragon's teeth, from which sprang the ancestors of the Spartans.) And the poet probably alludes to Tertullian's dictum (first echoed in Stouppe's letter), "Semen est sanguis Christianorum," usually translated (and expanded) as "The blood of the martyrs is the seed of the church."[36]

Tertullian's aphorism may have been especially compelling to Milton from a theological perspective.[37] For it seems to me that the sestet's description of the broadcasting of the victims' blood and ashes represents a kind of metaphorical Traducianism, a belief that, as we saw, states that the soul is physically transmitted from parents to their offspring. As such, the sestet may complement the poem's implicit Mortalism. In *De Doctrina* 1.7 Milton defends Traducianism, citing Tertullian, as well as Augustine, as an early advocate of the theory (YP 6:319). The sonnet's appropriation of the image of the martyrs is thus figurative, yet alive to the physicality inherent in Traducianism. When Milton enjoins God to sow the remains, the hoped-for action is analogous to Traducianism in that it presents a physical transfer of a spiritual substance: the remains will seed the Italian fields, from which will spring the next generation of the sect.

That the poet might have had a kind of Traducianism in mind here is suggested by the sestet's use of the Cadmus myth. Earlier in his career, Milton alluded to the myth (or its Ovidian analogue) in one of *Areopagitica*'s best-known passages, in which he concedes that postpublication censorship of books may be acceptable: "Books are not absolutely dead things, but do contain a potency of life in them to be as active as that soul was whose progeny they are; nay, they do preserve as in a vial the purest efficacy and extraction of that living intellect that bred them. I know they are as lively, and as vigorously productive, as those fabulous dragon's teeth, and being sown up and down, may chance to spring up armed men." Nonetheless, he advises caution in any such program: "as good almost kill a man as kill a good book. . . . Many a man lives a burden to the earth; but a good book is the precious life-blood of a master spirit, embalmed and treasured up on purpose to a life beyond life" (YP 2:492).

This passage strikes me as metaphorically Traducian: The soul of a book is bequeathed to it by its author, and its life-blood is preserved in the book's physical makeup. If the statement is informed by the doctrine, then this excerpt indicates that Milton already understood the Cadmus myth in Traducian terms some ten years prior to alluding to it in "Avenge O Lord." *Areopagitica* was published in 1644, which was, as we saw, just about the time his interest in Mortalism, and therefore Traducianism, commenced. Hence, the possibility that the sonnet is also assuming an imagined version of the doctrine, not in sown books but dispersed remains, is strengthened.

In any event, by suggesting that new Vaudois can spring up from the remains of the old ones, Milton parts company with other early modern Traducians such as Richard Overton, who attacked a doctrine that Milton adduces as support for Traducianism, namely, the Scholastic notion of the soul being wholly present in every part of the body. In his discussion of Traducianism, Overton mocks this supporting belief by reducing it to what is, for him, an absurdity: "[W]ere a man minced into Atoms, cut into innumerable bits, there would be so many innumerable whole Souls, else could it not be wholly in every part."[38] But for Milton, this is precisely the case, at least figuratively; the victims of the Piedmont massacre have been cut into bits, but if every bit contains the entire soul, God can take each one, no matter how small, and distribute it profitably.

It may be significant that God's action here is a comparatively detached one, for in *De Doctrina*'s account of Traducianism Milton argues that God has bestowed on all of creation the power to reproduce both physically and spiritually on its own, without the sort of divine intervention required by Traducianism's opposite, Creationism. Creationism, he believes, should be rejected: "If God still created every day as many souls as man's frequently unlawful passion creates bodies in every part of the world, then he would have left himself a huge and, in a way, a servile task, even after that sixth day of creation—a task which would still remain to be performed, and from which he would not be able to rest even one day in seven." He immediately follows this comment with a remarkable observation: "But in fact the force of the divine blessing, that each creature should reproduce in its own likeness, is as fully applicable to man as it is to all other animals; Gen. i, 22, 28. So God made the mother of all things living out of a simple rib, without having to breathe the breath of life a second time, Gen. ii, 22" (YP 6:319–20).

Here Milton argues that in Genesis, God first tells all animals to be fruitful and multiply (1:22), then issues the same command to humanity (1:28). Milton then adduces the creation of Eve from Adam's rib, suggesting, I think, that because of the prior command, Adam's body now contains a kind of native potency that can be used to help create Eve. He cannot, of course, procreate without a partner, but God can shape Eve from Adam's rib, which is itself vital. In other words, God works with a power already latent in the rib. The account of Eve's creation in *Paradise Lost,* Book Eight, expands on this implication. Adam recounts that God,

>   stooping opened my left side, and took
> From thence a rib, with cordial spirits warm,
> And life-blood streaming fresh; . . .
> The rib he formed and fashioned with his hands;
> Under his forming hands a creature grew.   (465–67, 469–70)

Significantly, there is no reference here to God imparting the breath of life a second time; instead, he takes a mere rib—albeit one still bloody and warm with vital spirits—and forms Eve from it.

The example of Adam's rib is especially pertinent for *Sonnet XVIII,* since it constitutes a precedent of what Milton asks for in the poem. That is, just as Adam's entire body contains a kind of potency, and inert portions of it can be used to help create Eve, so also God can sow the still-fresh remains of the Vaudois, from which will come a new generation. The victims are dead, body and soul, and will not awaken until the last day, but their remains constitute vital seeds. Such a belief could also account for the care and dignity that Milton imaginatively bestows on the blood and ashes as he enjoins God, in effect, to take them from the freezing Alps and bury them in the warm fields. For as Kerrigan points out, Mortalism "invests the body with extraordinary dignity . . . [It holds that] flesh and spirit lie down together in darkness. Not a shell or a husk, the corpse is the repository of all its former life."[39]

As commentators often point out, the scenario of the new generation rising up is characterized by anti-Catholic imagery, such as the references to the pope as the "Triple Tyrant" (12), which alludes to his three-tiered crown, and to his "sway" (11), which figures both the papacy's tyrannical domination and its precariousness. The new crop of Vaudois will learn God's ways in time to flee the "Babylonian woe," a phrase that recalls both the Babylon of Revelation and, for Protestants, the papacy. The fact that Milton envisions them as fleeing from their enemies is consonant with Mortalism. John Knott points out that the poet "could have introduced a different kind of apocalyptic perspective by rising to a vision of the Piedmontese reunited in a heavenly fold."[40] Instead, Mortalism may have led him to imagine a this-worldly deliverance for the new generation.

V

I have argued that Milton began experimenting with Mortalism in the revisions of *Sonnet XIV*, then adopted it as well as Traducianism in *Sonnet XVIII*. Does either doctrine figure in other pre–*Paradise Lost* poems? Christopher Hill and George McLoone have detected Mortalist traces in *Sonnet XXIII* ("Methought I Saw"), which was probably written three years after "Avenge O Lord." Hill remarks that while the poet's last sonnet "looks forward to Milton's reunion with his wife in heaven . . . this brings little consolation: the sonnet is about the pain of her absence in this world."[41] I would add that she is described as being brought back "from the grave," a kind of Lady Lazarus summoned from the tomb rather than called back from heaven. And what of the pre-1658 prose? In addition to the *Areopagitica* excerpt discussed earlier, other passages may evince Traducian or Mortalist imagery. Finding and assessing them is beyond the scope of this essay, but such an undertaking could further clarify the poet's theological development, particularly how and when he turned from orthodoxy to heterodoxy.

Marshall University

NOTES

1. Numerous critics, including Svendsen, have paid particular attention to the work's Old Testament allusions. For him, its imagery "create[s] a tone of religious indignation quite in keeping with . . . the Old Testament flavor of the opening lines." See "Milton's Sonnet on the Massacre in Piedmont," *Shakespeare Association Bulletin* 20 (1945): 147–55; quotation, 147. Charles Goldstein, "The Hebrew Element in Milton's Sonnet XVIII," *MQ* 3 (1975): 111–14, extends this line of inquiry by examining the work in terms of Hebrew catchphrases such as "thy truth" (*amitekha*), "of old" (*mi'qedem,* or *qedem*), and "forget not" (*al-tishkah*). In like manner, John R. Knott, "The Biblical Matrix of Milton's 'On the Late Massacre in Piemont,' " *Philological Quarterly* 62 (1983): 259–63, explicates the images of the scattered bones of line 2, which, he contends, recall various passages from the book of Jeremiah, and of God as shepherd (line 6), a common motif in both the psalms and the prophets. More recently, Jay Ruud, "Milton's Sonnet 18 and Psalm 137," *MQ* 26 (1992): 80–81, has argued that the poem's concluding phrase, "Babylonian woe," which is usually glossed in relation to Revelation 17:18—the verse alludes to the destruction of the whore of Babylon, commonly allegorized by early modern Protestants as the Roman Catholic Church—is better understood in terms of the curse that concludes Psalm 137, in which the psalmist prays that the Babylonians' children will be dashed against rocks.

My own reading of the poem shares some affinities with these studies, for in many respects Milton's understanding of Mortalism can be construed as Hebraic. While most historians agree that Mortalism is a Christian heresy that sprang up during the Reformation, Milton grounds it in the Old Testament's emphasis on the death of the body. His account of Mortalism in *De Doctrina* 1.13 focuses almost entirely on the claim that soul and body perish simultaneously, and he spends hardly any time on the Second Coming. Moreover, many of his proof-texts come from the Old Testament, and as I note in my main discussion, in *Paradise Lost* Adam intuits only the death of body and soul, without any reference to resurrection. Milton's emphasis on the Hebraic underpinnings of Mortalism anticipates the view expressed by literary historian Harold Fisch, who states that "the 'mortalist heresy' is at bottom one of those recurrent upsurges of original Hebraic doctrine which occur throughout the history of the Church" (quoted in William Kerrigan, "The Heretical Milton: From Assumption to Mortalism," *ELR* 5 (Winter 1975), 150).

Although not all interpreters have focused on the poem's imagery, language remains a pivotal concern for many of them. Bruce Boehrer's Foucaldian analysis in "Providence as Punishment in the Works of Milton: Sonnet 18 and the Waldensian State Papers," *South Atlantic Review* 54 (1989): 27–40, examines the ways the poem echoes Milton's state letters on the massacre. Kathryn Brock, "Milton's Sonnet XVIII and the Language of Controversy," *MQ* 16 (1982): 3–6, accounts for the ways the poet appropriates traditionally Catholic language in the sonnet. Stanley Fish, "Interpreting the Variorum," *CI* 2 (1976): 465–85, focuses on the meaning of "thy way" in the poem's closing line. So does George Bellis's trenchant critique of Fish in "Fish and Milton—Briefly," *ELN* 32 (1995): 23–34. For a speech-act approach, see J. S. Lawry, "Milton's Sonnet 18: 'A Holocaust,' " *MQ* 17 (1983): 11–14.

2. Milton tends to espouse the variation of Mortalism known as Thnetopsychism, which holds that the body and soul die, though certain passages in *De Doctrina Christiana* seem to support the alternative type, Psychopannychism, which states that soul and body merely sleep until the Last Day. In his useful study on early modern Mortalism, Norman Burns, *Christian Mortalism from Tyndale to Milton* (Cambridge, MA, 1972), helps to explain this apparent inconsistency: "Like Christians who since New Testament times have referred to the death of the body as a 'sleep' because they are confident of its resurrection, the Thnetopsychists may well have said that the soul 'sleeps' whenever they wanted to emphasize their faith that the soul will be raised to immortality on the Last Day" (18).

3. Shawcross's estimated dates for the solidification of Milton's Mortalist and Traducian views were proposed in an e-mail to me on 4 June 2004. Milton's Mortalism has not received extensive discussion in recent scholarship. Two exceptions are an article by Raymond Waddington, "Murder One: The Death of Abel. Blood, Soul, and Mortalism in *Paradise Lost*," in *Milton Studies* 41, ed. Albert C. Labriola (Pittsburgh, 2002), 76–93, and a recent collection of essays, *Milton and Heresy*, ed. John Rumrich and Stephen Dobranski (Cambridge, 1998). Though none of the contributions is specifically devoted to Mortalism, the opening paragraph of the book's introduction states that in *De Doctrina* Milton "insists on the common materiality and mortality of body and soul." Several chapters touch on the implications of the poet's monistic views; Rumrich's essay, for example, argues that monism buttresses the poet's Arianism: "For the monist materialist Milton . . . all creatures derive from God's own substance . . . The Son's material being originally may be more refined and exalted than that of other creatures, but eventually parakeets and pachyderms would also qualify as participants in the Godhead." God the Father, he continues, created the Son from his own substance, but the Son does not share the Father's essence. See Rumrich, "Milton's Arianism: Why It Matters," 75–92; quotation, 83. William Kerrigan's offering, "Milton's Kisses" (117–35), ventures a playful reading of Adam and Eve's kiss, described at *PL* 4.497–502. Although the couple does not actually make love until the end of Book Four, by describing the kiss in terms of Jupiter's impregnation of Juno, and by referring to Eve as a "matron" (501), Milton forecasts the later event. Kerrigan concludes that "the 'kisses pure' of John Milton, animate materialist, are the profoundest in our language, for they alone bear nature's power to create new human beings" (133).

4. Other Mortalist loci in *Paradise Lost* include 3.245, 247–49; 11.61–62, 64–65, 444–47; and 12.434–35. References to Milton's poetry (excepting his sonnets) come from *The Complete English Poetry of John Milton,* ed. John T. Shawcross (New York, 1963). Quotations from his sonnets are from *Milton's Sonnets,* ed. E. A. J. Honigmann (New York, 1966). Unless otherwise noted, references to Milton's prose are to *The Complete Prose Works of John Milton,* 8 vols., ed. Don M. Wolfe et al. (New Haven, 1953–82), hereafter designated as YP, with volume and page numbers given parenthetically in the text. All biblical references are to the Authorized Version.

5. Mary Ann Radzinowicz, *Toward "Samson Agonistes": The Growth of Milton's Mind* (Princeton, NJ, 1978), argues that Mortalism is "present in *Samson Agonistes* and simply underscore[s] the universality of its application to all men in all times. [In lines 91–94] Samson confirms . . . the indivisibility of body and soul. . . . [And] by what he both is allowed and not allowed to say of his son, Manoa confirms the mortalism. He notes positively that Samson's death is a freeing from bondage, a complete freeing shared by all men, and the final end of life whether it crown it or shadow it" (348). Anthony Low, *The Blaze of Noon* (New York, 1974), remarks that

> [t]he lack of references to Samson's being taken directly into heaven may also be relevant. Direct references are kept out by historical probability and poetic purpose, but plainer indirect reference could easily have been provided through the imagery, or through unconscious irony. . . . [B]y the time Milton wrote *The Christian Doctrine* . . . he became a mortalist. If the play was written after about 1658, then Milton would have assumed the death of Samson's soul along with his body, until he received eternal life at the Last Judgment. (225)

William Kerrigan, "Heretical," states that in the play "Samson is assumed to have perished in soul and body; no consolation of the orthodox sort will be achieved by his Old Testament father. . . . Like his author, Manoa is in key particulars a mortalist. We may be almost certain that Milton prepared this speech with the knowledge, never to be shared directly with his readers, that [the tragedy's closing elegy, 'Nothing is here for tears'] demonstrated the experiential adequacy of a doctrinal choice" (150). For Milton's discussion of Traducianism, see YP 6:321–22.

6. Barbara K. Lewalski, *The Life of John Milton: A Critical Biography* (Malden, MA, 2000), 424.

7. See Virginia Mollenkott, "Milton's Mortalism: Treatise vs. Poetry," *Seventeenth Century News* 36 (1968): 59; Burns, *Christian Mortalism,* 169; Kerrigan, "Heretical," 127; Waddington, "Murder One," 85. For Kerrigan's caveat, see "Heretical," 125 n. 1.

8. See Christopher Hill, *Milton and the English Revolution* (New York, 1979), 317.

9. Ibid., 323.

10. A. E. B. Coldiron, "Milton *in parvo:* Mortalism and Genre Transformation in Sonnet 14," *Milton Quarterly* 28 (1994): 1–10.

11. Burns, *Christian Mortalism,* 164, 172–79.

12. Ibid., 154.

13. Anna K. Nardo, *Milton's Sonnets and the Ideal Community* (Lincoln, NE, 1979), 58.

14. Honigmann, *Milton's Sonnets,* 136–37; Lewalski, *Life of John Milton,* 209; John Leonard, *John Milton: The Complete Poems* (New York, 1998), 694.

15. Honigmann, *Milton's Sonnets,* 135–36.

16. See Coldiron, "Milton *in parvo,*" 4. In an e-mail message to me on 4 June 2003, Shawcross made a similar point about possible Mortalist influences in the sonnet.

17. This section of my analysis is indebted to Shawcross, who in an e-mail message on 2 June 2004 brought to my attention the potentially Mortalist qualities of lines 5–8.

18. Coldiron, "Milton *in parvo,*" 7.

19. This portion of the Confession is cited by Nathaniel H. Henry, "Milton and Hobbes: Materialism and the Intermediate State," *SP* 48 (1951): 237. The parliamentary ordinance is quoted in Burns, *Christian Mortalism,* 16.

20. See Lewalski, *Life of John Milton,* 284–85.

21. Henry, "Milton and Hobbes," 248, was the first to suggest that Milton may have hidden this potentially controversial passage late in the poem to escape the censor.

22. See David Masson, *The Life of John Milton: Narrated in Connexion with the . . . History of His Time,* 6 vols. (1880; reprint, Gloucester, MA, 1965), 5:191.

23. William Hunter, "Milton and the Waldensians," *SEL* 11 (1971): 157.

24. Ibid., 159.

25. See *The Creeds of the Evangelical Protestant Churches,* ed. Philip Schaff (New York, 1919), 3:757–58.

26. Goldstein, "The Hebrew Element," traces the line to Psalm 79:10: "Wherefore should the heathen say, Where is their God? Let him be known among the heathen in our sight by the revenging of the blood of thy servants which is shed" (111).

27. Lewalski, *Life of John Milton,* 644 n. 38.

28. *The Works of John Milton,* 18 vols., ed. Frank Allen Patterson et al. (New York, 1931–38), 15:237.

29. Masson, *The Life of John Milton,* 5:43.

30. See Goldstein, "The Hebrew Element," 111.

31. Nearly all biblical allusions to the Book of Life have to do with salvation: If one's name is written in the book, one is saved; if God chooses to erase it, damnation ensues. See, for example, Exodus 32:32, Philippians 4:3, and Revelation 3:5. Revelation 20:12 complicates the meaning of the Book of Life somewhat by presenting the opening of not one but several books at the end of the age: "And I saw the dead, small and great, stand before God, and the books were opened; and another book was opened, which is the book of life. And the dead were judged out of those things

which were written in the books, according to their works." It would appear, then, that there were two sets of books, one with the names of the saved, and another with a record of their good works. It seems unlikely that the Waldensians would have needed to have their names written into the Book of Life, given that they were exemplary Christians. It may be, rather, that in the poem Milton refers to one of the volumes in which good works are set down, to suggest that the victims' groans can be counted as such.

32. Honigmann, *Milton's Sonnets,* 165.

33. Nardo, *Milton's Sonnets and the Ideal Community,* 134.

34. Ibid., 134.

35. Stouppe's remark is from *A Collection of Several Papers . . . Concerning the Bloody and Barbarous Massacres* (London, 1655), 2, and is quoted in Honigmann, *Milton's Sonnets,* 166.

36. The quotation is from Tertullian's *Apology,* in *The Ante-Nicene Fathers,* ed. Alexander Roberts and James Donaldson (Grand Rapids, MI, 1978), 177.

37. Traducianism was derived from Stoicism, which held that parents generate the souls as well as the bodies of their children. Tertullian seems to have been the first to apply the Stoic notion to the doctrine of original sin. He did so in reaction to Irenaeus, whose concepts on original sin he found vague and overly mystical. In the preface to his treatise *De Anima,* Tertullian contends that "[Adam], being given over to the death on account of his sin, the entire human race, tainted in their descent from him, were made a channel for transmitting his condemnation." And in the treatise proper, he remarks that "[e]very soul, by reason of its birth, has its nature in Adam until it is born again in Christ; moreover, it is unclean all the while that it remains [unbaptized]." See *The Ante-Nicene Fathers,* 177, 220.

Traducian sentiments may inform this church father's best-known quote about the blood of the martyrs, which is taken from the *Apology. De Anima's* preface refers to the *Apology,* which is cast in the form of an apologia, leading S. Thelwall, in *The Ante-Nicene Fathers,* 175 n. 1, to speculate that *De Anima* constitutes a kind of sequel to the *Apology.* If the two works are meant to be read together, then it is possible that Tertullian's statement on the blood of the martyrs is informed by his thinking about the soul's corporeality, even though he did not express that notion until the later treatise.

38. Quoted in Burns, *Christian Mortalism,* 174.

39. Kerrigan, "Heretical," 149.

40. Knott, "The Biblical Matrix," 262.

41. Hill, *Milton and the English Revolution,* 323. While McLoone, "Milton's Twenty-Third Sonnet: Love, Death, and the Mystical Body of the Church," *MQ* 34 (1990): 8–21, finds mortalism in the sestet, he adds that the wife "is both in the grave and in heaven simultaneously" (11).

THE AFTERLIFE OF THE WIDOWER'S DREAM: REREADING MILTON'S FINAL SONNET

Hugh J. Dawson

CRITICISM OF MILTON'S sonnet beginning "Methought I saw my late espoused saint" has had two main concerns, study of its internal dynamics and inquiry into the dream figure's identity.[1] The debate set off by William Riley Parker's proposal that the oneiric presence corresponds better with what little is known of the former Mary Powell than with the surviving information about the erstwhile Katherine Woodcock has apparently been settled by Anthony Low in refuting the chief argument made for the first wife—that only she outlived the quarantine period established by Leviticus 12:5 for effecting an ancient Jewish mother's postpartum cleansing—by noting that Milton twice wrote that the purification of mothers had been made supererogatory by Christ.[2] This essay returns to consideration of the poem's dynamics. It accepts that Milton may have begun from a real dream and studies his reworking of the poem's elements to argue that the much-ignored central lines contain his final appreciation of what seemed to have been a meeting with his wife, taking from his sleep experience fresh "trust" that they would know the joy of renewing their love in heaven.

Leo Spitzer's contribution to understanding the sonnet centers upon its female figure, insisting that the efforts to identify the "late espoused saint" were mistaken. For Spitzer, that image was of a type, not of a person, one derived from the *donna angelicata* figure Milton knew from having read "the two famous renowners of *Beatrice* and *Laura* who never wrote but honour of them to whom they devote their verse" (CM 3:303).[3] Whether or not one finds the question of her identity relevant, it is clear that Milton refers to the recent loss of one of his wives. All that he relates of the dream figure's history and character, and anticipates in their reunion, is framed in terms of the marital bond. Emphasizing the sonnet's autobiographical nature, forms of the first-person pronoun and possessive adjective appear nine times in a poem that from its first printing in 1673 has carried Milton's name. The author is the awakened dreamer, but nothing in the series of mental acts—neither his doubts concerning the reliability of his perceptions, the need to distinguish what was originally in the dream from what he added in recasting it in the poem, nor the psychology of his phantasmal experience—has exercised critics so much as the explication of the details with which he elaborated his memory of the episode.

Spitzer found that the sonnet resembles a triptych in which the panels represent paganism, the Old Testament, and the New; Milton's *donna angelicata* is portrayed within a "continuous rising movement," a "tripartite *crescendo* arrangement."[4] But the poem's pattern is far more complicated than this unilinear temporal progression. Those who miss Milton's distrust of his faculties while sleeping, signaled by the caveats implied in "Methought" and "fancied sight," or who overlook his important interruption of the narrative inevitably misread what is a very complicated report. They mistake much of the awakened poet's after-work for what was available to his dreaming mind. Far from being the sequential recital of sleep events that it at first seems, the poem is an intricate integration of fragments from the dream that have been enriched by many additions.

Low's remark that "all of Milton's sonnets between 1640 and 1660 are occasional in nature" reinforces Thomas Wheeler's argument for the proper point from which analysis of the poem should begin: "It will be wise to accept Milton's dream as a real dream," "Milton's dream was substantially what he said it was," and "it is prudent . . . to assume that Milton's dream was substantially as he described it." At the very least, this has the merit of taking the poet at his word. (It would certainly seem unlikely for the dream account to be nothing more than a mock autobiographical conceit sedulously contrived to build to a concluding display of self-pity.) Following Wheeler's advice that critics ought to proceed "in the light of what we know of Milton's mind," I will argue that, whether or not one finds the sleep episode to have been of the erotic type it so much resembles, the later mental activity registered in the sonnet is evidence that his wife's appearing to him in the dream had the effect of renewing his "trust" that they would meet again in the love of heaven, the faith that was to sustain him throughout his remaining years "in this dark world and wide" (*Sonnet XVI*, 2).[5]

Working backward from his remembered moment of awakening to isolate the sleep events from what the dreamer-become-poet later added reveals four stages of mental activity prior to Milton's making the technical decisions that shaped the poem he would publish, such as adoption of the Petrarchan sonnet form and the choice of appropriate diction: (1) the speaker's recollection of awakening; (2) his memory of a series of linked impressions that had been present to him in his sleep; (3) his performance of several sophisticated intellectual acts in summoning details from his mental reservoir and integrating these in a complicated elaboration of what he recalled from the oneiric sequence; and (4) his moving beyond the recall of the dream's details and his embellishment of them to make what appears in the two central lines, an affirmation of his devout "trust" that he was to be reunited with his wife in everlasting happiness after death.

What was chronologically the first in the series of mental actions is the subject of the poem's final line as the speaker recalls his awakening. Its three clauses report Milton's sense of being overwhelmed by the emotional over-load of that moment. There is no hint that he reverts to the dream in saying "she fled" with the implication that, like the ghost of Dido turning away from Aeneas in *Aeneid* 6.450–76, the figure of his "saint" behaved in any way that suggested she was spurning the man she had loved in her lifetime.[6] The compressed telling of the three simultaneous events is an attempt to re-create the confusion he felt on returning to reality, something he found far more difficult to credit than the almost tangible phantasm that had only a moment earlier been before his imagined vision.

The second order of mental activity is Milton's recall of several of the dream's elements: the image of a woman he hesitantly took to be his late wife; her drawing near, with her clearer form and movements increasing his confidence as to her identity; her having been "vested all in white" and "veiled"; and her inclining over him. Whatever else may have occurred in his sleep remains uncertain and must be distinguished from such additions as the description of Alcestis—"Rescued from death by force though pale and faint"—which derives from a literary text and could have become available to the poet only after he awoke and reverted to his store of learning. Examples of uncertainty within the dream are "Brought," with its implication of an escort in line 2—whether the suggestion is that his wife was led forward or borne to him, as Alcestis is commonly carried on a litter in stagings of Euripides's play—and "Came" in line 9—whether this word was intended to indicate that she drew near on her own initiative or at another's direction. The meaning of line 13's "inclined" is also ambiguous, referring either to the wife's posture or to what the sleeper took to be her intention. His recognition of her "Love, sweetness, goodness," and "delight" in lines 11–12 and his questioning of what his sight reported are mental actions that cannot be assigned fixed times. If they at first seem to be perceptions that had their origins within the dream, they seem on second thought at least as likely to have been acts performed at later times, possibly not until long after Milton regained consciousness.

The third category of mental activity is the addition of the many ele-ments of the report that would not have been present in the episode as it was recalled but must have been supplied in the retrospect of consciousness. The

first such intellectual action was epistemological scrutiny of the dream perceptions, a process that survived the confusion that attended awakening and
lingers in the doubtfulness of "Methought," the uncertainty of "my fancied
sight," and the hint of "as if" in Milton's memory of the moment when "as to
embrace me she inclined." The second of these intellectual actions was the
inclusion of matters stored in his reservoir of learning that he summoned up
after awakening—his recognition of the moral traits characteristic of a
"saint," his recalling the myth of Alcestis's rescue from the dead as drama-
tized by Euripides, his identifying Hercules as her deliverer, his citation of
the purification rite mandated by the "old Law," and his recall of the Gospel
promise of the eternal happiness awaiting the elect. The third group of such
mental acts includes the social and moral assessments in which Milton went
beyond fact-testing to make value judgments. Examples include his terming
his wife a "saint;" his reverence for the exemplary value of the myth of
Alcestis and Admetus; his appreciation of the expressional connotations of his
society's conventions of dress, color, and gesture; his awareness of the taboos
attaching to birth and death; and his respect for the long obsolete mandate of
Leviticus that required newly delivered mothers to undergo a ritual period of
purgation.

Besides these explicitly reported mental actions, there are others that
scholars, working from what is known of Milton's vast reading, have concluded very likely inform his allusions. These references include apparent
parallels between Alcestis's restoration to Admetus by "Jove's great son" Hercules and Jesus' redemption of his wife; between the figure in the dream and
Euripides's Alcestis, both of them silent wives and mothers who died pre-
maturely; between the love shown by the play's heroine for her husband and
that which his "late espoused saint" had demonstrated for him; between the
charity seen in Christ's death oblation and Alcestis's wife's willingness to
undergo the perils of childbirth and die in order that their child might have
life; and between the purificatory period required of Old Testament mothers
and the time of cleansing served by Alcestis, during which she is forbidden to
talk with others.[7]

Milton's last mental acts found deep personal meaning in the dream's
religious dimension. Sometime after he awoke, he reflected upon the event's
possible meaning, identified what he understood to have been the unspoken
message borne by his *donna angelicata,* and decided to include in the sonnet
the declaration of his renewed "trust" that he and his "saint" were destined to
share eternal happiness. This interpretation of the encounter accorded with
all that he remembered of his wife's character and the sum of his learning,
especially his appreciation of Jesus' salvific mission, which enabled the married elect to ascend to a sharing in the pure love of the heavenly communion.

This attempt to sort out the poem's stages of complication is not exhaustive, and its distinctions may at several points seem ill defined or overlapping. But neither completeness nor precision in treating the many details is so important as the disengagement of the core dream from its elaboration. Once one differentiates the kernel event from its enrichment in the poem and from proposals as to the sources of Milton's elaboration of his sleep experience, it becomes clear that the poet's learning has distracted his critics from distinguishing among the few images that he recalled from his sleep and the many decorative features with which he later enriched them.

Milton's report of his dream closely resembles scriptural and classical writers' accounts of such experiences. In terming sleep the near relative of death, Virgil employed a figure long popular among Greek and Roman poets, for whom dreams were the milieu in which souls of the dead met with those of the living.[8] Leaving Hades through the Gates of Somnus, the shades of the departed might, either on their own initiative or at the command of a god, present themselves to sleepers' minds. False dreams were said to have emerged by the Gate of Ivory, while those felt to be true were described as having come from the Gate of Horn.[9]

That the dream ended as "day brought back my night" may echo the tradition that credited morning dreams. As Milton knew from reading Virgil, Ovid, and Horace, oneiric experiences that occurred after midnight were thought prophetic.[10] Respect for this belief continued into the Middle Ages, as is seen in Dante's repeated references to it in the *Inferno* and in the three morning dreams, which very shortly prove to be true, in the *Purgatorio*. Closer to Milton's time, both Shakespeare and Ben Jonson refer to it.[11]

Dreams have prophetic and instructive functions in both the Old Testament (such as those of David and the pharaoh) and the New (from those in the infancy narrative of Saint Matthew's gospel [Matt. 1:20; 2:12–13, 19, and 22] to that of Pilate's wife [Matt. 27:19] and those of Saint Paul [Acts 16:9, 18:9]). Job 33:15–17 declares what appears to have been the widely held Old Testament understanding of the truth that may be revealed in dreams, a belief that continues in the New, as is seen in the magi's heeding the warning against their returning to Herod (Matt. 2:12). The clearest scriptural statement is Numbers 12:6: "If there be a Prophet of the Lord among you, I wil be knowen to him by a vision, & wil speake unto him by a dreame." The same advice as to the truth of dreams is heard in Adam's consolatory words to Eve: "God is also in sleep, and dreams advise, / Which he hath sent propitious, some great good / Presaging" (*PL* 12.611–13).[12]

Beyond conforming with the classical and biblical patterns of such experiences, Milton's account of his wife's visitation presents her as one whose appearing to him as a figure of innocence accorded with all that he remembered of her from their life together. Especially since she seems to have been mute throughout the dream-appearance, he could not have inferred anything concerning its promissory character until he awoke. While sleeping, his response would have been limited to the surprised thrill of meeting with an image that at first only uncertainly resembled his dim sense of his wife, his growing confidence that the shrouded figure was indeed hers, his increasing excitement as her image advanced toward him, and his gathering pleasure as he looked forward to her signaled "embrace."

Other commentators have discussed the sonnet's love theme. John J. Colaccio notes that the "persona regards the saint . . . with increasing conjugal affection" and finds that " 'my fancied sight' implies, in addition to the fact of his dream-vision, the persona's intense conjugal love as well, 'fancy' denoting the affections as well as the imagination." John C. Ulreich sees the failed "embrace" as reversing Orpheus's reaching out to Eurydice and argues that "Milton's identification with Orpheus defines the emotional content of the poem"; "the basic pattern of experience in the poem is that of Orphic myth."[13] However, neither critic sees the poem as the report of an erotic dream, although what it relates is very similar to such an experience. Upon examining the narratorial testimony, one recognizes this familiar sequence in the dream-drama in which the poet vividly represents an imagined passionate meeting with his wife. What very much resembles increasing sexual excitement appears in the deferral of the expected *volta*, as the convention of its occurring at or near the octave's close is ignored. Formal considerations yield to the pace of the dream in the interplay between the wife's silent but inviting advance and the sleeper's arousal as he infers from her approach that a consummation of their marriage may be at hand. His tense anticipation of that pleasure builds until the opening of the next-to-final line, where the adversative conjunction is succeeded by his pained interjection, "But O." The following temporal clause preserves the climax of the sleep episode when all movement is suspended with his wife "inclined" above him, a moment of arrest that increases the surprise at the dream's dissolve and the persona's being precipitated into despondency in the final line.

The "espoused saint" seems at first to have no personality beyond that of a devoted, self-sacrificing Puritan wife. Just as she is anonymous, she is featureless. The reader knows only that she was "vested all in white, pure as her mind: / Her face was veiled." Although this last clause has been taken to refer to the poet's blindness, the consonance of "vested" and "veiled" suggests that the paired verbals describe the dress of a figure who advanced with the maidenly reserve of a young wife nervously approaching her expectant husband, what Milton in *Paradise Lost* terms "innocence and virgin modesty" (8.501) and speaks of elsewhere as "the bashfull mutenes of a virgin"

(CM 3:394).[14] Though demure, the dream figure's manner is recalled as that of one who "Came . . . in her person," with all that the phrasing conveys of physical attractiveness. That her advance toward him was suffused with vital appeal is clear from the response of the widower recumbent upon what had been the couple's "genial bed" (*PL* 8.598). In reporting the "Love, sweetness, goodness" and "delight" that "shined" in the dream-image, the blind poet gives more than an imagined picture of his wife as an incarnation of virtue. He also intimates the attractiveness that, no matter his sightless condition, had drawn him to her in their times of marital intimacy. Adam's memory of the excitement experienced by his "internal sight" when he first saw Eve, also in a dream, deserves attention for its close variations of both the opening of the autobiographical poem—"Abstract as in a trance methought I saw [her]" —and its conclusion—when, as "She disappeared, and left me dark, I waked" (8.461, 462, 478). Just as remarkable is the recurrence only a few lines later of three principal nouns from the sonnet's lines 11 and 12—"love," "sweetness," and "delight," this last noun accompanied by a very significant modifier—in Adam's response to Eve's

> looks, which from that time infused
> Sweetness into my heart, unfelt before,
> And into all things from her air inspired
> The spirit of love and amorous delight.   (8.474–77)[15]

Those who take the sonnet to be about Milton's second wife read "my fancied sight" as a reference to the activity of his sleeping mind in supplying the dream-image with features of the spouse he had never seen.[16] But the phrase may as well refer to the pleasure due to his arousal's having been stimulated, no matter if only involuntarily, from within. The hesitation and passion of the climactic instant that linger in the "O" of the penultimate line tell of the dreaming poet's insurgent feeling. "As to embrace me she inclined," the veil (symbolizing virginal reserve), seems, in the odd way of dreams, to have slipped away unnoticed. (The revelation at this *paraesthesis* resembles the unveiling gesture since adopted into weddings, where the bride signals the abandonment of her last inhibition to giving herself to her spouse.) If "embrace" tells some of a kiss, the word suggests intimate relations at *Paradise Lost* 4.471, 771, and clearly refers to sexual consummation at 2.793 of that poem, as it does at *Samson Agonistes*, line 389.[17] At this instant, just as the yearning husband's expectation of again celebrating their love neared its climax, he "waked," and the figure of his wife evaporated without their having shared a word or touch, and consciousness recalled him to everyday life.

In fact, the nature of Milton's dream and his response will be forever unknown, and anyone venturing a reading of the sonnet along these lines must anticipate the objection that writing a poem about frustrated erotic experience was an unseemly project, one such as Milton cannot be thought to have undertaken. But a discreet poetic recall of a dreamed-of approach to sharing love with his wife would likely not have troubled readers of his time, who were much less embarrassed by the poetic muse than those of Queen Victoria's era. That the poem's reenactment of such excitement has for more than three centuries gone unremarked is its own proof of the decorum of a sonnet that, at least since Josiah Fenton in 1725 described it as one that "does honour to her memory," has been universally regarded as Milton's reverent memorialization of his marriage to the "saint" whose premature loss he mourns.[18]

Milton's response to the dream is not completely told, but moralists of the period followed medieval teaching on sleepers' reactions to phantasms appearing to the passive mind. If there were an emission like that thought to be condemned by Leviticus 15:16–18 and Deuteronomy 23:10–11, Milton would have regarded such an experience in the light of the patristic and Scholastic understanding that no fault attached to what took place when the full moral personality was not engaged. In writing of Christian poets' treatment of such events, Manfred Weidhorn explains that, so long as the excitement was neither deliberately stimulated nor prolonged—as is obviously intended by Admetus in Euripides's *Alcestis* in his pledging to hire craftsmen to fashion a sculpture of his wife so as to summon dream-memories of her—and the will did not accede to the mental suggestion and physical response, there was no culpability.[19] Dreams were involuntary mental intrusions brought about by "animal spirits that from pure blood arise / Like gentle breaths from rivers pure" (*PL* 4.805–6). Adam draws upon the same moral psychology that distinguished partial awareness of fantasies occurring in sleep from the full personality's engagement in the events of waking life in consoling Eve when she recounts her troubling dream: "What in sleep thou didst abhor to dream, / Waking thou never wilt consent to do." She should "be not sad. / Evil into the mind of god or man / May come and go, so unapproved, and leave / No spot or blame behind" (5.120–21, 116–19).[20]

Rather than playing to any prurient interest in the erotic memory-traces remaining in the poem, I will show that elements of the sleep episode were fused with Milton's conscious afterthoughts in the sonnet's religious statement. Finding its origin in dream excitement merely points to the start of a search into the import of his wife's appearing to him. Earlier readers have found in the sonnet echoes of the lines of *Paradise Lost* cited above when Adam, after believing he has been a witness to Eve's creation, awakes to discover that she has "disappeared, and left me dark." Although disappointed, he trusts that the dream will prove true, a belief that fires his resolve "To find [her], or for ever to deplore / Her loss and other pleasures all abjure." Happily, he finds her to be "Such as I saw her in my dream," and they come to know the joys of prelapsarian marriage (8.478, 479–80, 482). Milton awoke to the knowledge that his wife was dead, but she retains in the sonnet the image of the dream. At some time after he awoke, he experienced the consolation of faith that he would again have "sight" of the wife he had seemed to meet with during his sleep, but with the essential difference that they were to share in heaven a happiness far surpassing the "sum of earthly bliss" (8.522) experienced by Adam and Eve.

The poem is usually taken to do nothing more than relate Milton's memory of a vanished dream and his empty sense of loss, a reaction that many modern readers probably find complicated by the burden of "survivor guilt" at his having outlived a wife who died soon after giving birth to a child he had fathered.[21] With this kind of reading, the sonnet merely rehearses the illusion and the sleeper's awakening to self-pity. But a poem intended only to gratify a perverse pleasure by recycling the memory of his deception and lamenting the dream figure's abrupt disappearance would be wholly unlike what anyone familiar with Milton's character, philosophy of life, and writings would expect of him. It would surely have been an anomaly for him to have surrendered himself to fashioning what was no more than the elaboration of a fantasy that ends in surrender to maudlin despondency. One is not surprised when other poets memorialize their loss of loved ones in emotional love-death threnodies, but Milton's history of probing the many disappointments of his life for whatever they might tell of God's intention for him suggests that, soon after he awoke, he would have pondered what divine purpose might have lain hidden in his having been brought to the verge of expecting a renewal of marital love only to have that hope frustrated in his being returned to the sightless quotidian. The seriousness of his other sonnets—such as those in which he asks the reason for his late maturing, questions the meaning of his early blindness, addresses Cromwell and Vane on affairs of state, and justifies the enjoyment of leisure—argues this much: that it would have been in keeping with the personality of this famously introspective Puritan poet to have almost immediately set about searching into all he could remember of the dream to discover whatever personal meaning it might be thought to have held.

Not until the closing line tells of the speaker's awakening do readers learn that nothing of the preceding account was as it first seemed. Starting from the uncertainty of "Methought," they find that they must imitate Milton in searching within the dream, but with a new alertness to what was supplied after he recovered consciousness. Rereading reveals how much of the poem

is the elaboration of a very few sleep elements and brings the shock of
recognition on their discovering that surrendering attention to the narrative
rush had caused them to miss how much had been incorporated retrospectively and to overlook or at least undervalue a crucial departure from the
sleep sequence.

Midway through the sonnet, Milton breaks off telling of the dream to
insert an afterthought of an altogether different sort. Without their having
any relation to the six preceding lines or the six that follow, lines 7 and 8
interrupt the account of the figure's advance toward the dreamer to declare
his "trust" that they will meet "in heaven." These framed lines divide the
poem. In the earlier lines the wife is passive, a spectral presence perhaps in
need of others' care. She is immobile or nearly so as Milton sketches her
mythological and biblical analogues; the suggestion that she relies upon the
unnamed others who accompany her reinforces the sense of her likeness to
the "pale and faint" Alcestis. Following Milton's profession of belief, she
becomes volitional. One who had been "Brought to me" now "Came" to her
husband and "inclined" to "embrace" him in love, exciting his passion and
quickening his sense of their erotic rapport. The dreamer's response to the
appeal that "in her person shined / So clear, as in no face with more delight"
recalls Adam's response when Eve's "air inspired / The spirit of love and
amorous delight" (*PL* 8.476–77).

Besides its disregard of the narrative, the interruption is remarkable for
its departure from the structural patterns that the earlier and later sections
share: its abandonment of the progression from hesitant recognition to
crushing grief to admit the avowal of "trust"; its modal shift from narration to
creedal statement; and its rupture of temporal unity, as what is at all other
points a past-tense recall of the dream and its ending is suspended to include
this present-tense profession of a future expectation. The contrasts between
the content of the two lines and that of the rest of the poem are just as
striking. The truth of Christ's promise is opposed to the sleep-state's deceit,
eternal life to an evanescent dream, and "the joy of the unencumbered soul"
to the pain of one who has awakened to recognize his error and find he is still
subject to the vicissitudes of this life.[22]

Those persuaded to Parker's view that the poem is about the former
Mary Powell have taken Milton's report of his "saint" as having been "such, as
yet once more I trust to have / Full sight of her in heaven" to describe his
belief that he would then meet the only wife he had ever seen, for he was
totally blind by the time he married Katherine Woodcock. Readers like Low
who find the second wife the subject seem to these others to encounter an
irrefutable objection in the fact that Milton would not have described his
anticipated reunion with one he had never seen in terms of restored vision.

But the difficulty disappears when the lines are taken to refer, not to his expecting to recover sight of one seen in life, but to his trusting he would know the figure he intuited was his wife as he met her in his sleep. Just as Eve became present to Adam, Milton's wife would prove to be "Such as I saw her in my dream" (8.482). The possessive pronoun "Mine," reidentified by "such" two lines later, is the subject of a sentence with its predicate at the opening of the ninth line, where "Came" follows two intervening descriptive elements. The first recalls "the old Law" to stress the wife's spiritual purity and honor the Redemption that had released her from that edict. The other is a conclusion derived from her dream-semblance. She who "Came vested all in white" appeared then "as yet once more I trust to have / Full sight of her in heaven." Milton's Christian interpretation of the dream figure represents the sleep episode as a meeting with one whose "Love, sweetness, goodness in her person shined / So clear" that the radiant image afforded proof of her beatitude while contrasting with the "pale and faint" cast of the unredeemed Alcestis's body. The robe and veil of his "saint" have a double importance: In Revelation, white is the color of the gowns worn by the faithful souls who await the Judgment (Rev. 3:5, 6:11, 7:9, 7:13–14, 19:14), and it was the familiar liturgical symbol of faith. In the Mortalist view of the afterlife, the wife's soul would have been thought dead, but the significance of her dress so accorded with what Milton remembered of her exemplary life as to confirm what must have been his earlier belief that she was one of those souls to be gathered into bliss at the Resurrection.

Reading lines 7 and 8 as telling only of Milton's expecting to join his wife in heaven misses their polyvalence, for they admit at least equally of the understanding that "yet once more" relates, not to the rather remote infinitive "to have," but to "I trust," which the phrase immediately precedes. Taken in this sense, the collocation of the adverbial phrase with the subject and predicate enlarges one's sense of the meaning Milton took from his inquiry into the dream. The present tense tells both of his confidence in their future reunion and of his enjoying that faith while living. These words open *Lycidas:* "Yet once more, O ye laurels, and once more / . . . / I come to pluck your berries" (1, 3). The many attempts to clarify the allusion have brought no agreement, but they obviously refer to a resumption or new beginning.[23] They here imply that the oneiric encounter had brought a religious conversion in the rebirth of Milton's "trust" in ascending to a more purified love. That this word may be read as "faith" under another name appears from his elsewhere writing that "faith is also called . . . 'trust,' with the same meaning" (CM 15:397).[24] This avowal of regenerated belief, reached by the awakened poet's exercise of his reason as it was informed by his devout study, is chronologically and logically the last of the mental acts to be traced as he came to write the sonnet. His interrogation of the sleep encounter had brought a regeneration of the faith that must be every Christian's reliance "till God ere long / To his celestial consort us unite, / To live with him, and sing in endless morn of light" ("At a Solemn Music," 26–28).

The Redemption had won for the elect a love like that of the celestial creatures. Although Matthew 22:30 and Mark 12:25 declare that the saved will then no longer know marriage, both Evangelists' verses conclude with the promise that, in their immortal bodies, they will find themselves "as the Angels which are in heauen." The nature of that state was a vexing question for Milton, who understood with Adam that "heaven is for thee too high / To know what passes there" (8.172–73). Adam's early wish to know "Of their being / Who dwell in heaven" (5.455–56) and his later hesitant questioning imply the poet's curiosity concerning the evangelists' obscure promise of elect married souls' afterlife: "how their love / Express they, by looks only, or do they mix / Irradiance, virtual or immediate touch" (8.615–17)? Raphael seeks to fashion an answer proportioned to his auditor's experience by reverting to his rhetorical strategy of "likening spiritual to corporal forms, / As may express them best" (5.573–74) and finds in marital love an instructive means of teaching how those of his kind the "works of love . . . fulfill" (1.431):

> Whatever pure thou in the body enjoy'st
> (And pure thou wert created) we enjoy
> In eminence, and obstacle find none
> Of membrane, joint, or limb, exclusive bars:
> Easier than air with air, if spirits embrace,
> Total they mix, union of pure with pure
> Desiring; nor restrained conveyance need
> As flesh to mix with flesh, or soul with soul.[25]   (8.622–29)

Raphael's summary statement advises against useless speculation: "Let it suffice thee that thou know'st / Us happy, and without love no happiness." It is enough for those on Earth to "Be strong, live happy, and love" (8.620–21, 633).

If Raphael's report of celestial love is ambiguous in its metaphorical mingling of flesh and spirit, some clarification might be had from the fallen angels' gratification of what has become the raw lust that inflames the incestuous rapes related at *Paradise Lost* 2.763–67 and 792–96. Here is the antithesis of the love in heaven. The parodic debasement of marital love in scenes of erotic indulgence that repel the reader implies that the highest love requires a figure intimating its independence of physical pleasure and the experience of touch. So when Milton came to "measuring things in heaven by things on earth" (6.893) in the sonnet's image of the happiness to be shared by the married among the elect, he found the appropriate image in the promise he translated from 1 Corinthians 13:12: "We shall see with open eyes, not under a vaile" (CM 3:191) and represented the "trust" he took from the dream of his wife's embassy in terms of vision: he was to enjoy "Full sight of her in heaven without restraint."

Reading the sonnet with attention to the middle lines' anachronistic reaffirmation of religious belief finds it to possess a spiritual content that has until now been slighted. Even one who proposes such a reading resists its corollary, a much-diminished regard for the sonnet as a formal achievement. The poem so admired for its structural perfection now seems badly deformed by the intruded declaration of renewed belief. But, no matter the aesthetic sacrifice, the middle lines are the most fully considered and important of the sonnet. Their significance argues that appreciation of the poem cannot be had from readings predicated upon a narrative sequence that survives only by ignoring the interruption at the octave's close.

Rather than the integrity supplied by the sonnet form, it is the pattern of Milton's spiritual progress that unifies the poem. One observes a three-stage ascent as the movement of his thought corresponds with the Renaissance Neoplatonic humanists' ladder of love incorporated into Raphael's counseling of Adam in Book Eight of *Paradise Lost*. Milton's remembrance of his surprise on returning from the dream, the first category of mental activity sketched earlier, was the starting point for the ensuing pattern of growth. His next thought was the recall of the dream, in which his unreasoning animal faculties were captivated by the external beauty of a figure he took to be his wife, feeling what to Adam "seem[ed] such dear delight / Beyond all other" (8.579–82), although it did not deserve the name of love; it was no more than the base activity of the soul scorned by all thinkers in the Platonic tradition. Milton's recovered reason next passed to reflecting upon the married love he had known with his "late espoused saint" and the evidences of her virtue. The enhancement of her character performed in the second and third categories of mental actions that preceded his writing the poem—which were, in fact, one in that both ennobled the wife by relating her to positive cultural refer- ents—had its culmination in his analogizing her death with the sacrifices of Alcestis and Jesus. These first two stages of the widower's thought after he regained a sense of conscious life, the recall of the erotic dream's base excite- ment and his elaborating the rational love of his marriage, have their Neo- platonic parallel in the early lines of Raphael's instructing Adam in the ad- vances by which he must rise from delight in Eve's physical appeal to a reflective, mature, and human appreciation of her companionship:

> What higher in her society thou findst
> Attractive, human, rational, love still;
> In loving thou dost well, in passion not,
> Wherein true love consists not; love refines
> The thoughts, and heart enlarges, hath his seat
> In reason, and is judicious, is the scale
> By which to heavenly love thou mayst ascend.   (8.586–92)

The third stage of the Neoplatonic ascent intimated by Raphael in this final line is the advance testified to by Milton in the sonnet's middle lines, the progress from *philia*—the greatest love between mortals, which the recall of his marriage reminded him that his wife had then known—to his confident "trust" in the still higher love that he would share with his "saint" in the nonphysical, immaterial "sight" of heaven. The advance in love recorded in Milton's passage from animal arousal to spiritual quickening recalls Adam's summary of the archangel's teaching: love "Leads up to heaven, is both the way and guide" (8.613).[26]

Upon retracing Milton's mental actions and penetrating the accretions that had gathered between his awakening and writing the poem, one recognizes his advancement through the Neoplatonic gradations of love in the renewal of faith inspired by the agency of his *donna angelicata*. The manner whereby their transmuted bodies would be reunited remains obscure. Milton, like Adam, is resigned to accepting that the angels' mode of expressing their love, which would be that of the saved, lay beyond human knowing. To supply its faint likeness, Raphael has recourse to the figure of marital love, the happiness experienced by Adam and Eve that provokes Satan to envy at seeing the first couple as they "embracing slept," "Imparadised in one another's arms" (4.771, 506). Milton's sonnet engages the reader in his search within the dream that brought renewed "trust" that he would again know his "late espoused saint" in having "Full sight of her in heaven without restraint."

San Francisco, California

NOTES

1. Citations to *Paradise Lost* are to John Milton, *Paradise Lost,* 2nd ed., ed. Alastair Fowler (London, 1998). Citations to Milton's other poetry are to John Milton, *Complete Shorter Poems,* 2nd ed., ed. John Carey (London, 1997), where the poem beginning "Methought I saw my late espoused saint" is printed as "Sonnet XIX." Citations to Milton's prose are to *The Works of John Milton,* 18 vols., ed. Frank Allen Patterson (New York, 1931–38), hereafter cited as CM. Except where Milton's own translation is cited, biblical quotations are from the Geneva Bible: *A Facsimile of the 1560 Edition,* ed. Lloyd E. Berry (Madison, WI, 1969).

2. Anthony Low, "Milton's Last Sonnet," *MQ* 9 (1975): 80–82. Parker's argument is summarized and a bibliography of principal articles in the debate over the poem's subject is given in William Riley Parker, *Milton: A Biography,* 2nd ed., 2 vols., ed. Gordon Campbell (Oxford, 1996), 2:1045, 1247. Louis Schwartz, " 'Spot of child-bed taint': Seventeenth-Century Obstetrics in Milton's Sonnet 23 and *Paradise Lost* 8.462–78," *MQ* 27 (1993): 98–109, has noted that the father of a newborn had no role in the churching ritual and that, had Milton's first wife decided for it, she would have had her family's support. Churching is also discussed by Gerald Hammond, *Fleeting Things: English Poets and Poems 1616–1660* (Cambridge, MA, 1990), 217–18, 221–23. On the ancient purification requirement, see David R. Fabian, "Milton's 'Sonnet 23' and Leviticus XVIII.19," *Xavier University Studies* 5 (1966): 83–88.

3. Leo Spitzer, "Understanding Milton," in *Essays on English and American Literature,* ed. Anna Hatcher, 116–31 (Princeton, 1962).

4. Ibid., 126 n. 13, 125, and 124. Thomas Wheeler, "Milton's Twenty-Third Sonnet," *SP* 58 (1961): 513, sees the dream figure as "an ideal in the mind" rather than that of either wife. Milton's use of the *donna angelicata* figure is the subject of E. R. Gregory, "Milton's Protestant Sonnet Lady: Revisions in the *Donna Angelicata* Tradition," *Comparative Literature Studies* 33 (1996): 258–79.

By the Mortalist conception of the afterlife—which he terms "temporal death" and "a death like sleep, / A gentle wafting to immortal life" (*PL* 12.433 and 434–35)—Milton would seem to have thought his wife's soul dead until the Resurrection. Principal commentaries on his Mortalism include Denis Saurat, *Milton, Man and Thinker* (London, 1925), 310–22; Maurice Kelley, *This Great Argument: A Study of Milton's "De Doctrina Christiana" as a Gloss upon "Paradise Lost"* (Princeton, 1941), 32 and 153–55; and "Introduction," *The Complete Prose Works of John Milton,* 8 vols., ed. Don M. Wolfe et al. (New Haven, 1953–82), 6:91–95; George Newton Conklin, *Biblical Criticism and Heresy in Milton* (New York, 1949), 75–85; George Williamson, *Seventeenth-Century Contexts* (Chicago, 1969), 148–77; and C. A. Patrides, " 'Paradise Lost' and the Mortalist Heresy," *Notes and Queries* 4 (1957): 250–51. Norman T. Burns concludes that "mortalism plays an insignificant role in Milton's poetry and is not even hinted at before the publication of *Paradise Lost*" (*Christian Mortalism from Tyndale to Milton* [Cambridge, MA, 1972], 169). See also A. E. B. Coldiron, "Milton *in parvo*: Mortalism and Genre Transformation in Sonnet 14," *MQ* 28 (1994): 1–10.

5. Low, "Milton's Last Sonnet," 80; Wheeler, "Milton's Twenty-Third Sonnet," 511, 512, 515, 511. Low's comment was anticipated by E. A. J. Honigmann, *Milton's Sonnets* (New York, 1966), 49. Fabian, "Milton's 'Sonnet 23,' " recognizes the sexual appeal of the dream image but finds Milton exercising conscious control while dreaming: "His reluctance to share the embrace may be therefore attributed to an awareness that he must discipline his physical activity during the dream" (88). Something of this article's argument may be present in George H. McLoone, "Milton's Twenty-Third Sonnet: Love, Death, and the Mystical Body of the Church," *MQ* 24 (1990), who writes that the poem tells of Milton's response to his wife's "initiating consummation" and his conscious effort to "preserve the ego's selfish boundaries and delay redemptive, rather than merely physical, consummation." So, "the Saint's near-embrace of the speaker represents his wish for a consummation that is eschatological and ecclesiastical as well as sexual" (9, 17).

6. Thomas Stroup, "Aeneas' Vision of Creusa and Milton's Twenty-Third Sonnet," *Philological Quarterly* 39 (1960): 125–26, favoring Milton's first wife as the subject, argues the possible influence of *Aeneid* 2.792–94.

7. On Christian appropriations of the Hercules myth, see Marcel Simon, *Hercule et le Christianisme* (Paris, 1945). The same parallelism appears in *Ode on the Morning of Christ's Nativity,* 227–28; *The Passion,* 14; and *Paradise Regained* 4.563–68. On the term of silence in *Alcestis,* 1144–46, see Erna P. Trammell, "The Mute Alcestis," *Classical Journal* 37 (1941): 144–

50. The Greek sources of the myth and its reappearances in Western literature are traced in *The Oxford Guide to Classical Mythology in the Arts, 1300–1990s,* ed. Jane Davidson Reid (Oxford, 1993), 1:80–81. Milton knew the story from Euripides's drama, annotating its text in his copy of Paulus Stephanus's 1602 Geneva edition of Euripides and recommending it in *On Education* (CM 18:308 and 4:285). See also Maurice Kelley and Samuel D. Atkins, "Milton's Annotations of Euripides," *JEGP* 60 (1961): 680–87. The poem has clear parallels with the play. There Alcestis, who is recalled as the "best of wives" (*Alcestis,* 151–52, 241, 418, 1083), returns from death to instruct Admetus. The poem's first line so closely resembles lines 1066–67 of the play as to suggest a translation with the verb tense transposed into the past. "Jove's great son" in the sonnet's second line may have had its source in Hercules's terming himself a child of Zeus (1119–20). B. J. Sokol, who thinks the former Mary Powell is Milton's subject, provides valuable insights in "Euripides' *Alcestis* and the 'Saint' of Milton's Reparative Twenty-Third Sonnet," *SEL* 33 (1993):131–47.

8. *Aeneid* 6.278 and 522 follow the Greek description of Sleep as the brother of Death (Hesiod, *Theognis* 758–59 and Homer, *Iliad* 14.231). The relatedness of the two appears also at Homer, *Odyssey* 13.79–80; Cicero, *Tusculan Disputations* 1.38.92, and *De Divinatione* 1.30.63; and Ovid, *Amores* 2.9.41. In the *Convivio* 2.8.13, Dante wrote that "we constantly have direct evidence of our immortality in the prophetic perceptions we have in our dreams: they could not occur if no part of us were immortal, for, as careful reflection indicates, the source of such revelation, whether corporeal or incorporeal, must be immortal." See *The Banquet,* trans. Christopher Ryan (Saratoga, CA, 1989), 60.

9. Virgil, *Aeneid* 6.893–98; and Horace, *Odes* 3.27.41–42. See also Ross S. Kilpatrick, "The Stuff of Doors and Dreams (Vergil, *Aeneid* 6.893–98)," *Vergilius* 41 (1995): 63–70. The scholarly dispute as to the meaning of the two gates in Homer (*Odyssey* 19.562–67) is summarized by Patricia Cox Miller, *Dreams in Late Antiquity: Studies in the Imagination of a Culture* (Princeton, 1994), 15–17, 24–27.

10. Ovid, *Heroides* 19.195–96; and Horace, *Satires* 1.10.33. True dreams were thought to occur in the light sleep called *somnus* (*Aeneid* 1.353; 2.270; 3.151; 4.353, 466, 557; and 8.67), but those that appeared during the far deeper early sleep of exhaustion, *sopor,* were regarded as deceptive (*Aeneid* 3.173 and 10.642). On the distinction, see R. D. Williams's note to *Aeneid* 3.173 in *Aeneidos Liber Tertius* (Oxford, 1962).

11. *Inferno* 26.7–9, 33.26–27, 37; *Purgatorio* 9.13–19, 19.1–7, 27.91–99. On the tradition's appearance in these and other Dante texts, see Charles Speroni, "Dante's Prophetic Morning-Dreams," *Studies in Philology* 45 (1948): 50–59. Shakespeare alludes to the belief at 2 *Henry VI* 1.2.24, and Jonson ends *Love Restored* by writing that "all the morning dreames are true" and refers to the belief with evident seriousness in his correspondence. See *Ben Jonson,* 11 vols., ed. C. H. Herford and Percy and Evelyn Simpson (Oxford, 1925–52), 7:385, 10:537.

12. Manfred Weidhorn, *Dreams in Seventeenth-Century English Literature* (The Hague, 1970), 132–33, notes that, although he was often skeptical of others' reports of dreams, Milton—besides telling in *Paradise Lost* 3.29–32, 7.28–30, and 9.21–24, 47 of the inspiration he received at night and "when morn / Purples the east"—describes his dreams as a poetic resource in the Fifth Elegy, 10–20.

13. John J. Colaccio, "'A Death Like Sleep': The Christology of Milton's Twenty-Third Sonnet," in *Milton Studies,* vol. 6, ed. James D. Simmonds (Pittsburgh, 1974), 190, 189–90; and John C. Ulreich, "Typological Symbolism in Milton's Sonnet XXIII," *MQ* 8 (1974): 9–10.

14. This is not to suggest that Milton describes his wife in a white wedding gown, a custom dating only from the nineteenth century. Elizabeth K. Hill proposes that the wife's shade wears a burial shroud in "A Dream in the Long Valley: Some Psychological Aspects of Milton's Last Sonnet," *Greyfriar* 26 (1985): 3–13.

15. "Delight" appears three times in the twenty-five lines that soon follow (*PL* 8.576–600), in which Eve is described as the object of Adam's desire.

16. "My fancied sight" echoes "the cell / Of fancy my internal sight," the *cellula phantastica* that as "mimic fancy / Wakes to imitate" reason-governed thought (*PL* 8.460–61, 5.110–11).

17. Its sense at *Paradise Lost* 8.626 is designedly ambiguous.

18. Fenton's praise is quoted in *The Poetical Works of John Milton,* ed. Helen Darbishire (Oxford, 1952–55), 2:327.

19. Weidhorn, "Dreams and Guilt," *Harvard Theological Review* 58 (1965): 69–90; Steven F. Kruger, *Dreaming in the Middle Ages* (Cambridge, 1992), 44, 77. Euripides's Admetus pledges to order an image of his wife with the purpose of stirring memories of past marital happiness:

> Your form, in a replica fashioned by the skilled hands of craftsmen, will lie stretched out on the bed. On this I shall throw myself and wrapping my arms around it, while calling out your name, I shall seem to myself to gather my dear wife into my embrace, although I do not in fact hold her. This is, I recognize, a cold pleasure, but in this way I shall ease the grief of my soul. In my dreams you shall appear to please me; it is sweet to see in the night those who are dear, even if only briefly. (*Alcestis,* 348–56)

The translation is of the text of *Alcestis,* ed. A. M. Dale (Oxford, 1966).

20. On the operation of dreams, see also *Paradise Lost* 4.799–809, 5.100–113, 8.292–95, 8.460–63. This moral psychology figures also in 8.607–11 and in *Samson Agonistes* 1368: "Where the heart joins not, outward acts defile not." In his note to this line, Carey cites Aristotle, *Ethics* 3.1.1: "It is only voluntary actions for which praise and blame are given; those that are involuntary are condoned, and sometimes even pitied."

21. Schwartz, " 'Spot of child-bed taint,' " who thinks the first wife is the poem's subject, notes the likely guilt feelings (99–103).

22. The quoted phrase is from Cleanth Brooks and John Edward Hardy, *Poems of Mr. John Milton: The 1645 Edition with Essays in Analysis* (New York, 1951), 112.

23. Harris P. Fletcher, *The Complete Poetical Works of John Milton* (Boston, 1941), 115, read the lines as referring to a recent attempt at some verses on his mother's death. David Daiches, *Milton* (London, 1959), found Milton telling that "he has already begun his career as a poet because this is not the first time he has plucked the unripe berries" (76). For Edward W. Tayler, "*Lycidas* Yet Once More," *Huntington Library Quarterly* 41 (1978), "the words 'yet once more' must assuredly point toward previous poetic acts: *Comus* perhaps? the Nativity Ode? or even the 'Fair Infant Dying of a Cough'?" (105). Parker, *Milton,* thought the opening acknowledged Milton's "yet incomplete preparation. . . . [H]e had meant to write no more poetry until his muse had matured" (1:158).

24. Milton proceeds to clarify his sense of the Pauline term: " 'Trust' or 'confidence' seems rather to be a particular effect or degree of faith, or a firm hope, than faith itself, inasmuch as it is said to come 'by faith:' or perhaps by 'faith' in this passage we are to understand the doctrine on which this confidence is founded" (CM 15:397).

25. On the representations of sexual intercourse among angels and immortal human souls in *Paradise Lost,* see Hammond, *Fleeting Things,* 217–18, and Clive Hart and Kay Gilliland Stevenson, *Heaven and the Flesh: Images of Desire from the Renaissance to the Rococo* (Cambridge, 1995), 92–108.

26. On the Neoplatonic ladder of love, see Erwin Panofsky, *Studies in Iconology: Humanistic Themes in the Art of the Renaissance* (New York, 1962), 129–69, esp. 136–41. On its appearance in *Paradise Lost,* see Fowler's notes to 8.579–91.

MILTON'S TOAD, OR SATAN'S DREAM

Diana Treviño Benet

O NE OF THE MOST intriguing parts of *Paradise Lost* is the satanic dream, with its prologue and aftermath, in Books Four and Five. The section of the epic that begins with Satan "squat like a toad" at Eve's ear and concludes with Adam's comforting words to her raises trivial and substantial questions, but commentary has focused on one: what does the dream reveal about Eve's moral condition prior to her meeting with the serpent in Book Nine?[1] Essentially, there are two lines of thought on this issue, which has a long history. More than fifty years ago, E. M. W. Tillyard and, following him, Millicent Bell and others expressed the view that the dream shows Eve to be fallen or partly fallen. As Bell put it, "the rehearsal of Eve's dream already moves her across the border" into sin.[2] Other scholars, including Wayne Shumaker, John Diekhoff, Diane McColley, and Barbara Lewalski—with whom I agree—argue that Eve is sinless until she eats the forbidden fruit.[3]

The first reading, which also has more recent adherents, is characterized by the assumption that Eve is the author of the dream; from this premise, the conclusion follows that she is culpable, though without the agency of consciousness or will. Eve's moral status is crucial, but it cannot be determined by looking only at the dream proper and assuming that she is its source. Doing so scants Satan's important role in the process and ignores his intention as he squats by her ear. To clarify the rationale and significance of the dream sequence, I shall approach it by introducing two contemporary contexts with a common perception of Satan. Two literary dreams, in Richard Crashaw's translation of Marino's *Sospetto d'Herode* (1646) and in Abraham Cowley's *Davideis* (1656), and the animal-spirits theory of the era depict a Satan with awesome power over the individual. Satan's agents in these poems, using snakes, literally transfuse evil into sleeping men, a bit of dramatic business that might seem to be a simple metaphor for radical moral transformation. But the animal spirits theory elaborated by the contemporary scientific community promulgated satanic infection as a description of reality.

In the 1640s and 1650s, spurred by such discoveries as the circulation of the blood and the structure of the brain, scholars broadened the scope of their inquiries into areas that were, as yet, beyond their ken. In the culture of having more questions than answers or the means to acquire them, animal spirits became the explanation for many physical, intellectual, and spiritual phenomena. In this environment, the snakes of *Sospetto* and *Davideis* seemed to figure a physiological cause for moral behavior. Foregrounding the animal spirits that most readers ignore and referring to poems that define the spirits' significance in the cultural discourse of the seventeenth century will illuminate the dream sequence in *Paradise Lost*. Broadening our frame of reference to include the scene's literary and metaphysical contexts, we can understand it in a different way: By means of the entire dream episode, Milton seeks to establish Eve's innocence definitively in order to establish Satan's limitations, which are the limitations of the determinist view so popular among Milton's contemporaries, so repugnant to the libertarian author.

THE ANIMAL SPIRITS

A representative statement of the view that Eve's dream reveals her fallen condition is Manfred Weidhorn's, published in 1970:

> From a modern point of view . . . [the dream] reflects some of [Eve's] inner promptings. Prohibitions of any kind beget a restiveness and a desire to break down constraint, a desire sometimes fulfilled in dreams. . . . Hence this vision, by rehearsing Eve's thoughts and insidiously extending them, functions as a wish fulfillment. The angel who eats the fruit in the dream does what she herself wants to do. Her psyche dares at first to represent the forbidden action only as undertaken by someone else. It then musters the courage to exhibit Eve herself eating the fruit in the dream.[4]

More recently, Hugh MacCallum declares that Eve's "anxiety dream" reveals her "attraction (difficult to admit)" toward the forbidden act.[5] Her dream acknowledges desires and permits actions that consciousness cannot accept. An Eve whose dream reveals her fallen condition means that the toad Milton puts at her head in Book Four is, to all intents and purposes, unreal, part of a complex metaphor.

It may be difficult for modern readers not to identify the content of Eve's dream with her unconscious mind. Paradisal dreams convey messages to her and Adam from another world, a sphere of signification beyond their control. This dynamic is immensely suggestive for readers who assume a stratified model of consciousness and think of dream as self-communication that "rises" from the deeper to the conscious level, but is otherwise elusive. However, the elision of Eve's will by readers postulating a morally decisive level of mind that lies beneath her awareness is inconsistent with Milton's thought. Reason is fundamental to his theology. Looking to spirits theory and the contemporary poems that inform Milton's treatment of Eve's dream will enable us to understand it in a way that preserves her moral integrity and her innocence until she actually eats the forbidden fruit.

Barbara Lewalski and Stephen Fallon have documented Milton's knowledge of the interests of the nascent scientific communities at Cambridge and Oxford, with Fallon describing in detail the author's particular connection to the Cambridge Platonists. Lewalski shows that Milton was in touch, too, with Richard Jones, his former pupil, and his friend, Henry Oldenburg (Jones's tutor), during the time when these colleagues were pursuing studies at Oxford. Though the Oxford circle consisted mainly of royalists of the Church of England, Robert Boyle, an important member of the scientific group, was the brother of Lady Katherine Jones, Viscountess Ranelagh, Milton's good friend. At both Cambridge and Oxford there was great interest in animal spirits.[6]

Animal spirits were fluids thought to circulate around the nervous system. Galen had theorized that they originated in food. The stomach processed food into "chyle," which then went into the liver to be turned into blood containing an essential substance that was called "natural spirit." Some of the blood passed into the heart, which purified the natural spirits into vital spirits. This substance in turn flowed into the brain, where it was refined again to become the animal spirits.[7] The spirits might have been a quaint but ephemeral aspect of humoral theory, but the long-standing view that they were viable physiological entities was ensured by Galen's belief that the head (or brain) was the seat of the rational soul.

From antiquity, then, animal spirits were entwined with philosophical thinking on the soul. Later Christian thinkers theorized the *immortal* soul as the seat of reason and conscience, and by the mid-seventeenth century, Pierre Gassendi (1592–1655), a French philosopher, had proposed that the brain was its locus.[8] Thus, soul and animal spirits were intimately, physiologically, bound. During the seventeenth century, the spirits were ubiquitous as "scientific" explanations for everything imaginable. Though William Harvey, who had discovered the circulation of the blood in 1624, denied that spirits existed and declared that blood was the vital substance of the body, few agreed with him. To no avail, he complained later that the spirits did nothing but "serve as a common subterfuge of ignorance. For smatterers, not knowing what causes to assign to a happening, promptly say the spirits are responsible (thus introducing them upon every occasion). And like bad poets, they call this deus ex machina on to their stage to explain their plot and catastrophe." When Robert Burton wrote that the animal spirits were "a common tie or medium between the body and the soul," he was expressing the popularly held view.[9] The spirits were thought to carry the messages between body and soul that enabled sensation, movement, and (most significantly for our pur-

pose) thought. In other words, they were seen as the substance, the physiological "place," where the spiritual and the physical realms met and mingled.

Early in the seventeenth century, people believed that Satan could pen-
etrate the human body and invade the animal spirits because he was a spirit,
too. William Perkins, for instance, reminded readers in 1631 that "the Devill
is by nature a spirit, and therefore of great understanding, knowledge, and
capacity in all naturall things." Because of his "spirituall nature," Perkins
declared, Satan can "convey himself into the substance of the creature . . .
and being in the creature . . . he can worke therein." As the century and the
study of physiology progressed together, this spiritual observation gave way to
a revised formulation that combined physiology with religion. John Sutton
remarks that animal spirits, as "bearers of information between natural and
supernatural, visible and invisible, body and soul," understandably focused
early modern "concerns about the integrity of the message" because people
thought that "distemper or jarring in the spirits could pervert commands of
the will." The words of Milton's contemporary Anne Conway convey the
significance of potentially distempered or diseased spirits: "by these Spirits
which come from the Blood, we see, hear, smell, taste, feel, and think, yea
meditate, love, hate, and do all things whatsoever we do." She might have
said, also, that by these spirits we obey or disobey.[10]

To a reader today, the notion of Satan corrupting someone by penetrating her body and poisoning her bodily fluids is bound to seem fantastic, like a
weird, literal description of demonic possession. Indeed, possession and infected animal spirits both attribute to evil spirits the physiological ability to
control a person's behavior, rendering it involuntary; consequently, we might
conclude that hypothesizing corrupted animal spirits was an attempt at the-
orizing possession scientifically. But possession was relatively rare and usually
involved conspicuous physical symptoms such as convulsions or fainting;
satanic invasion of the spirits, on the other hand, seemed to Milton's contemporaries to be a fairly common and unobtrusive occurrence. Robert Burton
describes how Satan injects his poison into ordinary people: "[T]he devil is
still ready to corrupt, trouble, and divert our souls . . . he is a spirit, and hath
means and opportunity to mingle himself with our spirits, and sometimes
more slyly, sometimes more abruptly and openly, to suggest such devilish
thoughts into our hearts."[11] Animal spirits thus poisoned could be "unwel-
come bodily intrusions into the moral self": the possibility of harboring
tainted spirits within meant that it was impossible to know "whether current
cognitions and actions were caused by reason or by madness . . . by the Devil
or the [unpolluted] will."[12] As a "materialist monist" (in Fallon's phrase) who
thought of "spirit and matter as manifestations, differing in degree and not
qualitatively, of the one corporeal substance,"[13] Milton could not ignore the

popular notion that Satan could corrupt the rational soul by physical intervention. What was at stake was nothing less than the freedom of the will.

LITERARY DREAMS AND SNAKES

Milton probably located the first encounter of Satan and Eve in dream because divinely inspired dreams were conventional in ancient epic and, as
Josephine Roberts points out, because "the idea of Eve's temptation through
dreams had a long tradition in England extending back to the Anglo-Saxon
poem *Genesis B* (lines 564–67; 600–16)."[14] But the dream sequence in *Paradise Lost* also refers to two contemporary poems. The combination of satanic
intervention (in animal form), dream, and potential moral impact on the
dreamer was known to Milton from Richard Crashaw's translation of Marino's *Sospetto d'Herode* and Cowley's *Davideis*.

A difference between those poems and *Paradise Lost* involves the rep-
tile. In the poems of Crashaw and Cowley, a snake inspires poison into the
sleeper. Milton's Satan, obviously, cannot take the form of a snake before his
successful temptation of Eve. Since, however, toads were then thought to be
venomous, Milton creates a toad that attempts to inject venom into Eve as a
way of pointing to the satanic episodes fashioned by literary predecessors.
But the toad's appearance in *Paradise Lost* is not a simple tribute to its poetic
precursors. A look at the earlier poems will show why Milton objected to
their presentation of Satan.

In Crashaw's *Sospetto*, Vengeance, Satan's emissary and one of the
Furies, takes the form of Joseph, Herod's brother. In the dream she gives
Herod, she tells him of a newborn who is proclaimed the new Hebrew king,
Herod's successor. After she urges Herod to take action against the "He-
brewes royall stemme,"

> [H]er richest snake, which to her wrist
> For a beseeming bracelet shee had ty'd
> (A speciall Worme it was as ever kist
> The foamy lips of *Cerberus*) shee apply'd
> To the Kings Heart, the Snake no sooner hist,
> But vertue heard it, and away shee hy'd,
> Dire flames diffuse themselves through every veine,
> This done, Home to her Hell shee hy'd amaine.[15]

Crashaw's translation informs the reader that, long before, Herod had heard
"Prophecies" that sowed "doubts in his deep breast," fears that were revived
by the recent advent of "tributary Kings." The present dream has merely
"Shewed him his feares" (63). Even so, the dream is externally caused, and

the lines above identify the snake as the causal agent: it hisses and virtue flees. Flames of sin spread from Herod's heart, coursing through "every veine." He wakes in a "Sweat-bedewed Bed" and his "blood-swolne breast" "boyles" (60, 62); he rises "In rage, *My armes, give me my armes,* hee cryes" (60). Though the poison (of the "worme of jealous envy and unrest," 62) could be said to concretize the feelings the dream has stirred, the poem specifies that Satan is the source of the envy and the sin it inspires.

In Cowley's *Davideis*, Satan's servant, Envy, comes to Saul in a dream in the shape of Father Benjamin. She first tells the sleeping Saul to eliminate David because "Israel loves" the youth while Saul bears "but the *Name,* and empty *Title*" (1.269–70):

> With that she takes
> One of her worst, her best beloved *Snakes,*
> Softly, dear *Worm,* soft and unseen (said she)
> Into his bosom steal, and in it be
> My *Vice-Roy*. At that word she took her flight
> And her loose shape dissolv'ed into the *Night*.[16]

This dream is also externally caused. And once again, the snake's venom is the causal agent in the dreamer's behavior:

> The infected *King* leapt from his bed amaz'ed,
> Scarce knew himself at first, but round him gaz'd,
> And started back at piec'ed-up shapes, which feare
> And his distracted Fancy painted there.
>
> All thou hast said, *Great Vision*, is so true,
> That all which thou command'st, and more I'll do:
> Kill him? Yes *mighty Ghost*, the wretch shall dy,
> Though every *Star* in heav'en should it deny. (1.311–14, 327–30)

Saul believes he has been counseled in the dream by Benjamin, the patriarch of his tribe. Like Crashaw's Herod, Saul has physical symptoms of poisoning. In addition to the fantastic "shapes" he sees, his hair stands up on end and "Show'ers of cold sweat roll'd trembling down apace" (1.315–16). The venom, which concretizes the feelings Saul's dream created, is a metaphor for the envy that transforms him into a would-be murderer. But, again, the poem shows Satan (through his agent) to be the external cause of sin. Saul wakes ready to act as his poisoned heart dictates *because* he is "infected" by the snake from hell.

The dream-poison scenes fill in the space usually occupied in narrative by motivation.[17] Crashaw and Cowley supply a few details that might account for ordinary motive, but the sequence of events minimizes their importance;

both poems show an individual falling asleep in relative calm and innocence, experiencing a satanically produced dream, being poisoned, and waking infected, a sinner eager to act on murderous intentions. Though, as I suggested above, the poison could be a metaphor for wicked feelings attributable to Herod and Saul, the dream first creates those feelings, and then the poison, infused, is shown to take effect. In each case, rather than simply identifying the poison with the dreamer's hostile emotion, the poem suggests that the dream and venom, introduced by an external agent, cause the waking sin.

What is blurred or lost in the figurative language of these two accounts is the role of will in moral choice. If the snake infuses venom-sin into Herod and Saul, bypassing their rational minds, they can bear no moral responsibility. As the Father states in *Paradise Lost,* individuals merit neither blame nor praise, "Where only what they needs must do, appeard, / Not what they would" (3.105–6). The snake-poison metaphor, used to such dramatic effect by Cowley and Marino and Crashaw, came to acquire great significance from and in its cultural milieu. The emergent scientific community transmuted metaphor into a supposed reflection of reality; during the time Milton was composing *Paradise Lost,* as we have seen, current theories held that Satan could cause sin by entering the human body through the animal spirits.

MILTON'S TOAD

In *Paradise Lost* all creatures have the freedom to choose their moral direction. The epic includes another nocturnal temptation besides Eve's that begins with Satan speaking to a sleeper. There is no dream, though Milton uses diction reminiscent of Satan's interference with Herod and Saul: "So spake the false Archangel, and *infused* / Bad *influence into the unwary breast* / Of his associate" (5.694–96; emphasis added). But Milton specifies that Satan awakens Beelzebub (5.671–72), so diction notwithstanding, the text indicates that Beelzebub's reason is operative. Satan only suggests that the Father's "new Laws" may elicit new responses from his servants; he goes no further than warning that it is "not safe" (5.683) to say more. Satan does not try or need to persuade his confederate. Beelzebub himself generates the "new mind" that opposes the decree of heaven. His silence means that the moral "action" all takes place within him; the possibility of sin is hinted at by Satan, and the hint is seized upon by a will that accepts and embodies it— Beelzebub's will.

Bypassing the will or reason of people is a power that is accorded to God in *Samson Agonistes.* The Semichorus describes how God made the Philistines bring about their own death:

Among them he a spirit of phrenzie sent
Who hurt thir minds,
And urg'd them on with mad desire
To call in hast for their destroyer.   (1675–78)

The Philistines are unaware that calling for Samson summons their own destruction because their wills have been taken over, possessed by the heaven-sent spirit. Like Herod in *Sospetto* and Saul in *Davideis*, the Philistines' thoughts and actions are moved by an external force of which they are not aware. However, it is one thing for God to "hurt the minds" of the idolatrous Philistines with a supernaturally induced compulsion; it is quite another to attribute to Satan the power to introduce evil into a passive mind, override reason, and thereby engender sin.

But that is exactly what some of Milton's readers do. Harinder Singh Marjara, who recognizes the agency of the fallen angel, is also aware of the contemporary thinking about animal spirits. Like the scholars quoted above, however, Marjara sees Eve as "partly fallen before she actually ate the forbidden fruit" because, like them, he assumes that Eve is (at least in part) the source of her own dream: "Milton enables the reader to have a more comprehensive awareness of Eve's dream as caused by her own mind aided by Satan's evil influence."[18] The anachronistic psychologized model of dream (and mind) that leads Marjara and others to see Eve as wholly or partly fallen, along with his awareness of seventeenth-century beliefs about Satan's power over animal spirits, prompts him to describe a doubly vulnerable Eve. She is partly fallen because of her own unconscious desires and partly fallen because of Satan's physiological assault. In Marjara's reading, in other words, the archfiend succeeds in polluting Eve's animal spirits: Satan's "demonic influence does leave its spot behind, and Eve's animal spirits do take the taint" so that her "capacity to use reason is surely hampered." Though Marjara says the tainting does not make Eve's "behaviour *totally* deterministic"[19] (emphasis added), his interpretation means that she is not wholly free to choose her own course. Similarly, Neil Forsyth impugns Eve but also associates Satan with decisive influence: "Although hypnotists are said not to be able to make subjects do what they deeply abhor, the suggestions they can sow in the mind are often thought of as irresistible."[20] In these views, whether Eve's spirits are tainted or her mind receives irresistible suggestions, her reason has been hobbled.

Among scholars who think Eve is morally compromised in Book Four, Marjara is unusual in acknowledging a problem with this interpretation. He declares that seeing Eve in this light means that Adam is "wrong" when he tells her that evil leaves "No spot or blame behind" in the mind that does not accept it (5.117–19).[21] Marjara might have added that the epic narrator is also wrong, twice, in asserting that Eve is "innocent" when, following the dream, she prays with Adam (5.209), and that she is "yet sinless" when she goes off to work alone (9.569).

Reading the dream sequence more carefully and in the cultural contexts introduced above preserves the integrity of Eve's volition and, consequently, of her moral agency. By the combination of the toad, the dream, and the poison, Milton recalls the poetic treatments of Crashaw and Cowley. The dream scene in *Paradise Lost* is linked to *Sospetto* and *Davideis* by a number of similarities: the demonic poisonous animal, the voice that seems to waken the sleeper, the dream in which the evil spirit assumes a familiar guise, and the spirit's incitement of the dreamer to sin. The dreamer is silent and passive in all the accounts. There is a significant difference: neither Crashaw nor Cowley refers to the "animal spirits" in connection with the snake's venom. By using that technical phrase to describe Eve's bodily fluids, Milton deliberately refers to current theories about satanic invasion. He does so in order to deny absolutely the awesome power that they, along with the poetic accounts, attribute to Satan.

The dream sequence in *Paradise Lost* begins when the angels, alerted by Uriel, search for Satan in the garden and find him

> Squat like a Toad, close at the eare of Eve,
> Assaying by his Devilish art to reach
> The Organs of her Fancie, and with them forge
> Illusions as he list, Phantasms and Dreams,
> Or if, inspiring venom, he might taint
> Th'animal Spirits that from pure blood arise.   (4.800–805)

Milton does not question Satan's power over dreams; his "Wilde work" through "Fansie" (5.110–12) troubles even Christ in *Paradise Regained*: "at his head / The Tempter watch'd, and soon with ugly dreams / Disturb'd his sleep" (4.407–9). As for the demonic ability to dictate specific dreams, something that Crashaw and Cowley assume, Daniel Defoe observes in *The Political History of the Devil* (1726) that Milton's representation of how Satan "brought [Eve] to dream whatever he put into her Thoughts, by whispering to her vocally when she was asleep" is credible; "even now," he declares, whispering to a person in a deep sleep will produce dreams "of what you say."[22]

As satanic agents are the source of dreams that transform Crashaw's Herod and Cowley's Saul, Satan is the origin and producer of the dream Eve experiences and later describes to Adam. When Ithuriel's spear pokes the toad (4.810–11, 5.90–92), the dream's abrupt end points to its external source, as does Eve's immediate reaction. For the pre-Freudian perspective inflected with spirits theory, we turn again to Defoe:

> [Eve] wak'd with her Head fill'd with pleasing Ideas, and as some will have it, unlawful Desires; such, as to be sure she had never entertain'd before, fatally infused in her Dream, and suggested to her waking Soul, when the Organ Ear which convey'd them was doz'd and insensible; strange Fate of sleeping in *Paradise!* that we seem to have Notice but of two Sleeps there, and that in one a *Woman* should go out of him, and in the other, the *Devil* should come into her."[23]

Defoe's comment expresses the perspectives of Crashaw and Cowley and of spirit theorists: Satan "infused" particular ideas into the sleeping Eve, and "some" believe that she was infected thereby, the evidence of which is that she awakened with "unlawful Desires." Defoe is noncommittal about the tainting of Eve, though he does not doubt that Satan is responsible for the content of the dream: the ideas therein were "such, as to be sure [Eve] had never entertain'd before."

Satan, succeeds, then, in imparting the dream into the mind of the "insensible" Eve, but that is not all he attempts. The lines from Book Four quoted above specify that Satan hopes to accomplish one *or* both of two different possibilities. Besides creating dreams, the toad-Apostate is "Assaying," trying to inspire venom into the sleeper, just as the snakes did in *Sospetto* and *Davideis*. The text indicates Satan's uncertainty about his ability to poison Eve:

> Or if, inspiring venom, he might taint
> Th'animal Spirits that from pure blood arise
> Like gentle breaths from Rivers pure, thence raise
> At least distempered, discontented thoughts,
> Vaine hopes, vaine aimes, inordinate desires
> Blown up with high conceits ingendring pride.   (4.804–9)

Most commentators on Eve's dream, as I have said, ignore the toad, but the contexts we have adduced inform us that when Milton refers to Satan's effort to "taint" Eve's animal spirits there is nothing figurative about the possibility. As Dan Collins puts it, Satan intends "to inspire venom into [Eve's] mind, causing a distemper that could not be instantly cleared by an act of reason."[24] In the context of seventeenth-century discourse, Satan tries to corrupt the sleeping Eve. His hope is that her contaminated animal spirits will then give rise to thoughts, hopes, aims, and desires tending toward disorder, all of which, when animated by fanciful ideas, will create ("ingender") pride— Satan's own sin—in Eve. This paraphrase of the lines that elaborate on the desired action of the venom underlines their essential similarity to the descriptions of Crashaw and Cowley: the passivity of the victim who is physically tainted with sin. What Satan tries to do is to father (to "ingender") his sin in the sleeping woman by a rape upon her will.

Satan's power over reason or moral choice is exactly what Milton is not willing to concede to his contemporaries. He refers to the possibility of tainted animal spirits in order to refute the idea that Satan could hurt Eve's mind through an infusion of evil, circumventing reason and will by poisoning her bodily fluids. Details of the epic deny that Satan infects the unconscious woman. She tells Adam she dreamed of "offence and trouble" during the "irksome night" (5.34–35), and describes feeling with "damp horror chil'd" (5.65) when she saw the "angel" eat the forbidden fruit. In its conclusion, the dream is not pleasurable, either. Interrupted, it ends in confusion, and Eve, abandoned by her angelic guide, suddenly, in midflight, falls to the earth. As she describes it to Adam, she sheds a tear at the idea that she might have "offended" (5.135) merely by dreaming. Eve's response is utterly different from the reactions of the infected Herod and Saul to their satanic dreams. The text conveys no hint of Eve's attraction to or agreement with Satan's dream. Accordingly, Adam's comment that "Evil into the mind of God or Man / May come and go, so unapprov'd, and leave / No spot or blame behind" (5.117–19) declares her innocence, and his judgment is confirmed by the epic narrator with the statement, a few lines later, that "all was cleard" (5.136) by Adam's consoling words, with "cleard" meaning " 'to clear from the imputation of guilt, to free from accusation' (*OED* III.19)."[25]

According to seventeenth-century spirit theory, sin could spring from a physiological cause, unrecognized and involuntary, creating a "philosophico-moral difficulty" because "diabolical action on animal spirits works in exactly the same way as the action of the rational soul on the spirits is meant to in ordinary decision-making."[26] Milton's contemporaries would have seen Satan's effort to taint Eve's bodily fluids as a genuine threat. But at least some of them, if Robert Burton is any indication, would have agreed with the thinking of Adam and the poet:

The devil commonly suggests things opposite to nature, opposite to God and His Word, impious, absurd, such as a man would never of himself, or could not conceive, they strike terror and horror into the parties' own hearts. . . . such blasphemous, impious, unclean thoughts . . . proceed not from him, but from distempered humours, black fumes which offend his brain. . . . [They are] the devil's sins . . . which thou dost abhor, and didst never give consent to . . . yet [these sins] have not proceeded from a confirmed will in thee, but are of that nature which thou dost afterwards reject and abhor . . . as Satan labours to suggest, so must we strive not to give consent, and it will be sufficient.[27]

The notion that Satan could infect the unconscious individual with sin runs counter to the linchpin of Milton's moral philosophy, and he fashioned the dream episode in Books Four and Five to deny Satan's power to curtail the freedom of the will. Burton is as unwilling as Milton that Satan should be granted the power to pollute the innocent mind without its consent. The dream Eve describes in Book Five of *Paradise Lost* does not proceed from anything within herself; it takes its nature and particulars from its creator, bodying forth not Eve's fault but Satan's sin.

In spite of our efforts to read *Paradise Lost* according to the historical and theological perspectives that it assumes or articulates, we are occasionally aware that a modern or secular paradigm seems to account more persuasively for some aspect of plot, character, or motivation. Eve's dream seems to invite such an ahistorical approach: it is as if, somehow, Milton had composed a modern structure of interiority, motivation, and cause and effect that flows alongside the epic's theological framework. Knowing where the plot is going, we tend to see the dream as a sign that Eve is already moving, inescapably, toward the moment when she will eat the apple. Our assumptions about dreams make this reading seem natural, even commonsensical. But the obvious problem lies in the fact that the historical and the modern perspectives produce opposing interpretations whereby Eve is innocent or culpable.

Milton worked during a liminal period when science was starting to supersede theology as the primary frame of reference. As many scholars of varying education and abilities tried to formulate explanations for the workings of the mind and the body, and for the relationship between them, the animal spirits were called into service to account for every kind of phenomenon. Animal spirits that could be tainted, dreams that could be shaped—the world around the poet seemed to be constructing, willy-nilly, individuals powerless to determine their own moral character, at the mercy of Satan or other undetectable or unrecognized factors. These ideas were congruent with the indistinct but developing sense that there were forces underlying thought and action that were unknown and ungovernable, and that physiology played a significant role in the processes. It is not too much to say that spirit theory was an early expression of the concepts of the unconscious and of the biological contribution to behavior. It is not hard, either, to imagine why such ideas might have had a general appeal. They were a "new" explanation for the human propensity to sin. As such, they may have provided relief from the Calvinist rigors of the earlier seventeenth century, serving as a way to account, without guilt, for transgressive thought or action. But the idea of satanic invasion of the animal spirits is simply a metaphysically embellished determinism, and finally people need to believe in their own causal agency.

As time went on, the emphasis on vulnerable animal spirits gave way to the idea that the individual could and should endeavor to control the spirits.

But this development occurred in the late seventeenth and early eighteenth centuries;[28] before that elaboration of spirit theory, Milton wrote as he did about Eve's dream to respond to contemporary representations of Satan's power. These descriptions carried significant cultural weight because they followed upon religious teaching, agreed in the power they attributed to Satan, and issued from both poetic and scientific sources. Whatever Crashaw and Cowley meant, their poems seem to echo the thinking of the scientific establishment about morally vulnerable spirits. The poetic images they create seem to describe the very process by which Satan was thought to contaminate the passive individual with sin. Milton felt compelled to correct the error. *Paradise Lost* directly addresses readers who attribute too much power to Satan: "Happiness [is] in [man's] power left free to will / Left to his own free Will" (5.235–36). But it also addresses those who attribute too little power to the apostate. Satan is not, in the poem, a metaphor for Eve's own wayward desires or for any innate weakness—he is real. For the parameters of the danger he poses, both seventeenth-century and modern readers are referred to the description of the toad assaying whether "he might taint / Th'animal Spirits" (4.804–5). Though the apostate is a real threat, his venom, without the addition of conscious choice, is powerless to contaminate the passive Eve. In *Paradise Lost*, Milton challenged popular theories about the animal spirits in order to vindicate the complete freedom of all people to be "Authors to themselves in all / Both what they judge and what they choose" (3.122–23).

University of North Texas

NOTES

I would like to thank Judith Herz for helpful suggestions on an earlier version of this essay.

1. Quotations from *Paradise Lost, Paradise Regained*, and *Samson Agonistes* are from *The Riverside Milton*, ed. Roy Flannagan (Boston, 1998). Subsequent quotations are cited by book and line number in the text.

2. E. M. W. Tillyard, *Studies in Milton* (London, 1951), 12; Millicent Bell, "The Fallacy of the Fall in *Paradise Lost*," *PMLA* 68 (1953): 867. Others who believe that Eve is fallen or half-fallen include Northrop Frye, *The Return of Eden: Five Essays on Milton's Epics* (Toronto, 1965), 75; C. A. Patrides, *Milton and the Christian Tradition* (Oxford, 1966), 106; and Fredson Bowers, "Adam, Eve, and the Fall in *Paradise Lost*," *PMLA* 84 (1969): 269.

3. Wayne Shumaker, "The Fallacy of the Fall in *Paradise Lost*," *PMLA* 70 (1955): 1185–87, 1195–1202; John S. Diekhoff, "Eve's Dream and the Paradox of Fallible Perfection," *MQ* 4 (1970): 6; Diane K. McColley, *Milton's Eve* (Urbana, IL, 1983), 98–104; Barbara K. Lewalski,

"Innocence and Experience in Milton's 'Eden,' " in *New Essays on "Paradise Lost,"* ed. Thomas Kranidas (Berkeley and Los Angeles, 1969), 102–3. Other scholars who argue that Eve is innocent include H. V. S. Ogden, "The Crisis of *Paradise Lost* Reconsidered," *Philological Quarterly* 36 (1957): 3; Irene Samuel, "*Purgatorio* and the Dream of Eve," *JEGP* 63 (1964): 449; Stanley Fish, *Surprised by Sin: The Reader in "Paradise Lost"* (New York, 1967), 226; Dan Collins, "The Buoyant Mind in Milton's Eden," in *Milton Studies* 5, ed. James D. Simmonds (Pittsburgh, 1973), 236; and most recently, Kristin Pruitt, *Gender and the Power of Relationship: "United as one Individual Soul" in "Paradise Lost"* (Pittsburgh, 2003), 101.

4. Manfred Weidhorn, *Dreams in Seventeenth-Century English Literature* (The Hague, 1970), 149. Weidhorn's Freudian view that the dream shows Eve to be half-fallen is open about the psychological assumptions that some critics do not acknowledge or examine. A recent exception is Regina Schwartz, "The Toad at Eve's Ear: From Identification to Identity," in *Literary Milton: Text, Pretext, Context,* ed. Diana Treviño Benet and Michael Lieb, 1–21 (Pittsburgh, 1994).

5. Hugh MacCallum, *Milton and the Sons of God: The Divine Image in Milton's Epic Poetry* (Toronto, 1986), 139.

6. Stephen Fallon, *Milton among the Philosophers: Poetry and Materialism in Seventeenth-Century England* (Ithaca, NY, 1991), 50; Barbara K. Lewalski, *The Life of John Milton: A Critical Biography* (Oxford, 2000), 336–37. The history of the Oxford Circle and Robert Boyle's standing in it are detailed in Carl Zimmer, *Soul Made Flesh: The Discovery of the Brain—And How It Changed the World* (New York, 2004). For Fallon's discussion of Henry More and the animal spirits, see *Philosophers,* 72–74. Zimmer writes about interest in the spirits at Oxford (152–54).

7. Early spirit theory is summarized in Zimmer, *Soul Made Flesh,* 11–15.

8. Ibid., 29–30.

9. Harvey is quoted in ibid., 69. Robert Burton, *The Anatomy of Melancholy* (1658), ed. Holbrook Jackson (New York, 2001), 1.1, 148.

10. William Perkins, *A Discourse of the Damned Art of Witchcraft,* in *The Workes of that famous and worthy minister of Christ in the Universitie of Cambridge, Mr. William Perkins* (London, 1631), 610, 611; John Sutton, *Philosophy and Memory Traces: Descartes to Connectionism* (Cambridge, 1998), 37–38; Conway is quoted in Fallon, *Philosophers,* 121.

11. Burton, *Anatomy,* 3:417.

12. Sutton, *Philosophy and Memory Traces,* 198, 202–3.

13. Fallon, *Philosophers,* 102.

14. Josephine A. Roberts, "Diabolic Dreamscape in Lanyer and Milton," in *Teaching Tudor and Stuart Women Writers,* ed. Susanne Woods and Margaret P. Hannay (New York, 2000), 301.

15. *The Complete Poetry of Richard Crashaw,* ed. George Walton Williams (Garden City, NY, 1970), stanza 59. Subsequent quotations are cited by stanza numbers in the text.

16. *A Critical Edition of Abraham Cowley's "Davideis,"* ed. Gayle Shadduck (New York, 1987), 1.305–10; hereafter cited by book and line number in the text.

17. Weidhorn, "The Toad at Eve's Ear," 126, writes: "In the economy of the story such an event accounts for seemingly irrational behavior in the manner of primitive psychology. . . . Why should Herod want to kill Christ or Saul David?"

18. Harinder Singh Marjara, *Contemplation of Created Things: Science in "Paradise Lost"* (Toronto, 1992), 273.

19. Ibid., 273, 272, 274. Bowers, "Adam, Eve, and the Fall," also concludes that Satan accomplishes the "unconscious infection of Eve's animal spirits" (269). More recently, Sutton, *Philosophy,* 206, writes that Satan succeeds in poisoning Eve's animal spirits, but he does not reason from the complete dream sequence, basing his brief comment exclusively on 4.799–809 of *Paradise Lost* and later spirit theory.

20. Neil Forsyth, *The Satanic Epic* (Princeton, NJ, 2003), 165. Forsyth links Satan and his power in this episode to witchcraft (161–62).

21. Marjara, *Contemplation of Created Things,* 273.

22. Daniel Defoe, *The Political History of the Devil* (1726), ed. Irving N. Rothman and R. Michael Bowerman (New York, 2004), 152.

23. Ibid., 278.

24. Collins, "The Buoyant Mind," 236.

25. Quoted in Flannagan, *Riverside Milton,* 479.

26. Sutton, *Philosophy,* 207.

27. Burton, *Anatomy,* 3:418.

28. See Sutton, *Philosophy,* 192–202.

COMPOSING THE UNEASY STATION: CONFESSION AND ABSENCE IN *PARADISE REGAIN'D*

George H. McLoone

ALTHOUGH IT ADHERES to the same overall cosmography as *Paradise Lost*—heaven, earth, hell—Milton's second epic about temptation and obedience draws our attention to images that are not "there," not fully objectified in the narrative, as readers often note. Its central setting of the Holy Land has a more historical geography than the garden of *Paradise Lost*, but its coordinates, especially in the wilderness scenes, seem more subjective. Crucial images in the poem—illusory panoramas and tableaux, "mid air," the opening of heaven at the Jordan, the pathless wilderness, the "uneasie station" of the temple pinnacle, a soft, paradisal valley that seems both literal and figurative—further locate character and theme but at the same time sustain a sense of absence as somehow essential to the process of recovering Paradise. The effect complements the poem's seemingly uncertain or problematic structure, a narrative absence that has been variously regarded as hindering the reader's thematic awareness or, paradoxically, as engaging it.[1] In his opening declaration of theme, the narrator associates the key terms of Christian experience and the garden with an uncertain figure of Paradise, and predicts an outcome to trial and obedience that is edifying and perhaps aesthetic, but not objective—not the once happy garden and not the Paradise of heaven:

> I who e're while the happy Garden sung,
> By one mans disobedience lost, now sing
> Recover'd Paradise to all mankind,
> By one mans firm obedience fully tri'd
> Through all temptation, and the Tempter foil'd
> In all his wiles, defeated and repuls't,
> And *Eden* rais'd in the wast Wilderness. (1.1–7)

The narrator first expresses a motif of wilderness as a poetically edifying, or informing, absence by evoking Paradise as a remembered song echoed in his new song, then by locating the recovered Paradise in terms of the vacancy surrounding it—"*Eden* rais'd in the wast Wilderness" (1.7). The shift to "Eden" instead of "Paradise" at the end of the statement looks ahead to the end of the new poem, but at the same time it recalls the end of *Paradise Lost* where Adam and Eve, cast out of Paradise, "with wandring steps and slow, / Through *Eden* took thir solitarie way" (12.648–49). The new narrative of "Recover'd Paradise," too, ends paradoxically with an implied beginning of further, if better informed, trials and their consequent episodes of alienation and reconciliation. "Queller of Satan, on thy glorious work / Now enter, and begin to save mankind" (4.634–35), the angels sing encouragingly to the Son; but then, the narrator adds, "our Saviour meek / Sung Victor . . . unobserv'd / Home to his Mothers house private return'd" (4.636–39). The ending keeps the Fall as well as the redemption in view, and the prospect of absence—the uninscribed blanks and uncreating (or chaotic) moods challenging the providential imagination.

The poem's narrative uncertainty can be related to the problematic nexus of ideal and temporal verities in Christian experience generally, and to the Savior's role in reconciling a believer's concurrent prospects of eternity and of the moment in time. Examining this broad theme has led to a wealth of commentary celebrating the hero's magisterial ethics as well as his Trinitarian affiliation. Regarding the Son's victory in *Paradise Regain'd* complacently, however, may oversimplify the complex pilgrim voice also emerging in the poem—the gathering of soliloquies and recitals inscribing the moods of inconstant assurance and alienation consequent to sin. To be sure, historical aspects of Nonconformist literature and, to some extent, Puritan autobiography have been related to wilderness motifs in the text. Jane Melbourne, for example, has pointed out that wilderness motifs and the Exodus typology common to Puritan personal narrative, discourse, and preaching are reflected in the poem. She cites *Grace Abounding*, where Bunyan says he stayed long in a personal "Sinai" not only to experience a fear of the Lord but also to prepare his conversion account for ministry, and compares this subjective desert with that of *Paradise Regain'd*, where Jesus in the wilderness "descends" into himself, taking his mother's worrisome recollections with him as a mutual "wilderness of self." Returning to his mother's house at the end of the poem, the prior setting of a mother's anxiety ("Mary's wilderness"), is then his first saving act on behalf of fallen humanity. N. H. Keeble has commented that, for Milton, the biblical wilderness is integral to the design of Providence, and that the wilderness of the poem subsumes a variety of wilderness experiences in Commonwealth and Restoration history. Keeble also observes that the "lexicon of the wilderness" found in Thomas Ellwood's autobiographical vocabulary echoes throughout Puritan discourse, and in

Paradise Regain'd. Douglas Lanier has argued that the Son's wilderness journey is the occasion of planning how to "Publish" his office (*PR* 1.186–88), and, further, that his characterization is a projection of Milton's own vision of the "ideal author" as a composed and mysterious figure. With broader view, Ashraf H. A. Rushdy has considered Satan's and the Son's contrasting accounts of the redeemer's career as a clash of autobiographies having political implications, a struggle whose outcome illustrates Milton's ethic of self-knowledge (necessarily reflected in God-centered personal narrative) as prior to sanctified nationhood.[2]

Such critical insights regarding the wilderness motif could be developed further and with a somewhat different emphasis. The binary, or perhaps bipolar, image of the poem's wilderness journey centralizes absence as an epic crisis (or hazard) that, like mortality itself, exercises the providential imagination as a fallen as well as redeemed faculty. On the one hand, the undeniable image of a triumphant Son of God in the penultimate scene of the poem conveys assurance; on the other, a lingering sense of his predictable adversary along with the poem's final, approximate images—the Son reentering the fallen, sublunary world after a time of domestic seclusion—are not triumphant but contrasting, *penseroso,* as some readers also note, as if the hero were to contemplate the alienation as well as the fulfillment yet another journey entails. The poem's second paradise, then, involves fluctuating states of confidence and unease, but modalities consistent with the Puritan discourse of "experience"—personal interactions with Providence and its decrees. More specifically, Christian identity in the poem is enhanced by patterns of binary imagery also found in Puritan personal narrative—wandering and pilgrimage, falling and rising, absence and home—and the quasi-confessional soliloquies and recitals in the first two books enable the filial and pilgrim identity depicted in the last book.[3] Beginning with a brief survey of filial relationship, confessional relating, and the significance of the pinnacle crisis, the present argument then turns to a closer reading of confessional motifs in Books One and Two and in the climax of the poem in Book Four.

In Puritan culture, confessional narrative expresses and enables the uneasy, often anxious, process of composing the self. It aims to be the literary issue, or relation, of filial relationship—the affiliation predestined in "God's plot" (in Thomas Shepard's phrase) and unfolding in a believer's personal history that is experienced, composed (or revisited), and articulated as testimony. The Adversary is licensed by God to impede the issue as well as the course of articulation. Milton's hero is the "Son of God our Saviour" (4.636), as the narrator declares; but, "All men are Sons of God" in some sense, as Satan rightly albeit presumptuously observes (4.520), and "The Son of God I also am, or was, / And if I was, I am; relation stands" (4.518–19). Milton's poetic shaping of a "relation" that "stands" in the sense of a narrative issue enabling pilgrim identity, the "I was" that begets an "I am" in the poem, associates *Paradise Regain'd* with personal narrative. As in Puritan discourse generally, in doctrine and image the motivating force behind pilgrim identity in the poem is the Holy Spirit.[4] In more intense personal narratives, as in the poem, the Spirit's occasions may be expressed problematically, as a consciousness of absence, as longing or sighing rather than enthusiasm, or perhaps intermittently as longing and enthusiasm. Providence, God's oversight, foresight, and plot for the pilgrim journey, may also be experienced as dismay rather than guidance, especially when associated with the troublesome doctrine of predestination, one underlying prophetic moments in confessional narrative and in the poem. The Son's remote meditation and the Adversary's theater of distraction derive from the poem's Gospel sources, of course, mainly Matthew 4:1–11 and Luke 4:1–13. In Luke, the Son is "led by the Spirit into the wilderness," shown the world's kingdoms by Satan "in a moment of time" [*en stigma chronou*]—a phrase not in Matthew—before "answering" [*apocritheis*] Satan on the temple pinnacle, then returning to Galilee and embarking on a preaching ministry "in the power of the Spirit" [*en tae dunamei tou pneumatos*] (Luke 4:1, 5, 14; Authorized Version). A pinnacle scene is in both gospels, but in Luke's version it is the last temptation, a more dramatic positioning followed by Milton. The image or sense of the Son standing on the pinnacle while Satan falls is a Miltonic addition, as is the event of angels delivering the Son from the pinnacle to the gentle valley and banquet. In the last book of *Paradise Regain'd*, when Satan flies the Son out of the wilderness to Jerusalem, the temple pinnacle is at first another visionary or dreamlike station intended to misinform the realm of absence—an alienating port in air for false dilemmas and for standing and falling images of uncertain predication and spatiality. Unlike Satan's imperial and academic pantomimes, however, the pinnacle destination questions the worth of the Son's earlier, magisterial victories by its assault on his providential sense of self-authorship.

For many readers, the last ordeal of the poem seems to culminate in a clear declaration of the Son's prior, Trinitarian identity—the crisis for the hero as a man resolved by the hero as God. Satan here tells him "in scorn" (4.550),

> There stand, if thou wilt stand; to stand upright
> Will ask thee skill; I to thy Fathers house
> Have brought thee, and highest plac't, highest is best,
>
> Now shew thy Progeny; if not to stand,
> Cast thy self down; safely if Son of God:

For it is written, He will give command
Concerning thee to his Angels, in thir hands
They shall up lift thee, lest at any time
Thou chance to dash thy foot against a stone.   (4.551–59)

The Son spurns the apparent dilemma by asserting his divinity, then by standing in a divine or miraculous way that seems to suspend the law of gravity for him but enforce it for the Adversary: "To whom thus Jesus: also it is written, / Tempt not the Lord thy God, he said and stood. / But Satan smitten with amazement fell" (4.560–62).

A more deliberative school, one whose approach is closer to my own, doubts that the hero's peremptory statement, "Tempt not the Lord thy God," is a decisive claim to divinity, but allows that his nature throughout the poem may be implicitly divine as well as human, that his consciousness of his divinity is expressed elsewhere in the text (for example, 1.280–86), and that his standing on the pinnacle may well be miraculous. His sanctified humanity, however, embodies the poem's theme, and his "standing" on the Deuteronomy text, demonstrates what any obedient son of God—divine or human—should say if similarly tempted. The Son on the pinnacle, as elsewhere in the poem, triumphs mainly as a man, by human skill and by recalling Scripture in a way available to all who have received the Spirit. As Barbara Lewalski has discussed, the Son's appreciation of his divine nature is at first just as limited as that of his adversary, but this limitation, or challenge, is dramatically necessary for our appreciation of the Son's heroism as a human, one of us. The poem's significance, as well as its dramatic tension up to this point, is in the Son's "process of growth," one that is "not steady but fluctuating." The pinnacle scene, however, ends with the Son's "full understanding" of his divinity as well as of his mediating roles of prophet, priest, and king. His prophetic role and its application, Lewalski also observes, were common themes in the congregational ministry of Milton's Puritan contemporaries (for example, John Diodati, Richard Baxter, and William Perkins), who interpreted the wilderness temptations as a process consecrating Christ to the prophetic office.[5]

For Puritans, it might be added, the process of personal consecration to prophetic and priestly roles (roles available to all believers) included testimony and personal narrative, an extension of the "means" of public worship, Bible reading, and private soul-searching. Such private and public testimony was another way to deepen the spiritual insights of the composing self and, it was hoped, those of future auditors and readers in an immediate family, local congregation, or perhaps throughout the visible church. The practice was not unique to Milton's Puritan contemporaries, but one usually encouraged by them. The main experiential model for Puritan autobiographers (albeit a third-person narration) was, of course, Paul's conversion on the road to Damascus (Acts 9). Augustine's *Confessions* also remained an influence on both Catholic and Protestant autobiography; and, although the work may not have been accessible to radical sectarians of modest education, Puritan personal narrative often does exhibit an Augustinian kind of introspection.[6] If Milton was not familiar with these translations or with specific Puritan autobiographies such as Bunyan's *Grace Abounding*, he was surely aware of the trend of documenting personal religious experience—a "Puritan imperative," in John Stachniewski's phrase, "by which a sense of self was constructed." The imperative resulted in a structuring of consciousness against the anxieties of doubt and despair, as Stachniewski points out in his edition of *Grace Abounding*. He adds, however, that the modern critical tendency has been to find a more consistent narrative structure in conversion narratives than is warranted. On the one hand, a broadly sequential, or gradual, process of renovation derived from Paul underlies such narratives; on the other hand, "assurance" in them is often an unstable mood. *Grace Abounding* in particular reveals the "intimidatory theology," which interpreted backsliding as an indication of reprobation, "evidence that conversion had been temporary and inauthentic." Such narratives were also a test of the will in the composing itself, a process conducted with intense introspection to a degree "unprecedented in literature" since Augustine's *Confessions*.[7]

Puritans such as Baxter and Perkins, or the Quaker Thomas Ellwood (who claimed in his personal narrative to have given Milton the idea of a second poem about Paradise), often linked their formative episodes of pilgrim identity to the wilderness journeys of disestablished Christians as well as to the spiritually alienated condition of all descendants of Adam and Eve. In some Puritan congregations, the informal liturgy of the word included opportunities, even assignments, for prophecy and personal conversion testimony.[8] *Grace Abounding* (1666), as is often noted, probably began as Bunyan's narrative testimony for membership in the Bedford congregation before becoming a widely read extension of his ministry. In *The Preacher* (1656), William Chappell, Milton's first tutor at Cambridge, lists several New England Puritan discourses on the conversion experience as informative for his students preparing for ministry.[9] In conversion narratives themselves, returning "home" only to leave it, like summarizing "God's plot," or what can be known of it, inscribes an experiential wilderness mingling alienation with confidence. Milton's contemporary at Cambridge, Thomas Shepard, for example, describes the onset of his conversion as an anxious and contradictory experience. "The Lord began to call me home to the fellowship of grace," he believes, but his "many good affections" at this point are "blind and unconstant." He was still spiritually far from home: "Yet although I was troubled for this sin, I did not know my sinful nature all this while."[10] His alienation included a perverse, self-destructive impulse as well as a tendency to back-slide, and his articulation of salvation was uneasy. He was convinced of God's reality, then not, and recalls his second birth as an intermittent Genesis: "I felt it utterly insufficient to persuade my will of it unless it was by fits, when, as I thought, God's Spirit moved upon the chaos of those horrible thoughts." The burden of "perplexities" descended again; but, he continues, "when I was by them almost forced to make an end of myself and sinful life, and to be mine own executioner, the Lord came between the bridge and the water, and set me out of anguish of spirit." Over time, he recognizes a strengthening purpose in such experiences ("And thus God kept my heart exercised") and revisits them (sometimes revising earlier journal entries) to enable his minis-terial identity and to encourage members of his congregation.[11]

Similarly, in the fallen world of *Paradise Regain'd* the wilderness rather than home locates right-minded self-fashioning. For Adam and Eve's wayfar-ing descendants who regard the topography, the wilderness at first may seem a wasteland made worse by a sense of prior doom, but for true sons of God among them it can be mapped by a personal narrative wherein the sorting out of memory would eventually be the same exercise as the search for God in the self—as in Augustine's *Confessions,* where mnemonic peregrination is revisited as pilgrimage, perhaps through territory that at first glance is more wilderness than farm or town: "In those innumerable fields, and dens, and caves of my memory . . . I run and flit about, on this side, and on that side, mining into them so far as I am able, but can find no bottom. So great is the force of memory, so great is the force of life, even in man living as mortal. . . . I will pass beyond it, that I may approach unto thee, O sweet Light."[12]

Augustine's second, or deeper, look takes him simultaneously to a sense of the absence and mysterious presence of the Other, and implies a reformed aestheticism as one reflecting an alienated yet better informed self: "And behold thou wert within me, and I out of myself, where I made search for thee: I ugly rushed headlong upon those beautiful things thou hast made." The ugliness he found in the possessive imagination rather than in God's creation conveys the vacancy of an as yet unredeemed world encompassing the self; until, he adds, "thou discoveredst thy beams and shinedst unto me, and didst chase away my blindness." His new light implies in turn the ethos of a righteous autobiographer authoring his prophetic and ministerial identity, the pilgrim self: "He is thy best servant that looks not so much to hear that from thee which himself desired; as to will that rather, which from thee he heareth."[13]

Like mistaken desires for "beautiful things," complacent pilgrimage is blind, of course, when reaching home may seem assured or perhaps humanly determined, as in Bunyan's allegory of Ignorance in the last chapters of *The Pilgrim's Progress*. As Anne Bradstreet also writes in her poem on the consequences of the Fall, "Contemplations," in the calm waters of a prosperous voyage only a foolish mariner steers, "As if he had command of wind and tide, / And now become great master of the seas" (213–14).[14] In the personal narrative Bradstreet wrote for the benefit of her children, she would first disabuse them of the notions that signs are always evidence of grace or of election, or that her advice is the same as grace, which is a divine gift that cannot be passed from mother to child. Instead, she offers them a maternal image of one resigned to God's will; and, even if it means coming to an unhappy end, perhaps eternally, she affirms her trust in Providence: " 'Upon this Rock Christ Jesus will I build my faith, and if I perish, I perish.' "[15]

In *Grace Abounding*, Bunyan's prospect of a leap of faith is complicated by temptations to abandon the cause of Nonconformity as well as the doctrine of eternal life. Knowing that he could be sentenced to hang for unlicensed preaching, he fears his public example on the scaffold as well as death itself: "Satan laid hard at me," he states, "to beat me out of heart." Imagining the moment, he foresaw "a scrabling shift to clamber up the Ladder," an "occasion to the enemy to reproach the way of God and his People, for their timerousness." He found courage, though, in a compensating prospect of the gallows as platform: "an opportunity to speak my last words to a multitude which I thought would come to see me die," perhaps an opportunity for God to "convert one Soul by my very last words." His imprisonment, doubt, and fear are then subordinated to a mood of assurance by articulating the relation between word and way, Word and Providence:

At last this consideration fell with weight upon me, That it was for the Word and Way of God that I was in this condition, wherefore I was ingaged not to flinch a hairs breadth from it. . . .

I was bound, but he was free: yea, twas my dutie to stand to his Word, whether he would ever look upon me or no, or save me at the last. . . . I am for going on, and venturing my eternal state with Christ, whether I have comfort here or no; if God doth not come in, thought I, I will leap off the Ladder even blindfold into Eternitie, sink or swim, come heaven, come hell.[16]

His resolution seems to express a new or revised sense of providential identity. Earlier, however, he acknowledges that even after experiencing forgiveness he suffered from a perverse compulsion to commit an unpardonable sin, an utterance against the Holy Spirit. In his fear of the adversarial, uncreating word, a prospect of absence, he contemplated restraining his mouth, or worse: "I have been ready to clap my hand under my chin, to hold my mouth from opening; and to that end also I have had thoughts at times to leap with my head downward into some Muckhil-hole or other to keep my mouth from speaking."[17] Here his prospect of necessity is ironically a rejection of the Spirit's guidance, its articulation (joining and relating) of word and way, and his self-preserving yet self-destructive imaginings remind us that repentant believers as well as apostates could succumb to adversarial distortions of the religion of the heart and the Spirit.

Puritan detractors pointed to religious melancholy and self-murder as evidence of such an apparently skewed emphasis on the theology of election and its prophetic discourse. The case of William Doddington, a prominent Elizabethan Puritan who documented his despair before leaping off the bell tower of St. Sepulchre's, was well known and exploited by Catholic recusants in the pamphlet wars. Puritan reformers in turn pointed to apostate Protestants as cautionary examples, especially to the theologian Francis Spira, who succumbed to anxiety and delusion after returning to the Catholic fold. In a Baptist pamphlet of 1684 that seems to reflect the distractions of Milton's epic sinners, the suicidal fate of Protestant apostates is compared to that of the fallen angels: " 'Satan takes full Possession of them, and leads them into pernicious Error of Delusion.' "[18] In *Paradise Lost,* the prospect of a sinfully compulsive identity and consequent suicide also aggravates the fevered logic of newly repentant Eve after the Fall. Adam's ministerial response, however, reforms her catastrophic reasoning with a right application of the word and of the prophetic imagination—re-creative assurances that justify or rightly inscribe absence. Eve for a time means to rectify the Fall by ending life, intimacy, and progeny, and thereby frustrating Death's appetite for the human race: "Destruction with destruction to destroy" (10.1006), a sentiment that distantly echoes Moloch's hellish plea for a last, suicidal battle against the Almighty: "More destroy'd then thus / We should be quite abolisht and expire. / What fear we then?" (2.92–94). Adam observes the heedless resentment and confusion of motives in Eve's proposal, but also her capacity for right reason and prophetic understanding. In this instance, she has not been overwhelmed by the possessive voice of a levitating and seductive demon (who by now has already returned to hell). Rather, distracted by the prospect of endless regret, she cannot yet see recovered Paradise as a destination conceivably both godly and mortal:

> *Eve,* thy contempt of life and pleasure seems
> To argue in thee somthing more sublime
> And excellent then what thy mind contemns;
> But self-destruction therefore saught, refutes
> That excellence thought in thee, and implies,

> Not thy contempt, but anguish and regret
> For loss of life and pleasure overlov'd.   (10.1013–19)

A complex of edifying, selfish, and self-destructive motives often under-lies the modes of fallen discourse, needless to say, as is also implied in Adam's earlier romantic and damnable reaction to sinful Eve: "And mee with thee hath ruind, for with thee / Certain my resolution is to Die" (9.906–7). The later context (10.966–1096, however, is closer to the wilderness mode of the adopted, and it unfolds in a way that reshapes or composes repentance by referring desperation to the word as divine decree recalled and the Word as sanctified prospect. "Then let us seek / Som safer resolution," Adam coun-ters, "which methinks / I have in view, calling to mind with heed / Part of our Sentence, that thy Seed shall bruise / The Serpents head" (10.1028–32). In the second epic, the second Adam displays a similarly empowered memory of the word on the temple pinnacle.

In *Paradise Regain'd*, Satan's anxious concern with God's plot is fixated on the problematic significance of "Son of God," heard from the Father at the baptism event, and a simultaneous, mysterious sign of the Spirit, a dove descending—"what e'er it meant" (1.83)—into his supposed dominion of midair and the wide, fallen world. He returns to the appellative and the baptism event reductively but also compulsively, vainly exploring the pos-sibility that his dominion of air and ear (prospects, rumor, and oracles) is not yet at an end. Unlike the first epic, in the second epic his repeated negotia-tions of God's providential design and Word (the Son's freshly begotten iden-tity at the baptism) do not result in soliloquy or interior recital. Satan's confes-sional direction in the poem, his extended plea for the right of discovery, is away from knowing Providence by the Spirit's illumination and the means of searching the self, although he is an unintentional participant in God's plot.

Problematic reiterations of scriptural phrases, however, can be a trial for the saved as well, who may hear them compulsively as displaced echoes of conscience, or as the Adversary's attempts to confuse conscience. Bunyan's recurrent aural hallucination, for example, a voice that says "Sell Christ," signals to him not only a fear of apostasy but also the reprobate condition of a damned soul. The phrase, he knows, derives from Esau's foolish sale of his birthright for a simple meal (Gen. 27) and the episode's New Testament application (Heb. 12:16) to a foolish Christian who, in Bunyan's words, "shall cast off all those blessed beginnings of God that at present are upon him, in order to a new Birth."[19] Judas's betrayal of Jesus for money, his attempt to repent, and his suicide are perhaps implied (Matt. 26:14–16; 27:3–10). Bun-yan is sometimes comforted by more encouraging texts in grappling with the adversarial voice, but his conscience has been so lacerated by sin and guilt that assurance at times seems impossible: "Because my former frights and anguish were very sore and deep, therefore it did oft befall me still as it befalleth those that have been scared with fire, I thought every voice was fire, fire."[20] A more lasting peace of mind, however, is provided by an authoritative and providential experience of a voice also apparently derived from Scripture, although like the adversarial voice it is not a scriptural quotation. The heaven-descending pronouncement is illustrated by a subjective trope characteristic of *Grace Abounding,* an iconic figure that seems to hover somewhere between a metaphor and a visionary experience:

> But one day, as I was passing in the field, and that too with some dashes on my Conscience, fearing lest yet all was not right, suddenly this sentence fell upon my Soul, *Thy righteousness is in Heaven,* and methought withall, I saw with the eyes of my Soul Jesus Christ at Gods right hand, there, I say, as my Righteousness; so that wherever I was, or whatever I was doing, God could not say of me, *He wants my Righteousness,* for that was just before him. I also saw, moreover, that it was not my good frame of Heart that made my Righteousness better, nor yet my bad frame that made my Righteousness worse: for my Righteousness was Jesus Christ himself, *the same yesterday, to day, and for ever.* (Citing Heb. 13:8)[21]

The interleaving of actual and permanent Scripture with apparently unconscious scriptural derivatives, the glimpse of assurance through an uncertain mode of visionary discourse, and what is an implicit locating of the unseen, third person of the Trinitarian icon in the intuitive faculty of the narrator's soul conspire to ensure that providential testimony is construed as both subjective narrative, a mortal discourse, and narrative Other. Tracing or inscribing a native plain of alienation, the confessional pilgrim arrives at a *terminus ad quem* that is *a quo,* a ministerial outsetting subordinating both complacency and despair to the "sentence" and the Logos.

In *Paradise Regain'd,* when Satan returns to the troublesome phrase, "Son of God" and its iconic configuration, he would dissect word and image murderously. The Son, however, recalls and celebrates the mysterious revelation as sufficiently authorized and composed, as another beginning and begetting of providential design and relation:

> But as I rose out of the laving stream,
> Heav'n open'd her eternal doors, from whence
> The Spirit descended on me like a Dove,
> And last the sum of all, my Father's voice,
> Audibly heard from Heav'n, pronounc'd me his,
> Me his beloved Son, in whom alone
> He was well pleas'd; by which I knew the time
> Now full, that I no more should live obscure,

> But openly begin, as best becomes
> Th' Authority which I deriv'd from Heav'n.   (1.280–89)

In turn, the last lines of the Son's soliloquy demonstrate how his testimony enables prophetic and pilgrim identity, a second begetting of filial relation:

> And now by some strong motion I am led
> Into this Wilderness, to what intent
> I learn not yet, perhaps I need not know;
> For what concerns my knowledge God reveals.   (1.290–93)

The baptist had objected to the Son's submitting himself to the rite ("As much his greater"), until he was "hardly won" by what we can assume were the Son's winning words and charismatic presence (1.279). His convincing the baptist in this way demonstrates the Son's merit in acknowledging his new but mortal identity as a second Adam. His soliloquy then approximates a Trinitarian memory of primal creation, including images of new life, the Spirit, and the Father's voice (1.280–84). The sequence of images invites comparison with the events of the Nativity, the Annunciation, and the first begetting of the Son in heaven, as if the Son's narrative experience of filial relation included running back to fetch a golden age as well as trusting to a divinely ordained future.[22]

The baptismal landscape delineated earlier, where "the great Proclaimer with a voice / More awful than the sound of Trumpet, cri'd / Repentance, and Heav'ns Kingdom nigh at hand" (1.18–20), is at first objectified by the epic narrator. It has a geographic certainty along with an ordinary sense of filial relationship:

> to his great Baptism flock'd
> With aw the Regions round, and with them came
> From *Nazareth* the Son of *Joseph* deem'd
> To the flood *Jordan*, came as then obscure.   (1.21–24)

Consonant with the baptist's witnessing, however, is a mysterious, vertical reference—for Satan a shock of recognition that he would obfuscate with uncreating moods styled as airy empowerment (a displacement psychology similarly reflected by the "ugly dreams," unhinged winds, and "ruin reconcil'd" of the storm trial in the last book; 4.401–25). What seems a voice of confirming witness simultaneously orients and unsteadies the narrative's spatial compass:

> nor was long
> His witness unconfirm'd: on him baptiz'd

> Heav'n open'd, and in likeness of a Dove
> The Spirit descended, while the Fathers voice
> From Heav'n pronounc'd him his beloved Son.
> That heard the Adversary, who roving still
> About the world, at that assembly fam'd
> Would not be last, and with the voice divine
> Nigh Thunder-struck, th' exalted man, to whom
> Such high attest was giv'n, a while survey'd
> With wonder, then with envy fraught and rage
> Flies to his place, nor rests, but in mid air
> To Councel summons all his mighty Peers,
> Within thick Clouds and dark ten-fold involv'd,
> A gloomy Consistory; and them amidst
> With looks agast and sad.   (1.28–43)

To be sure, the divine voice at that point confirmed an extraordinary filial relationship, but at the same time it provoked the Adversary's voice, Satan's prosecutorial avatar derived from the Book of Job—a voice of doubt licensed by the Father. Satan's first epic journey, his "dismal expedition to find out / And ruin *Adam*," has been succeeded by "a calmer voyage" (1.101–3), a reconnaissance mission to determine this Son's power and authority, and aiming to ruin not by "force" but by "well couch't fraud, well-woven snares" (1.91–97). Of course, Satan had used fraud rather than force in *Paradise Lost* when seducing Eve—polluting air and speech "with Serpent Tongue / Organic, or impulse of vocal Air" (*PL* 9.529–30). Ironically, his "calmer" flight in *Paradise Regain'd* will end with his dispossession in air, when word and pinnacled image without guile or force are sufficient to cause his second fall.

In the early soliloquy, the Son also remembers a youthful self who read and contemplated laudable but temporal careers (1.200–226)—vocations influenced by his mother's encouragement to "matchless Deeds" and by her recital of the Nativity (1.227–58), but without his discovering her full intuition. His second reading of the prophetic scriptural texts is deeper, toward an original (or originating) voice of the Father and the Spirit, and the Trinitarian identity that is also his own "I am" (1.263). Through revisiting memory, his maternal sense of self matures, or is revised, into a scriptural self that is also the Word, a transcendent legacy of atonement that inscribes his relationship with the Father as eternal, and that transforms his soliloquy into divine pronouncement.[23] The riddle of the Sphinx, the devouring and dashed "*Theban* Monster" that will be figured in the pinnacle scene (4.572), not only discovered "man" as the right answer but also anticipated humanity's tragic identity, a psychic legacy of secret, tempting empowerment unconsciously intuited as weakness, the unstable compound of "forbidden" knowledge. In the poem's simile, Oedipus is not mentioned, only the satanically related monster and riddle: "That once found out and solv'd, for grief and spight / Cast her self headlong from th' *Ismenian* steep" (4.574–75). Indirectly, the simile will emphasize the abilities of the Son as a man destined to reverse Satan's adversarial status. Some sense of Oedipus's ironic victory in his answer to the Sphinx, however, and the preordained course of his own journey to "dread and anguish" (4.576) may also underlie the comparison.[24] The Son's discovery may allude to the divine "I am" of Exodus 3:14, but it more clearly echoes the heavenly Son sacrificially offering himself to the Father for humanity's sake in *Paradise Lost:* "I for this sake will leave / Thy bosom, and his glorie next to thee / Freely put off, and for him lastly die" (*PL* 3.238–40). The Son in *Paradise Regain'd* apparently has no conscious memory of a prior, heavenly existence. His conclusion, therefore, is prophetic in a ministerial as well as doctrinal sense—a sense of future completion of the self as it is derived from the right application of the word to the past and future journey, what was first heard in Mary's familiar voice and then in his reading of Scripture:

> This having heard, strait I again revolv'd
> The Law and Prophets, searching what was writ
> Concerning the Messiah, to our Scribes
> Known partly, and soon found of whom they spake
> I am; this chiefly, that my way must lie
> Through many a hard assay ev'n to the death,
> E're I the promis'd Kingdom can attain,
> Or work Redemption for mankind, whose sins
> Full weight must be transferr'd upon my head.   (1.259–67)

The Son's reading guided by the Spirit, his prophetic literacy, centralizes the prospect of mortality in the plot of renovation. Charting the promised kingdom means first taking on the burden, the heritage, of sin. This second, deeper exegesis implies the instability of the kingdom when construed as another earthly realm and, paradoxically, composes the more informed articulation of the kingdom as a state of absence qualified by expectation. Atonement as a route leading from and to the paradise within evokes the sobered attitude of penitent Adam and Eve at the end of *Paradise Lost,* when they enter the untraced territory of Eden and the historical world hand in hand. Here they are guided by Providence and prophecy, but are also seen wandering into a world of wildernesses where home is simultaneously a lost place as well as a present, trying reality relieved by moments of affection. In the fallen world, perhaps no one experiences any presence as fully informative as he or she might have, eventually, in an uncorrupted garden (as once imagined by Raphael in *PL* 5.491–505). For the Son, the better informed man, each secular abode depicted by Satan in *Paradise Regain'd* (thrones, cities, academies) reveals the present world ironically but prophetically: the world is absence, but it is also an image informing an interrogation of mores, and, at times, an adumbration of last things.

After the baptism event at the Jordan, the Son's next steps are deliberative and intentional and associated with fairly definite time and place:

> Mean while the Son of God, who yet some days
> Lodg'd in *Bethabara* where *John* baptiz'd,
> Musing and much revolving in his brest,
> How best the mighty work he might begin
> Of Saviour to mankind, and which way first
> Publish his God-like office now mature.   (1.183–88)

But, as he had done years before in the temple and later when he "again revolv'd / The Law and Prophets, searching what was writ / Concerning the Messiah" (1.259–61), the Son lets the domestic tether fall. He

> One day forth walk'd alone, the Spirit leading;
> And his deep thoughts, the better to converse
> With solitude, till far from track of men,
> Thought following thought, and step by step led on,
> He enter'd now the bordering Desert wild,
> And with dark shades and rocks environ'd round,
> His holy Meditations thus perus'd.   (1.189–95)

Here, in an unpromising, barren topography, he anticipates the brooding power of the Spirit influencing a second Genesis, a new testament. He ponders filial relation, we may assume, as part of the "mighty work" of salvation (1.186), the new life that he will in turn beget for fallen humanity in the wasteland at large. His self-authoring, monologic exploration is "holy," toward the Other, signifying his human nature's adoption by the Father, his internal experience of the Spirit, and the sanctifying course of his ministry and sacrificial death.

The Adversary's response to the mystery of divine affiliation is dialogic but transparently self-serving. As in the infernal councils of *Paradise Lost*, the consistory reflects his own hopeless vacancy, an unholy space in air for an antimatter of rhetoric aiming to obscure both providential insight and the design of re-creation. He has heard the "Fathers voice," the "voice divine," and its "high attest" of the Son at the Jordan, and is "Nigh Thunder-struck" (1.30–36). He had been "roving still / About the world" when he heard the voice (1.33–34), but now reacts by flight to "mid air" and acquiescent council, as cited above (1.38–43). He addresses the other fallen angels as lords of air as well as of panoramic earth—"O ancient Powers of Air and this wide world"— but he gravitates toward their permanent, infernal terminus and ironically undermines his own rhetoric of conquest: "For much more willingly I mention Air, / This our old Conquest, then [than] remember Hell / Our hated habitation" (1.44–47). Satan's seeming victories in *Paradise Lost* included conquests of air, which are encouraging memories after he is again "nigh Thunder-struck" and likely to fall headlong a second time. In *Paradise Lost,* he had flown from hell, where he saw himself imprisoned by the argument of force and not the force of argument, defeated by the heavenly Son who "so much the stronger prov'd / He with his Thunder" (*PL* 1.92–93). He rationalized then how the disaster left the fallen angels "in foresight much advanc't," and he thought yet "To wage by force or guile eternal Warr" (*PL* 1.119–22). His airy voyage out of hell and across the dominion of Chaos to earth brought him to Paradise and Eve. The second voyage, he now asserts, "Will waft me; and the way found prosperous once / Induces best to hope of like success" (1.104–5). The second context opposes two colloquies: bathetic "sad tidings" from hell's "great Dictator," leaving the "infernal Crew" amazed, "Distracted and surpriz'd with deep dismay" (1.107–9); and a heavenly prophecy developing the narrator's sublime yet ironic prospect that the Adversary will unknowingly enact the Father's decree:

> So to subvert whom he suspected rais'd
> To end his Raign on Earth so long enjoy'd:
> But contrary unweeting he fulfill'd
> The purpos'd Counsel pre-ordain'd and fixt
> Of the most High.   (1.124–28)

Satan's dismaying "impression" on the fallen angels (1.106) is smilingly countered by the Father's recital to Gabriel of a new page, a second annunciation coterminous with a second "message," a new conception of the Word (both scriptural and filial) relating to all sons of God:

> *Gabriel* this day by proof thou shalt behold,
> Thou and all Angels conversant on Earth
> With man or mens affairs, how I begin
> To verifie that solemn message late,
> On which I sent thee to the Virgin pure
> In *Galilee,* that she should bear a Son
> Great in Reknown, and call'd the Son of God.   (1.130–36)

The temptations of the Son that follow will "shew him worthy of his birth divine / And high prediction" (1.141–42), a predestined, sanctified articulation in telling contrast to the Adversary's abuse of speech—his "subtilty" and "cunning" expressing the same "cruel malice" that caused Adam and Eve's fall; "what the first man lost / By fallacy surpriz'd" (1.144–55), an impression now countered by final proof.

As a child, the Son saw himself "born to promote all truth," especially truth applied to "publick good," and his application of the scriptural word was mainly forensic and academic (1.204–5). At age twelve, he entered the temple as a prodigy not only to listen to "Teachers of our Law" but also to "propose / What might improve my knowledge or their own" (1.211–13). His ambition was magnified in turn by imaginings of "heroic acts" (1.216), including the liberation of Israel from Rome, then of the world at large by inspired rhetoric:

> To rescue *Israel* from the *Roman* yoke,
> Then to subdue and quell o're all the earth
> Brute violence and proud Tyrannick pow'r,
> Till truth were freed, and equity restor'd:
> Yet held it more humane, more heav'nly first
> By winning words to conquer willing hearts,
> And make perswasion do the work of fear.   (1.217–23)

The Son's youthful idealism, however, was not yet continuous with the Father's "high prediction" of saving deeds known to Mary. The kingdom of Israel, we know, will not be restored by Jesus, and truth will not be fully adumbrated by establishmentarian law (as also prophesied in *PL* 12.285–305). Mary was pleased at his formative vision, the Son recalls, at his "growing thoughts" that were "By words at times cast forth" (1.227–28), but she took him aside ("And said to me apart," 1.229) as if to reform this Socratic consciousness and voice with prophecy, a "high prediction" beyond dialectic:

> high are thy thoughts
> O Son, but nourish them and let them soar
> To what highth sacred vertue and true worth
> Can raise them, though above example high.   (1.229–32)

For Mary, the Son's prophetic office should derive from "sacred" virtue and culminate in expressing the Father's will, what is "above example high" in statecraft or perhaps in the Athenian *paedeia*. God's messenger "fore-told" his birth, then "fore-told" his endless dominion (1.238–39). A choir of angels celebrated the event and "told" shepherds "the Messiah now was born, / Where they might see him, and to thee they came" (1.245–46). A star "new grav'n in Heaven" was the "bright course" leading the wise men to the place (1.252–53). Later, "Just *Simeon* and Prophetic *Anna*, warn'd / By Vision," found him in the Jerusalem Temple and "spake / Before the Altar and the vested Priest / Like things of thee to all that present stood" (1.255–58). Mary and Anna also stand by means of these alternative, revised experiences of winning words, as will the Son himself on the temple pinnacle.

Mary's second experience of absence is simultaneous with the Son's first soliloquy in the desert, and with Andrew and Simon's waiting and sighing:

> Where winds with Reeds, and Osiers whisp'ring play
> Plain Fishermen, no greater men them call,
> Close in a Cottage low together got
> Thir unexpected loss and plaints out breath'd.   (2.26–29)

They see in their mind's eye something of the kingdoms Satan will show the Son—"Behold the Kings of th' Earth how they oppress / Thy chosen" (2.44–45)—but the context of their disappointed deliverance from earthly tyranny is revised even as they speak, as if the sustaining Spirit within (paradoxically reflected in "plaints out breath'd" and "whisp'ring play") were guiding their recital through absence, melancholy, and the "relapse / Unlook'd for" (2.30–31) toward a prophetic, alternative kingdom.[25] In their primary congregation of the second paradise, peregrinative testimony now begets hope, pilgrimage: "Thus they out of thir plaints new hope resume / To find whom at first they found unsought" (2.58–59). They have seen and talked with God's anointed revealed at the baptism by John, "his great Prophet" (2.50–51), and recollecting as much reshapes the psychology of "unexpected loss," their "perplexity and new amaze" (2.29, 38), into a mood of patient expectation and witness—"But let us wait; thus far he hath perform'd" (2.49)—and then into a gratifying intuition of the right narrative course of testimony: "Let us be glad of this, and all our fears / Lay on his Providence" (2.53–54). Although more private and alone, Mary apparently similarly converts perplexity to prophecy when she contemplates the Son's absence and then recalls the prodigious events of her past. Her insight, "To have conceiv'd of God" as one "highly favour'd, among women blest," and now "to sorrows . . . advanc't, / And fears as eminent" (2.67–70), at first locates her in the wilderness margin of fading expectations. Her "troubl'd thoughts, which she in sighs thus clad" (2.65), however, like the "plaints out breath'd" of Andrew and Simon, are reformed by her providential memory of "what remarkably had pass'd / Since first her Salutation heard" into "thoughts / meekly compos'd" (2.106–8), a reprise of divine relation that is continuous with the Son's "tracing the Desert wild" (2.109).

By Book Four, Satan's supposed dominion of middle air and its microcosm of prevaricating speech are, for him, simply the wilderness without hope or issue. As the narrator tells us, Satan is "Perplex'd and troubl'd at his bad success," the "perswasive Rhetoric / That sleek't his tongue, and won so much on *Eve*, / So little here, nay lost" (4.1, 4–6). The lofty, panoramic temptations of Rome and Athens that follow inevitably convey Satan's own reluctance to regard the empty center of his being—the damned Adversary as one "self deceiv'd" (4.7). Satan's "condition" for donating the world's kingdoms to the Son—"if thou wilt fall down, / And worship me as thy superior Lord" (1.166–67)—is a hopelessly inept utterance ironically foretelling his second fall away from the Son. The Son answers "with disdain" for Satan's "terms" (4.170, 173), but with patient acceptance of the Father's temporal "permission," a speech act, he knows, that will demonstrate how primary decrees of obedience, like those of Creation itself, are again crucial to human destiny:

> I never lik'd thy talk, thy offers less,
> Now both abhor, since thou hast dar'd to utter
> Th' abominable terms, impious condition;
> But I endure the time, till which expir'd,
> Thou hast permission on me. It is written
> The first of all Commandments, Thou shalt worship
> The Lord thy God, and only him shalt serve.   (4.171–77)

The Son's base contextualizing of "utter" (perhaps with its sense of "sell"), followed by his worthier tone and image—"It is written"—recalls the description of Satan's approach to him in Book One: "who first with curious eye / Perus'd him, then with words thus utter'd spake" (1.319–20) and the Son's telling, rhetorical question (a Reformation mainstay) regarding the word, taste, and temptation: "is it not written . . . Man lives not by bread only, but each Word / Proceeding from the mouth of God" (1.347, 349–50). Now, however, the Son's allusive image of temptation implies a providential entirety of narrative: "For this attempt bolder then that on *Eve* / . . . expect to rue" (4.180–81), and his peremptory subordination of Satan includes a command as well as a summary statement of one eternal identity: "Get thee behind me; plain thou now appear'st / That Evil one, Satan for ever damn'd" (4.193–94). If the seemingly deep, aesthetic textures of Rome and Athens do reflect something edifying in parts, they are nonetheless "built on nothing firm," as the Son says of the schools of Athens (4.292), and superfluous to "Light from above, from the fountain of light" (4.289). Rather, the primary story, like the primary decree, is that of the created, fallen, and redeemed self still dependent on the Father's mind (or intent), as the Son implies when he neatly folds the plot of first epic into the second:

> Alas what can they teach, and not mislead;
> Ignorant of themselves, of God much more,

And how the world began, and how man fell
Degraded by himself, on grace depending?   (4.309–12)

The climax of the poem depicts a paradise regained in middle air, an
image consistent with the wilderness topos but also with the confessional
attitude of true believers, Adam's "chosen Sons," who will eventually dwell
"secure, when time shall be / Of Tempter and Temptation without fear"
(4.614–17). A bad end to the wilderness journey, Satan would believe, is
owing to himself and to the Son's supposed prospect of either falling or
testing the Father, a kind of blasphemy: "I to thy Fathers house / Have
brought thee, and highest plac't, highest is best, / Now shew thy Progeny"
(4.552–54). Here, however, the Son does not show his progeny dialectically
or peremptorily, not by standing in a physical sense and not, of course, by
casting himself down. He demonstrates, or enacts, filial relation by recalling
what was "also" written, as if the permanent, scriptural command were continuous with his personal testimony, his prophetic position in time and in
eternity that is about to be witnessed: "To whom thus Jesus: also it is written, /
Tempt not the Lord thy God, he said and stood" (4.560–61). He stands and
Satan falls by means of the articulation of providential memory. What is
"also" written is, then, an epiphany of the composed self, a paradise regained
countering Satan's dubious utterances, categorical dissections, false dilemmas, and oracles, the erroneous, mythographic issue descending from Sin,
Death, and a paradise lost, and from misleading inscriptions of absence. The
Adversary's misapplication of Scripture represents the voices of the reprobate, and his fall is back to the tautological consistories of hell:

So strook with dread and anguish fell the Fiend,
And to his crew, that sat consulting, brought
Joyless triumphals of his hop't success,
Ruin, and desperation, and dismay.   (4.576–79)

The similes of Antaeus felled by Hercules—"Throttl'd at length in th'
Air" (4.568)—and the headlong falling Theban Sphinx (4.572–75) draw out
Satan's amazement in the manner of *Paradise Lost* and mythically relegate
his current domain of air to the prior epic's tragic measures of ruin. In a sense,
he falls backward through the narrative structure of the second epic toward
that of the first—past the Jerusalem temple and through classical simile, all
the way to consultative tautologies and obsessions, the abject episodes of
Paradise Lost he has attempted to impose on heaven, earth, and the Savior.
The Son is delivered to a place approximating the earthly Paradise and his
heavenly home, conveyed from the "uneasie station" through the now "blithe
Air" to a secure valley and innocent feast of heavenly food served by angels,

Who on their plumy Vans receiv'd him soft
From his uneasie station, and upbore
As on a floating couch through the blithe Air,
Then in a flowry valley set him down
On a green bank, and set before him spred
A table of Celestial Food, Divine,
Ambrosial, Fruits fetcht from the tree of life.   (4.583–89)

For all its spiritual authenticity and wholesome delights, however, the place is also comparable to what might have been, a heavenly earth imagined by Raphael for an obedient Adam and Eve—"when men / With Angels may participate," and "may at choice / Here or in Heav'nly Paradises dwell," as cited above (*PL* 5.493–503). The secure valley is not simply another mirage, but neither is it the altogether real world of the Son's prophetic ministry and mission existing uncomfortably beyond his return to his mother's house. Like the other quotations of "what is written" in the Gospel temptation narratives and in the poem, the soft, renovating landing is derived from Deuteronomy, from where the chosen are enjoined to "remember all the way which thy Lord God led thee these forty years in the wilderness, to humble thee, and to prove thee, to know what was in thine heart, whether thou wouldst keep his commandments or no," and to anticipate their eventual destination: "a good land, a land of brooks of water, of fountains and depths that spring out of valleys and hills, a land of wheat, and barley, of vines, and fig trees, and pomegranates, a land of olive oil, and honey, a land wherein thou shalt eat bread without scarceness" (8:2, 7–9). Milton's context, too, is a lyrical expression of the confessional mind reflecting on faith and obedience, a meditative image enabling the sustaining effects of memory configured as Providence. Unlike the forbidden tree that was freely accessible, the permitted tree of life became inaccessible, forbidden because of the Fall and guarded by vigilant angels. Now its fruit is freely, gracefully given, as was life at the first, and the Father's primary decrees are brought forward not strictly as mortal burden but as divine and filial relation, as both providential narrative and Trinitarian bond.

Freely standing on Scripture expresses an obedient mind, one that accepts all of God's decrees as just and, perhaps, as vocations to heroic action as well as to patient endurance. As the Father declared to the heavenly Son in *Paradise Lost* about the first sons of God, "Such I created all th'Ethereal Powers / And Spirits, both them who stood and them who faild; / Freely they stood who stood, and fell who fell" (3.100–102).

The Father's further distinction between foreknowledge and responsibility for Adam's fall, and his promise of mercy as well as justice set the prime narrative boundaries for the Son's atonement as well as for right reason

generally (*PL* 3.103–34). The context, however, begins with his observation
of Satan's hopeless case:

> Onely begotten Son, seest thou what rage
> Transports our adversarie, whom no bounds
> Prescrib'd, no barrs of Hell, nor all the chains
> Heapt on him there, nor yet the main Abyss
> Wide interrupt can hold; so bent he seems
> On desperat revenge, that shall redound
> Upon his own rebellious head.   (*PL* 3.80–86)

The Adversary is on his way to corrupt the world with serpent tongue—"By som
false guile" and "glozing lyes" (*PL* 3.92–93)—and the Father allows that the sins
of angels and humans, and their destinies, differ because of false witness:

> The first sort by thir own suggestion fell
> Self-tempted, self-deprav'd: Man falls deceiv'd
> By the other first: Man therefore shall find grace,
> The other none.   (*PL* 3.129–32)

The Adversary's proudly marginless imagination is a narrative ruin beyond any "bounds / Prescribed" that he would bring to earth and, in *Paradise
Regain'd,* to the Savior. Satan ostensibly begs clarification or definition of the
key terms of Providence, especially when they are articulated in the negative
spaces of the wilderness where righteous self-authorship begins. "Son of
God" is an epithet, he complains, "which bears no single sence"; as for
"Kingdom," whether "Real or Allegoric I discern not" (4.517, 390). On the
pinnacle, however, one step away from the abyss, the Son's application of the
scriptural word demonstrates the sure footing, the structural sufficiency, of
recalling the word as decree. Retrieving the text in this way is for Milton a
gesture of faith derived from a godly and truly creative imagination, one that
can reconcile the search for God in the self with the quest for identity in the
world. Satan's fear and loathing of the reconciling imagination embodied by
the Son, however, demonstrate the perpetual self-absorption of the damned.
The pinnacle scene in the poem conveys the challenge of relating an exemplary life by depicting the crisis of both sanctified and ignominious self-
authoring in midair, where one "relation stands" and another falls. Here,
relation obtains in the explorative and creative sense anticipated by the Son
in his soliloquy but is not comprehended by an amazed Satan, whose willful
narrative design merely reiterates his frustrated attempts to escape the divinely ordained decrees of heaven, earth, and hell, the ineluctable domains of
"I was" and "I am." The exemplary life, the Son's better mythos of the second
paradise, does not deny, or rationalize, the ruins of the first, of course, but

throws more light on them, especially the light of scriptural texts, in order to reveal both doctrine and the heart's core, the believer's true affections.

Along with the reminder of Satan's persuasive tongue that "won so much on Eve," the filial and testimonial senses of "relation" echo an uneasy station in *Paradise Lost*, where "*Eve* relates to *Adam* her troublesome dream" of a tempter and ascent, and where Raphael "relates at *Adams* request who that enemy is, and how he came to be so, beginning from his first revolt in Heaven" (from the argument to Book Five). Eve's anxious recollection of the dream was temporarily, somewhat complacently, resolved by Adam's doctrinal psychology. His analysis was both calming and cathartic for Eve, but it lingered as better informed irony in the epic narrator's attitude: something had entered Eve's sleep with a familiar voice but absent company, she tells Adam: "methought / Close at mine ear one call'd me forth to walk / With gentle voice, I thought it thine." "I rose as at thy call," she continues, "but found thee not." She walks alone to the tree of knowledge and meets an angel, "One shap'd and wing'd like one of those from Heav'n / By us oft seen." The angel insists, "Taste this, and be henceforth among the Gods / Thy self a Goddess, not to Earth confind, / But sometimes in the Air, as wee." In the dream, she succumbs to an appeal to appetite, if not yet to an exalted state, when the angel holds the forbidden fruit to her mouth: "the pleasant savourie smell / So quick'nd appetite, that I, methought, / Could not but taste" (5.35–86). The climax of her dream displays correlatives of false and true empowerment such as we see also in *Paradise Regain'd:*

> Forthwith up to the Clouds
> With him I flew, and underneath beheld
> The Earth outstretcht immense, a prospect wide
> And various: wondring at my flight and change
> To this high exaltation.   (*PL* 5.86–90)

In sleep, her dream's censor is not so much Adam remembered as herself, and in good conscience she abandons any lasting advantage from heeding the offending angel, falls, then happily wakes up:

> suddenly
> My Guide was gon, and I, me thought, sunk down,
> And fell asleep; but O how glad I wak'd
> To find this but a dream!   (*PL* 5.90–93)

When Eve is awake, Adam's consoling discourse to the "Best Image of my self and dearer half" on the psychology and ethics of the unconscious, the soul's "lesser Faculties" (*PL* 5.95–121), is rightly reasoned but ironically ominous in its application:

> Evil into the mind of God or Man
> May come and go, so unapprov'd, and leave
> No spot or blame behind: Which gives me hope
> That what in sleep thou didst abhorr to dream,
> Waking thou never wilt consent to do.   (*PL* 5.117–21)

On the one hand, the summary consonance of "Which," "what," "Waking," "wilt" enhances the irony of "never . . . consent"; on the other, the transience of unapproved evil, the gift of hope, and the concluding emphasis on freedom to choose sustain the recurrent second theme of *Paradise Lost*—renovation for sinners and the promise of a paradise regained by "one greater Man" (*PL* 1.4), the first theme of *Paradise Regain'd*. Excluding perversity from the dominion of the saved—the relegation of Satan to hell—is the second theme of *Paradise Regain'd*. Satan's fall from midair and the similes of the grander style also associate the Son with the prior battle in heaven. The choir of angels celebrates this triumphal aspect in turn and applies it to the founding of "A fairer Paradise" for Adam's "chosen Sons," as cited above,

>   whom thou
> A Saviour art come down to re-install,
> Where they shall dwell secure, when time shall be
> Of Tempter and Temptation without fear.   (4.614–17)

A downward yet exalting image, the Savior's descent from the temple reprises memories of the Incarnation and Nativity in the poem, and perhaps, too, the sinking and rising of the baptism that was "hardly won" from John at the Jordan. Before the time that shall be, however, even the temple setting is dubious and precarious, and the only secure dwelling is to live in the providential word—the overlapping contexts of Scripture, God's plot, and the personal narratives of the chosen. Satan may sojourn there as well, but he cannot abide there as fallen angel or as perverse locution forever. His narrative end in the poem is linked to the fate of mythic, unredeemable creatures of the imagination, although—as readers of the Gospel sources would very well know—he departs from the Son only "for a season" (Luke 4:13). Satan may seem to be free from hell at times, but is nonetheless enacting God's plot, as the Son and the Father have also reminded us. At first, the choir shifts the address of their ode directly to Satan and his eventual cosmic fall:

> But thou, Infernal Serpent, shalt not long
> Rule in the Clouds; like an Autumnal Star
> Or Lightning thou shalt fall from Heav'n trod down
> Under his feet.   (4.618–21)

They end, however, by prophesying his sublunary departures from the confessional imagination:

> hereafter learn with awe
> To dread the Son of God: he all unarm'd
> Shall chase thee with the terror of his voice
> From thy Demoniac holds, possession foul,
> Thee and thy Legions, yelling they shall fly,
> And beg to hide them in a herd of Swine,
> Lest he command them down into the deep
> Bound, and to torment sent before thir time.
> Hail Son of the most High, heir of both worlds,
> Queller of Satan, on thy glorious work
> Now enter, and begin to save mankind.   (4.625–35)

As editors note, the choir evokes the Gospel episode of the Gaderene demoniac, a man (in Matthew, two men) cured of madness when Jesus exorcises the demons possessing him. The demons plead to enter a herd of swine rather than return to the abyss, and the possessed swine run down a mountainside into a lake and drown. In Luke, the one man had been naked, living among tombs, and subject to chaining, but now in his right mind he sits at the master's feet and begs to stay with him. Jesus sends him on his way: " 'Return to thine own house, and show how great things God hath done unto thee,' " and the man "published [*karusson*] throughout the whole city how great things Jesus had done unto him" (Luke 8:26–39). The positioning of the passage and its aural sequence of fiendish voices yielding to divine order and praise—"terror," "yelling," "beg," "command," "Hail"—summarize the effects of judgment on both the damned and the saved in God's plot. The Son's "glorious work" as "heir of both worlds," heaven and the fallen world, is to share that vision of Providence with Adam and Eve's descendants and to enable their reflective self-authorship and testimony. The more edifying images of the Gaderene episode in Luke—the healing power of mercy and the newly composed self sent on the Lord's mission of testimony—are not in the angel's song, and the later significance of the Son's retracing his steps in the poem's last lines—"hee unobserv'd / Home to his Mothers house private return'd"—is not stated. We know, however, that this station, too, will be a point of departure, or descent, of the Word into experience and into singular, personal contexts.[26] The return journey is not strictly metaphorical or visionary; but, like the Son's saving mission in the Gospel, it traces the condition of absence by which we define home.

Marymount University

NOTES

1. See the brief survey of criticism in Jeffrey B. Morris, "Disorientation and Disruption in *Paradise Regained*," *Milton Studies* 26, ed. James D. Simmonds (Pittsburgh, 1990), 219. Morris argues that the narrative's "formal disorientation" (220) compels the reader to shift attention from setting to speech, a more appropriately theological orientation. James M. Pearce, "The Theology of Representation: The Meta-Argument of *Paradise Regained*," *Milton Studies* 24, ed. James D. Simmonds (Pittsburgh, 1988), on the other hand, regards the arrangement of the poem as "unrhetorical," its structure unfolding not as a "drama of inquiry" but as a "drama of contemplation," enabling us to see the "highest image of human possibility" (295, 283). Alinda Sumers-Ingraham, "John Milton's *Paradise Regained* and the Genre of the Puritan Spiritual Biography" (Ph.D. diss., The George Washington University, 1984), 25–69, has also surveyed the "problem of structure" as a recurrent issue in criticism of the poem. Her argument is that Puritan spiritual biography as influenced by the Book of Job was in turn an influence on the sequence and meaning of temptation in the poem.

Sanford Budick, *The Dividing Muse: Images of Sacred Disjunction in Milton's Poetry* (New Haven, 1985), contends that the imprecise, nonreferential language patterns of *Paradise Regain'd* generate a sense of extraordinary, divine space, displacing ordinary phenomenology, and thereby establish the ideal pattern of Christian experience. Compare his observations on the Son's retirement from action in a wilderness "zone of absence," an image contributing to the poem's paradigmatic symbolism of "disjoined fulfillment" (137, 145). Quotations from Milton's poetry are taken from *The Complete Poetry of John Milton*, ed. John T. Shawcross (New York, 1971).

2. Jane Melbourne, "Self-Doubt in the Wilderness in *Paradise Regain'd*," *SEL* 34 (1994): 138, 149. N. H. Keeble, "Wilderness Exercises: Adversity, Temptation, and Trial in *Paradise Regain'd*," *Milton Studies* 42, *"Paradise Regained" in Context: Genre, Politics, Religion,* ed. Albert C. Labriola and David Loewenstein (Pittsburgh, 2002), 96. Douglas Lanier, " 'Unmarkt, Unknown': *Paradise Regained* and the Return of the Expressed," *Criticism* 37, no. 2 (1995): 187–212. Ashraf H. A. Rushdy, "Of *Paradise Regained:* The Interpretation of Career," *Milton Studies* 24, ed. James D. Simmonds (Pittsburgh, 1988), 253–75, and *The Empty Garden: The Subject of Late Milton* (Pittsburgh, 1992), 117–90. See also Marshall Grossman, *"Authors to Themselves": Milton and the Revelation of History* (Cambridge, 1987), and Margot Todd, "Puritan Self-Fashioning: The Diary of Samuel Ward," *Journal of British Studies* 31 (1992): 236–64. Both Grossman and Todd acknowledge Stephen Greenblatt, *Renaissance Self-Fashioning: From More to Shakespeare* (Chicago, 1980).

3. Compare Albert Cook, "Imaging in *Paradise Regained*," *Milton Studies* 21, ed. James D. Simmonds (Pittsburgh, 1985), 215–27. With a different emphasis, Cook surveys a pattern of contrasting images in the poem and lists rocks and air, light and dark, hunger and food, desert and vegetation, martial display and peace. See also Barbara K. Lewalski, *Milton's Brief Epic: The Genre, Meaning, and Art of "Paradise Regained"* (Providence, RI, 1966), 336–41.

4. See Geoffrey F. Nuttall, *The Holy Spirit in Puritan Faith and Experience* (1947; reprint, Chicago, 1992). Across the Puritan spectrum, as Nuttall emphasizes, the basis of truly Christian identity was a personal experience of the Spirit, and, citing John 3:8, "the Spirit blew where it listed" [*to pneuma hopou thelei pnei*] (177). Experiencing the Spirit was, of course, joined to the "means" of the scriptural word, as Nuttall explains (20–33), and such encounters are reflected in confessional testimony.

We may compare with Milton's autobiographical ethos in *The Reason of Church-Government* (1642), in *Complete Prose Works of John Milton*, 8 vols., ed. Don M. Wolfe et al. (New

Haven, 1953–82), 1:820–21, one that forges a ministerial "covnant" with English readers suffering from prelatical tyranny, and that will generate future literary works deriving from "devout prayer to that eternall Spirit who can enrich with all utterance and knowledge, and sends out his Seraphim with the hallow'd fire of his Altar to touch and purify the lips of whom he pleases," an image perhaps combining Isaiah 6:6–8 with John 3:8. See the brief survey of references in the poetry as well as prose in William B. Hunter, "Spirit," in *A Milton Encyclopedia,* vol. 8, ed. William B. Hunter et al. (Lewisburg, PA, 1978), and Hunter's conclusion (36–37): "It seems clear that Milton testifies to its operation in his own life." Milton's autobiographical statements, of course, indicate his belief in Providence, but are not intimately spiritual, not detailing any course of spiritual development or providential "experiences," as pointed out by Hunter, "Autobiography," in *A Milton Encyclopedia,* 1:118–19.

5. Lewalski, *Milton's Brief Epic,* 133–35, 163, 183–88.

6. See Paul Delany, *British Autobiography in the Seventeenth Century* (New York, 1969), 30–32. Puritans without Latin, however, might have been gratified by the publication of William Watts's "Protestant" English translation, one promoted as untainted by the Roman Catholicism of another translator, Sir Tobias Matthew. Watts's title is indicative: *Saint Augustines Confessions translated: and with some marginal notes illustrated. Wherin, Divers Antiquities are explained; and the marginall notes of a former Popish Translation answered* (London, 1631). Sir Tobias Matthew, *The Confessions of the incomparable doctour S. Augustine, translated into English. Together with a large Preface, etc.* (St. Omer, 1620). The Matthew translation, along with others, as Delany notes, was reprinted throughout the century.

7. John Bunyan, *Grace Abounding* (Oxford, 1998), xix, xxvii–xxviii. Compare Delany, *British Autobiography,* 92, on Bunyan's ability in *Grace Abounding* to interrogate complacently happy endings, "the skill he uses to persuade us that the outcome of his struggles really was doubtful." Stachniewski, *The Persecutory Imagination* (Oxford, 1991), relates the disturbingly strict Calvinism found in some Reformation autobiography to the complex psychologies of guilt found in Marlowe's *Dr. Faustus,* Donne's *Holy Sonnets,* and *Paradise Lost.* He argues that despite the apparent Arminianism of *Paradise Lost* and Milton's intent to show Adam and Eve as free to choose their spiritual destiny, the darker aspects of Calvin's theology ineluctably work their way into the poem. In a comment on *Paradise Regain'd* (373–75), Stachniewski remarks that Satan knows he is simply acting out a preordained "mode of self destruction." See also Leopold Damrosch Jr., *God's Plot and Man's Stories: Studies in the Fictional Imagination from Milton to Fielding* (Chicago, 1985), on Calvinist doctrine and its influence on *Paradise Lost,* on Puritan autobiography, and on the eighteenth-century English novel. Damrosch emphasizes Milton's sense of a comprehensive mythology as one necessarily depicting the good as circumscribed by evil, and observes, the " 'paradise within thee' " promised by Michael to Adam and Eve near the end of *Paradise Lost* (12.587) will not be " 'happier far' " than the prelapsarian garden, but only "happier than the wreckage of fallen Eden" (115).

8. See John Cotton, *The Doctrine of the Church* (London, 1644), 6; and Nuttall, *Holy Spirit,* 85.

9. Originally *Methodus Concionandi* (London, 1648). Under the heading, "On True Conversion" in the English translation, Chappell lists only Thomas Shepard, Thomas Hooker (the Connecticut patriarch), and John Cotton as recommended authors. *The Preacher* [1656] (Menston, 1971), [216]. Compare Perry Miller, *The New England Mind* (Cambridge, MA, 1939), 27.

10. Milton arrived at Christ's College in 1625, and Shepard was at Emmanuel College from 1620 to 1627. I do not know of any evidence that he knew Shepard particularly. The quotation from Shepard's autobiography, "My Birth and Life," is from *God's Plot: Puritan Spirituality in Thomas Shepard's Cambridge,* edited by Michael McGiffert (Amherst, MA, 1994), 42–43.

11. *Certain Select Cases Resolved,* excerpted in McGiffert, *God's Plot,* 46.

12. Augustine, *Confessions: With an English Translation by William Watts,* 2 vols. (Cambridge, MA, 2000), 2:123.

13. Ibid., 2:147, 141–45.

14. *The Works of Anne Bradstreet,* ed. Jeannine Hensley (Cambridge, MA, 1967), 213.

15. Quoted in Daniel B. Shea, *Spiritual Autobiography in Early America* (Princeton, NJ, 1968), 114–18.

16. Bunyan, *Grace Abounding,* 91–92.

17. Ibid., 31.

18. See Michael Macdonald and Terence R. Murphey, *Sleepless Souls: Suicide in Early-Modern England* (Oxford, 1990), 64–67. Compare Stachniewski, *The Persecutory Imagination,* 37–40, 49–52, 320, on despair and suicide in Puritanism; and Elizabeth Pope, *Paradise Regained: The Tradition and the Poem* (1947; reprint, New York, 1962), 87–101. Pope surveys several seventeenth-century interpretations of the Gospel pinnacle as including a temptation to suicide, but discounts their influence on the exegetical tradition underlying the poem. Nonetheless, Milton's poetic interest in the pathology and sin in prior contexts should be noted. In *Paradise Lost,* Eve proposes suicide to Adam as a means to put a stop to sin and death (10.966–1006), as discussed below; and, as observed by Alastair Fowler in his commentary on the passage, in *The Poems of John Milton,* ed. John Carey and Alastair Fowler (New York, 1972), Milton cites passages on suicide by Dante and Sidney under the heading "Death self-inflicted" in his Commonplace Book (976). Milton would also have been aware of satanic characterizations of self-murder and their precipitous settings in Shakespeare (for example, *Hamlet* 1.4.69–78; *Lear* 4.6.1–79); Milton apparently studied some of the legal and economic ramifications. In their comparison of the judicial policies of the Stuart and Commonwealth regimes regarding suicide, Macdonald and Murphey, *Sleepless Souls,* 116–17, mention Milton's secretarial assignment to examine the self-murder and forfeited property law, and ways to discourage *non compis mentis* verdicts in favor of the strict enforcement of forfeiture.

19. Bunyan, *Grace Abounding,* 65.

20. Ibid., 65; compare Delany, *British Autobiography,* 91.

21. Bunyan, *Grace Abounding,* 65–66.

22. Milton's *Ode on the Morning of Christ's Nativity* may be compared; for example, lines 133–35: "For if such holy Song / Enwrap our fancy long, / Time will run back, and fetch the age of gold." The Nativity ode also locates the doomsday seat of divine judgment in midair, Satan's supposed dominion in *Paradise Regain'd:* "When at the worlds last session, / The dreadfull Judge in middle Air shall spread his throne" (163–64). Compare Rushdy, *The Empty Garden,* 271–72, on the sense of deferral in both poems, and J. Martin Evans, "The Poetry of Absence," in *The Miltonic Moment* (Lexington, KY, 1998), 11–37. Evans regards the imagery of the Nativity ode as Puritan in its negativity.

23. Compare John Shawcross, *Paradise Regain'd: "Worthy T'Have Not Remain'd So Long Unsung"* (Pittsburgh, 1988), 63–69, who analyzes the Son's mature, magisterial identity in the poem as one taking on the Father's "energy" but still influenced by Mary's spiritual "meekness."

24. Compare Damrosch, *God's Plot,* 115–16, on the simile and on the difference between Sophoclean and Christian guilt: "For the Greek, knowledge, even if terrible, is the path to enlightenment. For the Christian it is the path to death, and can only be repaired by a myth which is 'to the Greeks foolishness' (1 Corinthians 1:23). Oedipus becomes a god; Christ becomes a man."

25. For some Puritans, prayers in the Spirit were sometimes expressed as spontaneous sighs and groans. See Nuttall, *Holy Spirit,* 65–66, 72.

26. Marjorie O'Rourke Boyle, "Home to Mother: Regaining Milton's Paradise," *MP* 97

(2000): 499–527, has argued that the final image of the poem is an implied prolongation of action, an effect influenced by Luke where the closure of the wilderness and temptation pericope is intentionally "prospective." Further, the poem's ending suggests a classical motif of homecoming as beginning (as in the *Odyssey*'s last books and in Pindar's odes), and a body of medieval contemplative texts in which celebrations marking the final stages of meditation are figured in terms of arriving at Mary's house.

THE GROTESQUE IN *AREOPAGITICA*

Markus Klinge

A $REOPAGITICA$ IS $MISREAD$ by many modern critics who consider its proposals purely from a political vantage point and ignore its aesthetic background and polemic techniques. My new reading of the tract places it in the context of the grotesque, and I will aim to arrive at a more cohesive reading by forwarding a radical new suggestion: *Areopagitica* may purport, on the surface, to call for an instant revocation of the 1643 Licensing Order; however, its polemical techniques suggest that Milton is not primarily aiming at an immediate political effect. I believe he intends, rather, to influence his readers in the medium or long term. *Areopagitica* is not a political piece as such; although it uses some of the techniques associated with controversial prose, it does not aim to convince by stringent logic or by current political expedience. Rather, it works on the reader's aesthetic sensibilities. As a consequence, *Areopagitica* should not be read as a philosophical exposé, but as a subtle attempt to change minds and to soften strong, preexisting convictions. In the first half of the twentieth century, William Haller pointed out with reference to *Areopagitica* that "Milton wrote not a pamphlet but a poem."[1] I feel that many modern critics have forgotten this, and I believe it is time for a reevaluation.

Throughout the twentieth century, there has been increased criticism of *Areopagitica* as an exponent of tolerance and of freedom of the press.[2] In comparison to pamphleteers such as Roger Williams, John Goodwin, William Walwyn, Henry Richardson, or John Lilburne, some scholars have pointed out that Milton is far less radical in his proposals, arguing for a lesser degree of toleration and a lesser degree of unlicensed printing.[3] Others argue that Milton's tract contains a series of logical inconsistencies that ultimately renders a Tolerationist reading one-sided.[4] John Illo and Willmoore Kendall even claim that *Areopagitica* is not advocating toleration or freedom of the press at all.[5]

Some critics have attempted to explain Milton's apparent logical inconsistencies. Arthur E. Barker suggests that Milton's understanding of the freedom of the press is limited by the concept of Christian liberty.[6] Ernest Sirluck, Christopher Hill, Stephen Burt, and Christopher Kendrick see *Areopagitica* as a strategic document that aims to gather the largest possible support from a disparate readership.[7] Joseph Wittreich suggests that Milton employs irony in order to teach, Henry Limouze thinks that the tract's incongruity is based on an evolving distinction between individual and public licensing, and Harry Smallenburg sees *Areopagitica*'s incongruity as a reflection on the nature of truth. Abbe Blum suggests that Milton is torn as a result of the "interdependence of author and authority," Stephen Dobranski points out that Milton should be seen as a collaborative author and inconsistent human being, and John Schaeffer proposes that the tract's incongruities are transcended in the image of the Eucharist.[8] Stanley Fish sees *Areopagitica* as only peripherally concerned with licensing, and primarily with illustrating the indifference of books; in other words, instead of relying on outside influences, readers must learn to become part of the "incorporate body" of truth.[9] Martin Dzelzainis offers a more cohesive analysis of *Areopagitica* by placing Milton's views on toleration in the context of classical republicanism.[10]

Despite all attempts at vindication, the enthusiasm of earlier Miltonists has given way to widespread acknowledgment of *Areopagitica*'s limitations, and even among those favorably disposed toward Milton, support can at times appear a little half-hearted.[11] However, from almost all sides of the modern critical spectrum, there has been agreement in one respect: *Areopagitica* is now seen as a fundamentally incongruous text that defies easy categorization.

There is one problem with this new orthodoxy, however: for some three hundred years after its publication, readers must have misunderstood Milton's tract. Illo believes that the earlier enthusiasm for *Areopagitica*'s tolerance and freedom of the press was based on selective passages and promulgated through successive generations until it became what he calls the "myth of the *Areopagitica.*"[12] He implies that earlier readers were somehow carried away by the poetic genius of *Paradise Lost* and started to attribute to Milton an ingenuity in the fields of philosophy and politics that he never possessed. Critics who acknowledge incongruities in *Areopagitica* have tacitly accepted the validity of the "Milton myth," even if they do not subscribe to Illo's reevaluative approach.

But how could generations of Milton readers have gotten it so completely wrong? The theory of the Milton myth does not fully explain the extent of the misreading: if Milton worship had a large impact on the way the prose works were read, one would expect similar myths to emerge for other works that also contain passages attractive to the modern mind. Yet no other Milton myth exists, especially not on a comparable scale. Furthermore, the incongruities in *Areopagitica* should make it an unsuitable text to refer to when freedom of the press is actively debated (rather than just celebrated).

During subsequent years, when more coherent and recent texts on freedom of the press were available, there should have been no need to invoke the spirit of such an incongruous (and hence vulnerable) text. Yet Charles Blount and William Denton appropriated *Areopagitica* for their antilicensing arguments in 1679 and 1681, Mirabeau translated *Areopagitica* into French just before the 1789 revolution, and E. M. Forster invoked its spirit in 1944 when Churchill intended to curtail the freedom of the press.[13] All of these writers were engaged in debates about freedom of the press, in which they could not afford to present their positions with obvious flaws. How is it possible that they failed to notice those passages in which Milton talks about the burning of books? Or the simile in which Milton compares books to "Dragons teeth" on which a "vigilant eye" (2:492) must be kept? Or the passages in which he exempts Catholics, Anglicans, and *jure divino* Presbyterians from general toleration?

What I suggest is that they did *not* get it wrong. Rather, many modern critics have put *Areopagitica* into an inappropriate context by scrutinizing it as if it were a pamphlet with an immediate political aim, with clear philosophical ideas, a methodical approach, and constructive suggestions. *Areopagitica* does deal with matters of political and philosophical concern, and Milton does exploit some of the methods associated with such texts. However, he deals with the issues in a fundamentally different way: within Milton's overall technique, the incongruity that characterizes part of *Areopagitica*'s argument is deliberate and strategic and marks the tract as a preliminary document. Analyzing Milton's handling of the grotesque gives, in this context, vital clues about how *Areopagitica* should be read.

THE HISTORICAL CONTEXT

The seventeen months between the passing of the Licensing Order in June 1643 and the publication of *Areopagitica* in November 1644 were marked by political and religious controversy among parliamentarians. The unity against the common royalist foe had started to crumple even earlier, but by 1643 three distinct groups were beginning to emerge: first, the Presbyterians; second, the supporters of the Gathered Churches, the early Independent movement; and, third, smaller and less homogeneous as a group, the radicals. The most sizeable and important of these groups were the Presbyterians, and their majority in Parliament and in the Westminster Assembly carried such anti-Tolerationist legislation as the 1643 Licensing Order. At the same time, the Presbyterians were divided between the strict and highly intolerant *jure divino* faction, which dominated the Westminster Assembly, and the more moderate Erastians, who held the majority in the House of Commons.

The most important political and religious question of 1643 and 1644 was whether the supporters of the Gathered Churches, a minority both in the Assembly and in Parliament, could persuade the Erastians to vouchsafe their toleration. To this purpose the five "dissenting brethren," central opposition figures in the Westminster Assembly, published in spring 1643 the *Apologeticall Narration,* a manifesto of their beliefs twinned with a plea for toleration. Polemically, the *Apologeticall Narration* proved highly effective in that it obtained a considerable degree of approval from its target group, the moderate Presbyterians and the Erastians: Charles Herle, the Presbyterian licensor of the *Apologeticall Narration* found it *"so full of peaceablenesse, modesty, and candour . . . : That . . . I think it every way fit for the Presse,"* and John Selden, one of the leaders of the Erastians, even defended it in Parliament.[14]

The *Apologeticall Narration* had two further effects: it infuriated the *jure divino* Presbyterians, who felt outmaneuvered, and, on the other end of the spectrum, it encouraged the radicals, who pleaded for an even greater degree of toleration. In the course of 1643–1644, the debate heated up considerably, and although there were still attempts to forge a union of moderates, it became increasingly apparent that a settlement between Presbyterians and supporters of Gathered Churches would not be reached. The positions had become entrenched and would culminate in the more open and direct confrontations between Independents and Presbyterians in the years immediately following. If the radicals had ever entertained any realistic aspirations for wide-ranging toleration, by autumn 1644 it had become clear to them that their hopes would be disappointed. Radical Tolerationists such as Roger Williams were aware of the limited political impact their tracts were likely to have. In *Bloudy Tenent,* he points out defiantly: "I confesse I have little hopes . . . that this Discourse against the *doctrine* of *persecution* for cause of *conscience* should passe currant . . . yet *liberavi animam meam,* I have not hid within my *breast* my *souls* belief."[15]

Where does Milton fit into this political and religious landscape? Ernest Sirluck and his followers place Milton in the camp of the moderates. They suggest that Milton's presentational inconsistencies were a strategic attempt to forge a coalition between Erastians and Independents. Sirluck argues, for example, that Milton aims to win over the Erastians by avoiding any comment on the issue of separation between church and state. His interpretation is still followed by many critics today, but criticism has increased: Stephen Dobranski, for example, points out that Sirluck's "dialectical method cannot accommodate *Areopagitica*'s complex historical implications."[16] I endorse such reservations; however, I disagree with Sirluck on an even more fundamental level. Sirluck implies that Milton's tract is written with a moderate and conciliatory tone similar to that used by the dissenting brethren, and that therefore *Areopagitica* contains an immediate political agenda. I will show that the exact opposite is true, and that instead of appealing to an Erastian audience, *Areopagitica* was much more likely to alienate it. In fact, it not only alienated the moderate Presbyterians, but also the conciliatory supporters of the Gathered Churches, and even some of the radicals.

One of the problems with Sirluck's reading is that outside of *Areopagitica,* Milton was not conciliatory or moderate as far as toleration or freedom of the press were concerned; he had an immediate and highly personal interest in both issues. His divorce tract had made him notorious, had occasioned a direct complaint from the Company of Stationers, and would ultimately lead to an official examination by the House of Lords.[17] Milton's name and his ideas on divorce were widely used by prominent intolerationist Presbyterians such as Herbert Palmer, Daniel Featley, Ephraim Pagitt, and Robert Baillie, who aimed to persuade the more lenient moderates to fall into line with them. Moderate Presbyterians such as John Bachiler and Erastians such as William Prynne also expressed reservations.[18] The postscript of *The Judgement of Martin Bucer,* published only a few months before *Areopagitica,* implies a level of personal anger, which suggests that Milton had little time for an accommodation with the Presbyterian anti-Tolerationists. He denounces the anti-Tolerationists as "this working mystery of ignorance and ecclesiastical thraldom, which under new shapes and disguises begins afresh to grow upon us" (2:479).[19] The commonplace grotesque motifs of the metamorphosing shape and disguise, as well as the direct association of the anti-Tolerationists with the prelates, indicate a vehemence that stands in sharp contrast to the polemics of the moderates. To deal with this complication, Christopher Hill, who subscribes to Sirluck's reading, suggests that Milton's tract displays "tactical moderation,"[20] a strategic wiliness that is motivated by a seventeenth-century form of realpolitik, and which hides Milton's real convictions.

Such a reading is highly unlikely. In arguing for mutual toleration and for a revocation of the 1643 Licensing Order, Milton is repeating arguments that had been in the public domain for well over a year without having had any real political effect. It is difficult to imagine that Milton could have thought that his own, relatively late contribution to the debate would be more successful than his predecessors'. If Roger Williams, who had spent the early 1640s in America, could gauge the likely impact of his proposals, it seems plausible that Milton, who had actively participated in the political altercations of the 1640s, possessed similar political acumen. Like Williams, Milton was fighting for a cause that, from a political perspective, seemed lost for the time being. However, unlike Williams, Milton was not defiant in his approach, but aimed to influence his readers in the medium and long term.

The seemingly straightforward call for an (instant) revocation of the Licensing Order was merely a formal point of departure, a concession to both the genre and the spirit of his contemporary readers. In reality, Milton's practical proposals for press control were much less straightforward and indeed much more difficult to discern.

THE FIGURE OF THE ORATOR

While Christopher Hill's assertion of tactical wiliness is misleading as far as *Areopagitica*'s political agenda is concerned, it is still important because it indicates a common reading experience. Hill's comment implies a certain apprehensiveness toward the persona of the author, which is also felt by other readers—albeit often for different reasons.[21] It is not easy, after all, to trust a person who appears to be acting *tactically* and whose words cannot, therefore, be taken at face value, even if you agree with some of the tenets they expound. A mixture of approval and apprehension can also be seen in the only known contemporary response to *Areopagitica,* by a German-speaking correspondent of Samuel Hartlib:

Miltons discours hat unterschiedliche guete Notiones in sich, so seind auch seine expressiones an vielen orten scharpf und ingenios. Ist aber über all fast all zu satyrisch, auch wegen seines all zu affectaten styli an vielen orten ohne ursach gar obscur.

[Milton's discourse contains notions of disparate quality; thus in many passages his expressions are astute and ingenious. However it is almost everywhere all too satirical, and many passages are obscure without cause, as a result of his all too affected style.][22]

On the one hand, the correspondent judges the tract as brilliantly argued and, one may infer, argumentatively convincing. On the other hand, Hartlib's correspondent is alienated on two accounts: he objects to a satirical tone that is too aggressive, and to stylistically elaborate passages that obscure the tract's argumentative exposition. In fact, beyond the admiration for Milton's line of argument, Hartlib's correspondence also displays a certain exasperation with *Areopagitica*'s "obscure" passages, as they seem to serve no obvious purpose (that is, they are "obscure without cause"), and merely diminish the tract's persuasiveness and its overall appeal.

Neither criticism reflects stylistic blunders and shortcomings, as Hartlib's correspondent assumes, but they are, in fact, part of a deliberate strategy that aims to prevent a direct identification with the authorial persona and with the argument he presents. This is particularly true if one considers the largest group of Milton's projected readership in Parliament, the Erastian faction. Within this section I will show that Milton's authorial persona is constructed in a manner that makes him appear incongruous, his argumentative positions fluctuating and at times even suspect or downright devious. To illustrate his technique, I shall look at the author's persona and at the party allegiances he signals, at his technique of grotesque satire, and at the stance he takes on press control.

Milton's authorial self-presentation seems conventional at first sight. He follows the traditional practice of rhetoric as defined by Cicero, Quintilian, and Aristotle, and aims to illustrate his own authority as orator and his qualification to speak.[23] At the same time, Milton attempts to secure the benevolence of his imagined parliamentarian audience for a speech that contains, after all, a critical, epideictic undercurrent. The stance Milton assumes in the exordium is particularly suitable in this context. He poses in the guise of the "privat Orator" in the style of Isocrates and Dion Prusaeus (2:489), and by doing this he gives the impression of being an isolated philosopher-orator-scholar whose private contemplation convinces him of the correctness of a particular policy. As a precedence for private oratory, he

> could name him who from his private house wrote that discourse to the Parlament of *Athens,* that perswades them to change the forme of *Democraty* which was then establisht. Such honour was done in those dayes to men who profest the study of wisdome and eloquence, not only in their own Country, but in other Lands, that Cities and Siniories heard them gladly, and with great respect, if they had ought in publick to admonish the State. Thus did *Dion Prusaeus* a stranger and a privat Orator counsell the *Rhodians* against a former Edict. . . . But if from the industry of a life wholly dedicated to studious labours, and those naturall endowments haply not the worst for two and fifty degrees of northern latitude, so much must be derogated, as to count me not equall to any of those who had this priviledge, I would obtain to be thought not so inferior, as your selves are superior to the most of them who receiv'd their counsell. (2:489–90)

Milton emphasizes the philosophical detachment in both his prototypes: clearly, neither Isocrates, writing from "his private house," nor Dion Prusaeus, "a stranger and privat Orator," are at the head of a party of angry discontents. Instead, both seem of scholarly and retiring disposition, and the *private* nature of their political comments are given particular emphasis.

The Miltonic persona whose life is described as "wholly dedicated to studious labours," and who also professes a sole interest in the "publick good" (2:486), pretends to philosophical detachment to a similar degree. In fact, Milton stresses at the very onset of his tract that the only reason he renders *Areopagitica* in the form of a pamphlet is because he lacks "accesse" to Parliament "in a *private* condition" (2:486; italics mine). The implication is that *Areopagitica* is only in the public domain out of sheer necessity; it is still at heart a private speech written for a private occasion.[24] The effect of this pose is reassuring for a parliamentary readership, at least at first sight: crit-icism may be voiced, but the author's intentions are neither publicly adver-sarial nor seditious.

Areopagitica's exordium also gives the impression that the speech will be epideictic, as far as the *genus orationis* is concerned. The subject matter seems to be praise and exhortation: thus, Milton applauds the "laudable deeds" and the "indefatigable vertues" of Parliament, includes a short justifi-cation for flattery (487–88), and progresses to giving the "plainest advice" (488), exhorting Parliament to "judg[e] over again that Order which ye have ordain'd to *regulate Printing*" (490–91). The word with which he chooses to label his own speech in the exordium is telling: *Areopagitica* is a "Homily" (491). This implies a didactic and benevolent intent. It seems that Milton wants to show Parliament its error of judgment and hopes that it will mend its ways speedily.

By the time the reader arrives at page 23, however, the pose of the orator has changed substantially. Milton now expresses his incredulity at

what words of complaint I heard among lerned men . . . utterd in time of Parlament against an order of licencing; and that so generally, that when I had disclos'd my self a companion of their discontent, I might say, if without envy, that he whom an honest *quaestorship* had indear'd to the *Sicilians,* was not more by them importun'd against *Verres,* then the favourable opinion which I had among many who honour ye, and are known and respected by ye, loaded me with entreaties and perswasions; that I would not despair to lay together that which just reason should bring into my mind, toward the removal of an undeserved thraldom upon lerning. . . . And in their name I shall for neither friend nor foe conceal what the generall murmur is. (2:539)

Suddenly, it seems, Milton is no longer an isolated, "privat Orator," or a "stranger," but he is in fact the mouthpiece of a general discontent, speaking not just *for* others, but at their request and "in their name." If parliamentary readers were reassured by the pose Milton had assumed in his exordium, they may at this point be much more unsettled. In fact, the diction of the passage is almost conspiratorial: Milton discloses his discontent to his com-panions, he is privy to seditious murmurings, and he is embroiled in a large-scale controversy that involves both friends and foes. The implications of this tone are even more worrying if the allusion to Cicero is explored further: Milton has cast off the guise of the retiring, secluded, private orator, and adopts instead a highly public and adversarial stance. The implication of Milton's allusion is this: like Cicero, Milton has been approached by the victims of a corrupt and tyrannical administration, and, just as in Cicero's case, the powerful nature of their adversary enforces a certain amount of clandestine behavior. Who is the corrupt and tyrannical Verres in this com-

parison? The inference is that he is a conglomerate of all the powerful supporters of licensing, that is, the anti-Tolerationist *jure divino* Presbyterians of
the Westminster Assembly as well as the supporters of licensing in Parliament, including most of the Erastians.

The Cicero allusion has not only altered Milton's pose, but also the
nature of the speech: it is now no longer epideictic, didactic, and benevolent
but, rather, forensic, accusatory, and angry. The Miltonic persona, then, appears as incongruous, and to some extent also devious: an Erastian reader, for
example, may have been lured into a false set of expectations, and might be
discontented to discover that the author is in fact much more openly hostile
than he had initially pretended. A radical reader, by contrast, may also be
disappointed by Milton's shifting authorial stance. The initial appeasement of
Parliament may well have surprised and dismayed such a reader, especially
because the postscript to *Martin Bucer* had given hope for a more overtly
confrontational approach. In both cases a direct identification with the authorial persona is prevented.

Milton claims as his models Isocrates, Dion Prusaeus, and Cicero, but
none of them reflects Milton's position in the Toleration debate accurately.
This apparent contradiction enhances the feeling of authorial deviousness.
Milton's divorce tracts had made him a notorious exploiter of the freedom of
the press in the eyes of the anti-Tolerationists, and even the more moderate
Erastians were unlikely to approve of publications such as *The Doctrine and
Discipline of Divorce.* For Milton to pretend, in this context, that his position
was that of a "privat Orator" writing from his "own private house" gives a
highly inaccurate impression. Milton's name was already in the public domain, and his aversion to licensing was not so much born out of abstract and
secluded contemplations, but rather from the real practical persecution of his
own writings, as the postscript to *Martin Bucer* implies.

The Cicero comparison is inaccurate for the same reasons. In Cicero's
case, his righteousness and his love for an old-fashioned, Roman virtue had
convinced him to become involved in the persecution of Verres. He had
nothing to gain from the case (other than fame), and he was not one who was
suppressed or exploited by the rule of Verres. Forensic and angry Cicero's
speeches may be, but he is never personally affected by the outcome of the
trial. Milton's case in the Toleration debate is not like Cicero's; in fact, it
resembles much more closely that of the unjustly persecuted Sicilians.

What the reader is left with is an uncertain picture of Milton as author of
Areopagitica. His pose may appeal to some readers at some time, but it will
alienate those same readers at another point in the tract. Hartlib's correspondent had complained of an inexplicable lack of clarity in *Areopagitica;* Chris-

topher Hill of "tactical moderation": I believe that the way in which Milton has constructed his authorial persona encourages such reading experiences.

PARTY ALLIANCES

The feeling of an incongruous authorial position is further encouraged by the conflicting party allegiances *Areopagitica* signals. One bewildering feature of Milton's tract is that he simply seems to ignore what goes on around him.[25] He names neither friends nor opponents, and he also fails to engage, directly, with the current state of the Toleration debate.[26] As a consequence, it becomes difficult to place the figure of the author in the political and religious landscape. For a partisan reader, aware of the Toleration debate and of its political implications, this is problematic: a straightforward identification or rejection is not possible, and therefore political hints and implications become significant. These signals, however, are not only difficult to decipher, but they are actually contradictory.

Initially, for example, Milton seems to appeal to the Presbyterians and Erastians in Parliament. Thus, he refers to the part he played in the anti-episcopal debate as an opponent of Bishop Joseph Hall and as a defender of Smectymnuus (2:488).[27] All the five Smectymnuans were central Presbyterian figures in the early 1640s and were widely admired for their early and courageous stance in the victorious struggle against episcopacy. By alluding to his defense of Smectymnuus, Milton presents himself, momentarily, as an old comrade-at-arms of the Presbyterian faction. It is a pose that furnishes him with prestige, and in turn colors his criticism of the parliamentary Licensing Order, carried by the Presbyterian majority, with a feeling of goodwill: "he who freely magnifies what hath been nobly done, and fears not to declare as freely what might be done better, gives ye the best cov'nant of his fidelity; and that his loyalest affection and his hope waits on your proceedings. His highest praising is not flattery, and his plainest advice is a kinde of praising" (2:488).

The tone of goodwill toward Parliament is communicated here with words such as "fidelity," "loyalty," "affection," "praise." Taken in isolation, the Presbyterian credentials and the elevated praise of Parliament suggest Erastian sympathies.

Other passages, however, signal support for the early Independent movement and for the radicals, and Milton even employs some of the polemics associated with these parties. Milton indicates his approval, for example, through his use of two biblical proof-texts: Saint Paul's dictum, "Prove all things, hold fast that which is good" (Thess. 5:21, YP 2:511–12), and the wheat-and-tare parable (Matt. 13:24–30, YP 2:514). Both texts suggest that toleration is divinely sanctioned, and their scriptural implications feature widely in tracts by Independent and radical Tolerationists.[28] The fact that Milton also uses these texts (and the standard Tolerationist arguments they are associated with) signals an implicit party alliance. As a consequence, an informed seventeenth-century reader would be torn in several directions: on the surface, there seems to be a new, detached, and independent appeal; underneath, however, Milton is actively engaging with the debate and appealing to the sympathies of disparate and disunited parties. A feeling of authorial evasiveness results, and I suggest that the difficulties a reader experiences when trying to locate the author's political allegiances are, in fact, the result of a specific design.

The confusing position Milton's authorial persona takes in the controversy between the new and the old is perhaps the best indicator of how Milton constructs deliberately conflicting signals within the current political atmosphere. Analyzing an author's stance toward the old and the new in 1643 and 1644 is particularly useful in this context because the implications for an author's party alliance are straightforward: Presbyterians, both *jure divino* and Erastian, support the old, early Independents, and radicals support the new. Presbyterian opinions on church government are fundamentally based on the notion of a restoration of the original, biblical form of church government—they are not based on innovation. The idea of new discoveries in divinity was seen as an affront, especially by *jure divino* Presbyterians.[29] Even William Prynne, who as an Erastian did not subscribe to the *jure divino* principle, and who believed that a certain degree of Christian freedom was permissible in church government, denies categorically that such a liberty included new forms not yet discovered: "*THE OLD IS BETTER:* Old *Presbytery,* old unlordly *Episcopacy,* are (no doubt) far better for us then *New Independency.*"[30]

Milton's position is curious within the context of this debate. Initially it appears that he goes to some length to distance himself from advocacy of the new. Thus, he explains that the freedom of the press is not a novel invention, but is based on the best ancient precedents: "I might defend my selfe with ease, if any should accuse me of being new or insolent, did they but know how much better I find ye esteem it to imitate the old and elegant humanity of Greece, then the barbarick pride of a *Hunnish* and *Norwegian* statelines" (2:489).

The antithesis "new or insolent" and "old and elegant" indicates that Milton—despite foreseeing potential misunderstandings—considers his own proposals as based on tradition and antiquity. The bias for the old seems clear enough, and *Areopagitica* seems to adopt a Presbyterian (and Erastian) approach within the present debate. However, the fact that Milton's "old and elegant" precedent is based on pagan Athens rather than on early church or Reformation history already indicates a considerable yet implicit deviation from the received manner with which Presbyterians conducted their arguments. A further deviation from the Presbyterian position occurs only a few pages later, when Milton suggests that licensing might hinder "the discovery that might bee yet further made both in religious and civill Wisdome" (2: 491–92). Although Milton avoids the word "new," a certain hostility to the Presbyterian position becomes evident. The inference is that while Milton's own argument for freedom of the press is not novel in itself, a revocation of the Licensing Order would enable others to make precisely the sort of discoveries in "religious and civill Wisdome" from which he had seemingly distanced himself. A certain fluidity of logic in Milton's argument becomes evident.

Later in the tract, when Milton presents his vision of England as "a Nation of Prophets, of Sages, and of Worthies," his support for the new is unequivocal: "there be pens and heads there, sitting by their studious lamps, musing, searching, revolving new notions and idea's wherewith to present, as with their homage and their fealty the approaching Reformation" (2:554). Milton's earlier rejection of what is "new or insolent" has come full circle, and he even mentions with approval the controversial adjective "new."[31] The fact that this transition is not explicated within the tract seems somewhat underhanded even for a modern reader, and it must have appeared all the more so for a readership that was attentive to such key distinctions as the question of "old" and "new." Again, a feeling of authorial deviousness and tacit manipulation emerges. Although Milton's position makes it difficult for a contemporary reader to gauge his specific party alliance, the subtleness with which he modulates his stance in the debate between the new and the old indicates that Milton is pursuing a particular strategy that makes his authorial persona look appealing in one passage, less appealing in another, and rather slippery and metamorphosing if analyzed as a whole.

GROTESQUE SATIRE

Another characteristic that makes it difficult to place the Miltonic persona is *Areopagitica*'s technique of grotesque satire, and the increasing hostility with which it portrays the anti-Tolerationists. In order to estimate the relative severity of Milton's grotesque satire, and the impact its polemics were likely to have, it is important to assess the state of the Toleration debate in the autumn of 1644. In this section I aim to explore the grotesque structures Milton sets up in his satire, and to illustrate that the technique, in the existing climate of the debate, was unlikely to secure wide support from moderate English Presbyterians. Indeed, the severity of the satire even managed to dismay a reader like Hartlib's correspondent, who was otherwise convinced by the gist of Milton's argument.

The central document of the early stages of the Toleration debate is the *Apologeticall Narration,* not only in terms of its argumentation, but also as far as the drawing of polemic and stylistic frontiers is concerned. In some way its authors, the five dissenting brethren, were attempting exactly what Sirluck asserts of *Areopagitica*—the forging of a coalition between the moderate, Erastian Presbyterian and the early Independent movement. In a minority in the Westminster Assembly, they address Parliament directly (and also the people at large), thus signaling an Erastian bias that ultimately opposes the theocratic pretensions of the Scottish *jure divino* majority in the Assembly. The manner in which the brethren forward their argument is deliberately nonconfrontational: even the genre—a mixture of autobiographical apology and historical narration—steers away from the vehement polemics usual in Renaissance religious controversies.[32] Polemically, the *Apologeticall Narration* proved highly effective by obtaining a considerable degree of approval from its target group, the moderate Presbyterians and the Erastians. Charles Herle, the Presbyterian licensor of the *Apologeticall Narration,* found it "so full of peaceablenesse, modesty, and candour . . . : That . . . I think it every way fit for the Presse," and John Selden, one of the leaders of the Erastians, defended it in Parliament.[33]

In fact, the pose of humility is one of the major polemic points of appeal for the Tolerationists, especially in comparison to the more vehement replies contributed by *jure divino* Presbyterians such as Adam Steuart, Robert Baillie, or Thomas Edwards. Thus, Walwyn commends the "spirit of meeknes"; Hezekiah Woodward aims to render his own "words as *smooth as oyle,* and *as soft as Butter*"; Henry Robinson asks "in all meeknesse" for mutual restraint; *A Coole Conference* comments on "the Apologie; whose words are milde, and soft . . . [its] bullets can do no hurt, can make no battery"; the anonymous *A Reply of Two of the Brethren to A. S.* calls it a "poor meek thing" and mockingly compares Adam Steuart's *Observations* on the *Apologeticall Narration* to "a man with a Pole-axe, knocking a man on the head to kill a flie lighting on his beard."[34] Williams also comments on the stylistic difference between the Tolerationists and the anti-Tolerationists: "These *Arguments* against . . . *persecution,* and the *Answer* pleading for it, written (as *Love* hopes) from godly *intentions, hearts,* and *hands,* yet in a marvellous different *stile* and *manner.* The *Arguments* against *persecution* in *milke,* the *Answer* for it (as I may say) in *bloud.*"[35]

Williams's assessment is a little simplistic as some of the more extreme supporters of toleration also vent their anger in vehemence.[36] However, in general, the Tolerationists avoid overtly divisive, violent outbursts and the use of grotesque satire; even the most radical Tolerationists such as Robinson or Williams refrain from stylistic provocation, and even as the debate heats up the Tolerationists only rarely employ vehement, grotesque satire. Instead, the mode of Marprelatian mockery is revived in a series of pamphlets leveled at the *jure divino* Presbyterians.[37] While not excessively vehement, this Marprelatian mode is much more provocative than the earlier style of humility: it is clearly not an intention of these tracts to accommodate the moderates or to offer the possibility of a coalition between radicals, Independents, and Erastians. Critical responders such as Sidrach Simpson, one of the authors of the *Apologeticall Narration,* testify that even the instigators of the Toleration debate had misgivings about the increasingly provocative manner with which the controversy was conducted.

How foule things were reported of Christ and *Paul?* How boldly were the Primitive Christians calumniated, that if all things were not believed by all, yet some thing might be believed by some. . . . So have the Papists dealt with *Luther, Calvin, Beza, Perkins, Whitaker* and others: so dealt *Martin* Mar-prelate (as he called himselfe) for the Presbiteriall government against Episcopacy. But as that course was not blessed by God to reformation, or to mitigation of the Bishops wrath; so neither was it liked or approved by the grave and wise ones of his owne opinion.[38]

It seems that in order to appeal to moderate and conciliatory readers, as Simpson does in his *The Anatomist Anatomis'd,* what is also needed—and indeed almost expected—is a denunciation of radicals at both ends of the religious spectrum. Thomas Hill, a conciliatory supporter of Presbyterianism, displays such a technique in *The Season for Englands Selfe-Reflection* when he suggests that *"There seemes to bee some* good hopes *of a faire* accommodation" between the Independents and the Presbyterians. At the same time, however, he explicitly excludes the more radical fringe views of the debate, rejecting not only strict *jure divino* Presbyterianism but also the proposals for universal toleration.[39]

With the polemical stage set out, it becomes possible to assess Milton's contribution to the debate in terms of its style. A defining aspect of *Areopagitica*'s polemics is that it refrains from the *ad hominem;* Milton does not link his debate to any of the combatants, and he also refrains from using the Marprelate mode, which he had helped to resurrect earlier in his anti-episcopal pamphlets.[40] Indeed, to some extent *Areopagitica* contains the hallmarks of the earlier phase of the Toleration debate, the practical and conciliatory aspects of style with which the debate was instigated in the *Apologeticall Narration.* Like that pamphlet's narrative, or like Woodward's epistolary contribution, Milton uses an uncommon literary genre for a polemical religious dispute in choosing the form of the printed oration. A further similarity is that Milton, as part of his overall strategy, employs the themes of humility, meekness, and mildness, and attributes them to his own authorial persona and to Parliament, his addressee. Milton's tone is apologetic from the outset. He hopes to illustrate that his authorial motives are "blamelesse" (2:487), and he works toward his "owne acquittall" (488). Parliament is "milde and equall" (488), and the author apologizes that he should "thus farre presume upon the meek demeanour of [Parliament's] civill and gentle greatnesse" (489). Indeed, despite indicating that the purpose of the pamphlet is the voicing of a "grievance" (487), the conclusion of Milton's *exordium* seems to offer implicit concessions to the argument for censorship, and Parliament's reasons for passing the ordinance:

I deny not, but that it is of greatest concernment in the Church and Commonwealth, to have a vigilant eye how Bookes demeane themselves, as well as men; and thereafter to confine, imprison, and do sharpest justice on them as malefactors: For Books are not absolutely dead things, but doe contain a potencie of life in them to be as active as the soule was whose progeny they are; nay they do preserve as in a violl the purest efficacie and extraction of that living intellect that bred them. . . . And yet on the other hand unlesse warinesse be us'd, as good almost kill a Man as kill a good Book; who kills a Man kills a reasonable creature, Gods Image; but hee who destroyes a good Booke, kills reason it selfe, kills the Image of God, as it were in the eye. (2:492)

Taken in isolation, the plea in this passage does not seem to be for freedom of the press, nor does Milton attack the intellectual premises behind the Licensing Order. Although Milton vaguely intimates that press control should take place after publication ("thereafter"), the central concern of the passage is that extreme care should be taken in the process of censoring: the implication is that good books have an exponential power to exceed their authors' natural goodness, but Milton intimates in this metaphor, conversely, that books also have the potential to exceed ordinary humans in wickedness. The inference seems to be that if good books are the image of reason and of God himself, dangerous books must be destroyed all the more urgently because they are the epitome of evil. Later on, when Milton expounds his theory of the usefulness of adversities, these inferences turn out to be wrongly deducted (as I intend to show), but at this stage the violence of Milton's demand to "confine, imprison, and do sharpest justice on" books seems to present a polemical concession to the supporters of licensing. Hence, the above passage enhances the conciliatory tone that dominates the early parts of *Areopagitica,* and heightens the similarity to the style of the *Apologeticall Narration.*

However, the ending of Milton's narrative digression signals a change in tone, which may have come as a surprise for contemporary readers.[41] When Milton's history arrives at the point at which licensing is conceived and born, the plain narrative style, appropriate for historical narrations, and also for historical digressions within deliberative orations (see 7:501), gives way to vehement satire leveled against licensing and its progenitor, Counter-Reformation Catholicism. The reader cannot help being taken aback by the unexpected barrage of grotesque images Milton draws up. These are images of disguise and play-acting: the Council of Trent needs unmasking (2:501), the prelates are the Catholic's "Eccho," and their "gay imitation" copies Catholics "apishly" (2:504). There are anatomic images of torture, in which licensing is "a violation" to "many an old good Author" and "rake[s]" through their "entralls" (2:503), or in which Juno (as figuration of licensing) stifles a natural birth (2:505), thus cruelly prolonging the labor pains (see YP 2:505 n. 68). There is an unnatural "engendring" between the Council of Trent and the Spanish Inquisition (2:503), and there are "womb[s]" that issue "Monster[s]" (2:505).

Milton also employs the typical grotesque mixture of the sinister and horrifying and the insubstantial and ludicrous. Thus, from one perspective the birth of licensing and its effects on good authors are portentous, monstrous, and sinister: "the Councell of Trent, and the Spanish Inquisition engendring together brought forth, or perfeted those Catalogues, and expurging Indexes that rake through the entralls of many an old good Author, with a violation wors then any could be offer'd to his tomb" (2:502–3). Milton uses the grotesque motif of the monstrous birth, the images of disembowelling and of the defiling of graves to illustrate the full horror and perverseness of licensing. By contrast, however, the Catholic licensors, who by logical continuation of the image should appear as sadistic torturers, turn out to be specimens of the ludicrous grotesque. The "2 or 3 glutton Friers" (2:503), Milton's first example of typical licensors, may still have some small remnant of menace through the implied image of their physical bulk. However, his last example, in which five personified *"Imprimaturs"* are seen "complementing and ducking each to other with their shav'n reverences" in the "Piatza of one Title page" (2:504) is almost entirely farcical and makes the licensors look spineless and petty.[42] The author, who "stands by in perplexity at the foot of his Epistle," waiting to find out whether he "shall to the Presse or to the spunge," is part of the grotesquely comic image, and he is a long way removed in imagery from the "old good Author" whose "entralls" are "rake[d] through" by the "expurging Indexes."

This tendency is further enhanced by Milton's use of the ridiculous grotesque in his description of hell and the satanic. Thus, Milton laconically comments on a book with imprimaturs from four different licensors: "Sure they have a conceit, if he of the bottomlesse pit had not long since broke prison, that this quadruple exorcism would barre him down" (2:504). To add to the farcical nature of his comment, Milton complements the image of breaking from the "bottomlesse pit" with the eccentricity of Claudius's proposed legislature on flatulence: "I feare their [the Catholic licensors'] next designe will be to get into their custody the licencing of that which they say *Claudius* intended, but went not through with" (2:504). In the end, the potential menace of hell becomes harmless in the image of "new limbo's, and new hells," "sought out" by Catholics so that "they might include [Protestant] Books also within the number of their damned" (2:506). This is a hell without substance, and it holds little terror.

The mixture of the comic and the frightening, of the insubstantial and the threatening exists in conjunction with more conventional grotesque images and disorients the reader to some extent. What started as a serious and scholarly historical digression into the history of censorship with the aim of indirect social criticism, develops into a sequence of grotesque images that contrasts sharply with the scholarly and historical tone of the earlier passages.

While the historical outline of censorship is problematic in its stylistic development, it is also circumlocutory in its polemic target.[43] For although Milton includes the "Prelats, and their Chaplaines" and their "apishly Romanizing" (2:504) approach to licensing, the main thrust of the grotesque polemics is aimed at Catholicism and at licensing. The Parliament, the anti-Tolerationist Presbyterians, and the reestablishment of licensing in 1643, which are, after all, the logical continuation of the increasingly grotesque history of licensing, are exempt here from Milton's direct criticism. However, the implications of Milton's history and the development of his style are severe, as they indicate polemical possibilities of grotesque satire that distinctly break with the tradition of restrained criticism as instigated in the *Apologeticall Narration.* At this stage of his pamphlet, Milton still labors to illustrate that any association between the historical grotesqueness of licensing and the English supporters of licensing is merely accidental and due to insufficient information (see 2:507). However, although the connection between Catholics, prelates, and the Presbyterians is only tentative, the fact that Milton suggests an association at all indicates, even at this stage in *Areopagitica,* a certain polemic belligerence.

And yet, the association of the Presbyterians with the prelates, offensive as it is, is not innovative in itself, as many of the more outspoken Tolerationist tracts were quick to utilize the same association.[44] What is new in Milton's tract is that he opens up the possibility for vehement, Reformation-style grotesque satire: although not explicitly realized in the historical digression, the potential for a more vehement rejection of anti-Tolerationism can already be felt.

As *Areopagitica* progresses, Milton labors to enhance and underpin the tentative link that he establishes between Roman Catholicism, the Anglican prelates, and the anti-Tolerationist Puritans: thus, in a *reductio ad absurdum,* Milton points out that, for licensing to operate properly, indexes of forbidden books would have to be established, and that, to keep public morality controlled, Parliament would have to send visitors to all parishes in order to assess and enforce uniformity (see YP 2:524 n. 140). The polemic link between such measures and the notorious Catholic *Indexes of Prohibited Books* and the *Index of Expurgations,* the Spanish Inquisition, and the much-hated Laudian visitors must have been highly obnoxious for many moderate readers. Although the association is again tentative in that it is merely hypothetical, the polemic link becomes increasingly established in the reader's mind, and, as *Areopagitica* progresses, Milton makes the comparison even more prominent; thus, he sardonically points out that the question of licensing "will soon put it out of controversie that Bishops and Presbyters are the same to us both name and thing" (2:539), and he even compares the anti-Tolerationist Presbyterians to the widely detested and recently abolished Star Chamber, the Laudian instrument of power, used for the suppression of Puritanism (2:569). Through the associative link between Catholics, prelates, and anti-Tolerationist Presbyterians, the explicit and vehemently grotesque satire Milton had leveled at Catholicism and at licensing in general becomes relevant for the way in which the reader perceives the anti-Tolerationists. The incomplete and increasingly grotesque history of censorship is completed in the reader's mind, and the real target of Milton's grotesque satire and its current application becomes evident. Later in the tract, the link becomes clearer still:

But if neither the check that *Moses* gave to young *Joshua,* nor the countermand which our Saviour gave to young *John,* who was so ready to prohibit those whom he thought unlicenc't, be not anough to admonish our Elders how unacceptable to God their testy mood of prohibiting is, if neither their own remembrance what evill hath abounded in the Church by this lett of licencing, and what good they themselves have begun by transgressing it, be not anough, but that they will perswade, and execute the most *Dominican* part of the Inquisition over us, and are already with one foot in the stirrup so active at suppressing, it would be no unequall distribution in the first place to suppresse the suppressors themselves; whom the change of their condition hath puft up, more then their late experience of harder times hath made wise. (2:568–69)

The grotesqueness of the Presbyterians is emphasized through the association with the Dominican friars of the Inquisition, but also through the image of metamorphosis, the "change of their condition," and the image of being grotesquely "puft up." Furthermore, Milton illustrates the threat the

Presbyterians pose to the people at the heart of society through his eques-
trian image, which sees the "Elders . . . with one foot in the stirrup."

The fact that Milton employs vehement and severe polemics that include grotesque Reformation-style satire puts him stylistically outside the
camp of the moderates. In this context it is also significant that *Areopagitica*
contains only an explicit exclusion of Catholics from toleration. The fact that
Milton does not condemn the radicals on the other side of the religious and
political spectrum, such as Williams or Robinson, also suggests that *Areopagitica* cannot appeal immediately to Erastians, as it lacks one of the essential
characteristics of conciliatory pamphlets in the current state of the debate. It
is difficult to reconcile the tract's initial humble and conciliatory approach
with the vehemence and aggressiveness that surface as the tract progresses.
Again, a feeling of authorial deviousness is evoked, and a direct identification
with the author is prevented.

Press Control

If the nature of *Areopagitica*'s grotesque satire makes it unlikely that a pragmatic and conciliatory political motivation was Milton's primary intention,
the disjointed way the tract portrays the question of press control adds to this
impression. The imprecise manner of Milton's depiction of press control has
caused some exasperation among modern critics: Illo, for example, suggests
that it is impossible to ascertain what form of press control Milton actually
wanted.[45]

Within this section I aim to show that the critical uncertainty about Milton's
views on press control is part of *Areopagitica*'s overall technique of presenting
fluid and metamorphosing positions. At the intellectual center of Milton's portrayal of press control lies the question of how bad books, that is, books that need
to be suppressed, can be identified. *Areopagitica* presents its readers with a
series of historical and theoretical models of press control, which are held up to
analysis. While some are rejected outright, many others are presented with at
least partial approval. And yet Milton also implies that none of these models is
sufficient for distinguishing bad books from good ones.

I have divided the different models of press control featured in *Areopagitica* into four main categories and have arranged them sequentially from
most severe to least severe. Such an arrangement is in some way misleading
because it suggests a systematic and logical distinction that is, in fact, missing
in the tract. There is considerable logical overlap, and models can also appear
in conjunction with each other. What my division shows, however, is that the
way in which *Areopagitica* explores press control is difficult to grasp if stringent logical or polemical rules are applied.

The first model of press control presented in *Areopagitica* is the quasi-Catholic model, based on prepublication licensing and executed by professional licensors. Milton shows that this system is the de facto model of press control in the Commonwealth, following the 1643 Licensing Order, and he unequivocally rejects this system as repressive. Its most extreme and absurd form is the practice of licensing by multiple imprimaturs "under the hands of 2 or 3 glutton Friers" (2:503), and objection to this manner of licensing is, of course, *Areopagitica*'s formal theme. Hence, its negative presentation, which often comprises grotesque satire, is not surprising. At first it seems that Milton's proposal for remedying the crisis is merely a reestablishment of the *status ante quo:* freedom of the press should be reestablished much as it had been in the period before the passing of the Licensing Order.[46] All that he demands, it seems at first, is that the parliamentary order should be "call'd in" (2:488), thus allowing the previous practice of publishing to continue.

However, the second model of press control presented in *Areopagitica* poses a significant alteration to previous practice. This model identifies bad books on the basis of their contents, and the classical Athenian system is its paradigm. Only two particular types of books are "take– notice of" by the Athenian "Magistrate": those that are "blasphemous and Atheisticall, or Libellous" (2:494). All other writings, including presumably (but not explicitly) heretical and seditious ones, appear to be permitted. The high praise Milton bestows on the Athenian model suggests that an emulation of such a system would be a worthwhile endeavor. However, the Athenian model is more liberal than the previous practice of press control, in which Parliament, theoretically, possessed an absolute right to ban any book it saw fit.[47] By allowing press control for the categories of "atheistic" or "libelous" only, Milton's Athenian model, if transferred, curtails Parliament's rights substantially and narrows the scope of governmental interference in publishing.

Despite the distinctive liberalization the Athenian model presents, Milton never clearly distinguishes the method of censorship by content and the pre-1643 practice of press control. The conflation of these two distinct models can be seen, for example, when Milton points out that,

as for regulating the Presse, let no man think to have the honour of advising ye better then your selves have done in that Order publisht next before this, that no book be Printed, unlesse the Printers and the Authors name, or at least the Printers be register'd. Those which otherwise come forth, if they be found mischievous and libellous, the fire and the executioner will be the timeliest and the most effectuall remedy, that mans prevention can use. (2:569)

Rhetorically, Milton's proposal is a plea for reestablishing the *status ante quo*. Logically, however, Milton's proposals mix the Athenian model with the previous method of press control practiced in the Commonwealth. Thus, while the exclusion of anonymously or illegally published pamphlets is taken from pre-1643 Commonwealth practice, Milton proposes essentially a much more liberal system of press control based on content, like the Athenian model. Nevertheless, Milton never explicitly distinguishes these rival models and the fundamentally diverging approaches they imply.

However, despite Milton's high praise, and despite being more liberal than the *status ante quo,* the Athenian model is also shown to be insufficient, especially if rigidly and logically applied. A little later in the tract, Milton includes among the number of books that should be permitted Luigi Pulci's *Il Morgante Maggiore* (511), which laid its author open to charges of atheism, heresy, and mockery of religion;[48] the works of Pietro Aretino (518), one of the most notorious literary blackmailers and gossip-mongers of the Italian Renaissance, and the plays of Aristophanes, to whom even Milton refers as a "malicious libeller" (2:523).[49] It appears that what many would consider to be atheistic and libelous writings should not be silenced after all. The boundaries of freedom of publication that the Athenian model sets up are pushed further back—they are open to debate and apparently governed by a certain interpretative flexibility. It seems, then, that the Athenian model is not as suitable an instrument for identifying bad books as it had appeared at first. By suggesting that a further, individual assessment is needed even within the categories of "atheist" and "libel," Milton erodes demarcations that had previously appeared as absolute. Milton's comments infer that a second intellectual process is needed in order to save all those books that are good, despite falling into categories that would formally designate them as bad.

Milton's position is further complicated by a second model of press control, also based on content. The paradigm of this is the system of censorship practiced in early Christian Rome. In this model, the "Books of those whom they took to be grand Hereticks were examin'd, refuted, and condemn'd in the generall Councels; and not till then were prohibited" (2:500–501). The model extends the categories for "bad books" and includes now also severe cases of heresy. However, Milton's interjection, *"those whom they took to be* grand Hereticks" (italics mine), indicates a certain apprehensiveness. In itself, such a cautious stance is not surprising, as much of Milton's earlier prose expresses severe reservations about the views and practices of the early church, especially after the Constantinian conversion (compare *Of Reformation,* 1:558, 560). In fact, the early Roman Christian model of censorship is prefaced with the derogatory interjection: "From hence we shall meet with little else but tyranny in the Roman Empire, that we may not marvell, if not so often bad, as good Books were silenc't" (2:499–500). Milton suggests that the Athenian and late Roman Republican models, in which only libels and atheistic writings are prosecuted, are preferable in comparison. However, despite the seeming inferiority of the early Christian model, the author also expresses broad approval when he points out: "By this time the Emperors were become Christians, whose discipline in this point [that is, of licensing] I doe not finde to have bin more severe then what was formerly in practice" (500).

What is most surprising is that this second submodel of censorship by content, which Milton (partially) approves, is similar to the de facto press control system in force in the Commonwealth prior to the 1643 Licensing Order. The early Roman Christian model of censorship, which focuses on "grand Hereticks," and which is decided on by "the generall Councels," conforms practically to the *status ante quo* (even if it does not theoretically): regulation of the press concentrated largely on religiously controversial or heretical writings, and books were called in and burned by parliamentary order rather than by professional licensors. This happened, for example, in the case of the *Book of Sports* in May 1643, and even after the Licensing Order was passed, direct censorship by Parliament was still carried out for books like Roger Williams's *Bloudy Tenent* (August 1644).[50] By contrast, the ancient Greek model of censorship, which focused on atheistic and libelous writings only and was executed by the *Areopagi,* a council of judges (rather than a general council), did not resemble the *status ante quo* of the Commonwealth as closely.

As a consequence, a disparity of authorial allegiances seemed to arise: on the one hand, Milton recommended a calling-in of the 1643 Licensing Order and a restoration of previous practice; on the other hand, the historical censorship system that most closely resembled the previous status quo was only tentatively approved, and incurred strictures as severe as: "we may not marvell, if not so often bad, as good Books were silenc't." The fact that *Areopagitica* signals at least some partial agreement with tenets of publications that Parliament had banned (the *Book of Sports* and the *Bloudy Tenent*) also indicates that Milton cannot have approved, unequivocally, of a system of censorship that resulted in persecution in these two cases. By comparison, the Athenian system is portrayed with more approval. Despite this, the reader senses by inference that censorship by a careful parliamentary process is preferable to a system of professional licensors, and that the overall effect of the early Christian system of censorship is still largely beneficial, if not ideal.

However, Milton's portrayal of the Athenian and of the early Christian models suggests that there is a fundamental problem with all systems that base press control on content: they cannot be relied on when it comes to distinguishing good books from bad ones. The system of early Christian society, Milton admits, is only slightly more severe than the original Athenian model, and yet it bans good and bad books indiscriminately. This circumstance suggests that censorship by content can only be as good as the society that employs this model and the authorities that execute it. Whereas in well-educated, ancient Athens, the system seemed to work relatively well, in a corrupt Roman Christian society a very similar system led to arbitrary persecution of both good and bad books.

The third model of press control in *Areopagitica* takes an intellectually different approach and proposes to distinguish bad books by their bad effects. In the opening of his tract, Milton points out that in the "Church and Commonwealth . . . a vigilant eye" should be kept on books since they can be "as vigorously productive, as those fabulous Dragons teeth; and being sown up and down, may chance to spring up armed men" (2:492). The implication seems to be that censorship for seditious and divisive pamphlets and for those that incite civil unrest is appropriate, and indeed desirable. Tacitly, however, the Cadmus myth alters the nature of the pre-1643 practice of press control[51] by suggesting that books should be judged by their effects. These effects must, of course, be monitored by the "vigilant eye" of state and church, but the conditional nature of "*may chance* to spring up armed men" (italics mine), suggests that official interference need only occur if the "Dragons teeth" turn out to have a volatile effect; otherwise, circulation can be left undisturbed. In such a system of press control, there is also no longer the need to single out particular contents for censorship: any type of book can be published as long as there are no bad effects.[52]

In order to operate such a model of press control, assessment must take place after publication, that is, after the effects of a book have become sufficiently clear. As part of the logical framework of this third model of press control, Milton suggests that prepublication licensing is unnatural, while postpublication press control is needed, and indeed highly commendable: "If it prov'd a Monster, who denies, but that it was justly burnt, or sunk into the Sea. But that a Book . . . should be to stand before a Jury ere it be borne to the World, and undergo yet in darknesse the judgement of *Radamanth* and his Collegues, . . . was never heard before" (2:505–6).

Many modern critics see Milton's real position in this insistence on postpublication press control, and it is indeed true that its importance is stressed in several passages of the tract.[53] The above quotation, with its grotesque imagery, is a particularly forceful and memorable formulation of this position. However, the model in which press control is based on the effect of books presents only another implicit shift in the imprecise nature with which Milton discusses the appropriate boundaries of press control.

As in the discussion of the second model of press control, the central question for an assessment of this third method is: what success is there in identifying and eliminating bad books? As was the case with earlier models, *Areopagitica* contains passages that lavish praise on the third model, but there are also passages that implicitly challenge the model's efficiency. For example, before agreeing that monstrous books should indeed be condemned and burned, Milton points out:

> As for the burning of those Ephesian books by St. *Pauls* converts, tis reply'd the books were magick, the Syriack so renders them. It was a privat act, a voluntary act, and leaves us to a voluntary imitation: the men in remorse burnt those books which were their own; *the Magistrat by this example is not appointed*: these men practiz'd the books, another might perhaps have read them in some sort usefully. (2:514; italics mine)

The last subclause of this quotation throws into doubt the entire process of press control by effect, and also challenges its practicability. If there are some readers who can peruse the same pagan, magical books "in some sort usefully," while others consider them as extremely dangerous for themselves, how can a central government unequivocally ascertain whether a given book has a bad effect? In the example cited, such a judgment has to be made for each particular reader, and the implication seems to be that, ultimately, only the readers themselves are capable of making that judgment. It seems that governmental press control on the basis of books' effects also fails in distinguishing bad books and good books in all cases. Again, the reader is struck by the seeming logical inconsistency of Milton's discursive position.

While undermining the efficiency of the third model of press control, the above quotation also illustrates the nature of the fourth model of press control contained in *Areopagitica*. By insisting that the burning of the magical books was a private act only, Milton denies anti-Tolerationist Presbyterians a polemically useful precedent by which press control could be legitimized scripturally. The implication of Milton's reading of Acts 19:19 seems to be that if the magistrates have no legitimacy to act as censors, the entire process is open to be dealt with according to Christian liberty.

The fourth model of censorship is marked by Milton's suggestion that any type of press control should be nonobligatory and administered voluntarily by the readers and owners of books themselves. At times, this fourth model may go so far that Milton seems to suggest that there is no need for governmental interference at all, and that all tracts, no matter what their content, can have a potentially beneficial effect:

> Since therefore the knowledge and survay of vice is in this world so necessary to the constituting of human vertue, and the scanning of error to the confirmation of truth, how can we more safely, and with lesse danger scout into the regions of sin and falsity then by reading all manner of tractats, and hearing all manner of reason? (2:516–17)

The formulation "all manner of tractats" here is so wide-ranging that it seems to include all dangerous, heretical and seditious books, and transcends the question of pre- or postpublication press control. Indeed, so wide-ranging is the potential benefit of reading books in this passage that there is no longer a need to single out, as the Athenian model had done, atheistic or libelous books. Within this model even the reading of Catholic propaganda is permissible, both to the learned and to the ignorant, as their perusal is essential for scholars and can do no harm to the lay community:[54] "It will be hard to instance where any ignorant man hath bin ever seduc't by Papisticall book in English, unlesse it were commended and expounded to him by some of that Clergy: and indeed all such tractats whether false or true are as the Prophesie of *Isaiah* was to the *Eunuch*, not to be *understood without a guide*" (2:519).

There are two subcategories in the fourth model of censorship outlined in *Areopagitica*. In the first one, all that Milton seems to insist on is the importance of good guidance as a supplement to reading dangerous books. Evidence of such good guides can be seen in the figure of Isaiah in the above quotation, or in the figure of Saint Paul in the reference to Acts 19, cited above. The implication is that Paul's converts turn against their own magical books and burn them as a consequence of his good guidance in religion. In practical terms it is quite difficult to gauge how this demand for guidance would affect press control in the Commonwealth, but because Milton continually stresses Parliament's role as guide of the nation, some sort of governmental warning may be what is in his mind. Thus, Milton points out that badly educated and ill-prepared readers "well may be exhorted to forbear, but hinder'd forcibly they cannot be" (2:521). Such a method of providing nonobligatory guidance would be similar to that which Milton had tentatively approved in the primitive churches: "The primitive Councels and Bishops were wont only to declare what Books were not commendable, passing no furder, but leaving it to each ones conscience to read or to lay by" (2:501).

Although this manner of press control by nonobligatory guidance is frequently endorsed, *Areopagitica* also contains passages that indicate the dangers of any explicit, official guidance or governmental interference. Thus, Milton rejects "an implicit faith" and points out that "a man may be a heretick in the truth; and if he beleeve things only because his Pastor sayes so, or the Assembly so determins, without knowing other reason, though his belief be true, yet the very truth he holds, becomes his heresie" (2:543). It seems, then, that the reader is once again faced with conflicting information, and that the system of self-regulation combined with nonobligatory governmental advice seems broadly beneficial, and yet flawed.

In the second category of the self-regulatory model of press control,

Milton argues that a wide-ranging education alone can fortify against evil books. The implication is that in an ideal society with educated and responsible citizens, no governmental interference is necessary at all.

> If it be true, that a wise man like a good refiner can gather gold out of the drossiest volume, and that a fool will be a fool with the best book, yea or without book, there is no reason that we should deprive a wise man of any advantage to his wisdome, while we seek to restrain from a fool, that which being restrain'd will be no hindrance to his folly. (2:521)

Well-educated readers can distinguish between good and bad contents for themselves, and so no press control is needed. They can also keep in check, without outside guidance, the potentially bad effects of such books. Such a system seems in many ways ideal, but even for this model *Areopagitica* contains a counterexample in the figure of the "acute and distinct *Arminius*," who "was perverted meerly by the perusing of a namelesse discours writt'n at *Delf*, which at first he took in hand to confute" (2:519–20). Even a discerning, cautious, and well-educated reader such as Arminius cannot fully shield himself against potential seduction of a bad book.

In fact, at times Milton even suggests that the very attempt to single out bad books is futile and based on fundamental misconceptions of good and evil:

> Good and evill we know in the field of this World grow up together almost inseparably; and the knowledge of good is so involv'd and interwoven with the knowledge of evill, and in so many cunning resemblances hardly to be discern'd, that those confused seeds which were impos'd on *Psyche* as an incessant labour to cull out, and sort asunder, were not more intermixt. It was from out the rinde of one apple tasted, that the knowledge of good and evill as two twins cleaving together leapt forth into the World. (2:514)

If the difference between good and evil can often "hardly . . . be discern'd," a press control system that aims to identify and eliminate bad books is fundamentally flawed. Indeed, if knowledge of evil is essential for an understanding of good itself, all forms of censorship have to be considered as counterproductive. Nevertheless, the question remains whether there are any books that are so evil that they are guaranteed to produce only negative effects. I shall defer the answer to this question until later in this essay, when I have analyzed the concept of "grotesque truth." For now, I shall concentrate on the impact of Milton's portrayal of censorship for *Areopagitica* as a whole.

For the reader, the overall effect of Milton's technique is a feeling of considerable imprecision and vagueness. There is no clear distinction between the different models, and no systematic discussion of their benefits and shortcomings. Nevertheless, certain demarcations can be sensed beyond which press control becomes malevolent. It seems quite clear, for example, that the Roman Catholic system of licensing is extremely undesirable, and that the Licensing Order of June 1643 is similarly deficient. Among the other suggestions voiced in the course of the tract, the reestablishment of the status quo prior to the Licensing Order has perhaps the largest polemical impact. However, in terms of its logical argument, *Areopagitica* contains an additional three models of censorship that are more liberal than the previous practice, and their presentations often carry considerable prestige—and yet each of them is seen to be faulty as well. The result is that despite presenting a polemical unity, *Areopagitica* is marked by a logical and methodological fluidity and imprecision that confounds the reader. In this context, *Areopagitica* diverges considerably from the expectations raised by analytical or constructive political pamphlets.

The construction of such a wide-ranging net of press control schemes furnishes the tract with a highly complex incongruity. This suggests that the vacillating of the authorial position may not just be accidental, but in fact a deliberate strategy: it is part of an argumentative structure that is based on metamorphosis and modulation rather than precision of argument. The effect is that while a polemic point is being made, the matter of press control is increasingly complicated. What had seemed a relatively easy choice between the anti-Tolerationist model of licensing on the one hand, and the unqualified call for freedom of the press on the other, is made complex and problematic because the reader is confronted not only with incongruous positions but also with an authorial guidance that is at times highly tentative.

GROTESQUE TRUTH

Milton not only complicates the issue of press control, he also complicates the concept of truth. Milton uses a metamorphosing technique in portraying truth similar to what he had used in his portrayal of censorship. However, the outcome is not one of deliberate vacillation and tentative guidance, but of slowly turning the concept of truth into a grotesque entity.

The call for peace and truth is one of the central battle cries of the Tolerationist debate,[55] and Milton, by portraying truth in an incongruous and metamorphosing manner, again transcends common polemics. Thus in *Areopagitica,* truth metamorphoses from an Amazon-style warrior and wrestler who grapples with Falsehood (2:561) to a town under siege, "beleaguer'd" (554) and in need of champion defenders; truth is also described as merchandise (535–36) and compared to a "streaming fountain" (2:543). The increasingly incongruous and constantly metamorphosing concept of truth is summed up with the use of explicitly grotesque imagery: truth, if constricted, is like the Roman god most closely associated with metamorphosis, Proteus, and when "caught & bound . . . she turns herself into all shapes, except her own" (563). Milton heightens the grotesqueness of this image by suggesting that at times "it is not impossible" for truth to "have more shapes than one" (563). One of the central passages in *Areopagitica* that illustrates Milton's grotesque conception of truth is the myth of Isis and Osiris, derived from Plutarch's *Moralia:*

Truth indeed came once into the world with her divine Master, and was a perfect shape most glorious to look on: but when he ascended, and his Apostles after him were laid asleep, then strait arose a wicked race of deceivers, who as that story goes of the *AEgyptian Typhon* with his conspirators, how they dealt with the good *Osiris,* took the virgin Truth, hewd her lovely form into a thousand peeces, and scatter'd them to the four winds. From that time ever since, the sad friends of Truth, such as durst appear, imitating the carefull search that *Isis* made for the mangl'd body of *Osiris,* went up and down gathering up limb by limb still as they could find them. We have not yet found them all, Lords and Commons, nor ever shall doe, till her Masters second comming; he shall bring together every joynt and member, and shall mould them into an immortall feature of lovelines and perfection. (2:549)

Here the grotesqueness of the mangled and fragmented body of Truth is heightened by a sexual inversion of the image. While Truth is a virgin, the figure of Osiris is male in Plutarch's original myth, with the dismembered body, reassembled by Isis, missing only its genitals.

The notion of truth as a grotesque entity is one of the most innovative aspects of *Areopagitica* within the Toleration debate. The central ideas, however, which allow Milton to develop this new concept, are very much part of the debate. Indeed, a considerable complication of the concept of truth existed even prior to *Areopagitica*'s publication. The trigger for this development lies in the new-old debate, and in the central charge which the anti-Tolerationist Presbyterians leveled against the Independents, that by allowing alteration of received religious concepts they paved the way for the rule of opinion, which, in turn, constituted a grotesque reversal of the natural order.[56] To answer this charge, a conceptual development of truth (and opinion) became paramount. John Goodwin, for example, denies the grotesque and parasitic nature of opinion and imagines it instead as a quasiplanetary satellite to truth,[57] while Roger Williams complicates the concept of truth even further, and places it into a Neoplatonic frame of reference:

Peace. 'Tis lamentably true (*blessed Truth*) the *foundations* of the *World* have long been out of course: the *Gates* of *Earth* and *Hell* have conspired together to intercept our joyfull *meeting* and our holy *kisses:* . . .

Truth. The like enquiries in my flights and travells have I made for *Peace,* and still am told, she hath left the *Earth,* and fled to *Heaven.*

Peace. Deare *Truth,* What is the *Earth* but a *dungeon of darknesse,* where *Truth* is not?

Truth. And what's the *Peace* thereof but a fleeting *dreame,* thine *Ape* and *Counterfeit?*[258]

The images of truth and peace as figures that can either dwell in heaven or on Earth, the notion of the Earth as a *"dungeon of darknesse"* and as an *"Ape* and *Counterfeit,"* conjures up Platonic imagery associated with the theory of ideas. Plato uses the image of the cave in order to teach the nature of philosophical enlightenment (7.514a–515b). For Plato it is the duty of those persons who have escaped from the cave and have become accustomed to "look directly at the sun itself" (516b) to return and instruct those remaining in the darkness. The obvious political application of Williams's Neoplatonic allegory is that the more truth and peace are harassed, constrained, or attacked, the more difficult it becomes for mortals to find access to enlightenment, and the more grotesque society becomes.

Like Williams's conception of truth, Milton's is close to the Platonic notion of the *daimon,* a half-divine, half-earthly mediator. Truth, symbolized in *Areopagitica* by Osiris, has a dual nature: one is epitomized in the image of that "perfect shape most glorious to look on," and it is associated with the first and the second coming of its "divine Master." The second nature of truth is captured in the grotesque image of the dismembered carcass of Osiris. This Neoplatonic slant in Milton's concept of truth can also be seen in the adaptation of 1 Corinthians 13:12 (see YP 2:549 n. 221): "he who thinks we are to pitch our tent here, and have attain'd the utmost prospect of reformation, that the mortall glasse wherein we contemplate, can shew us, till we come to *beatific* vision, that man by this very opinion declares, that he is yet farre short of Truth."

Contained in this image is a radical polemic reversal of the relationship between truth and opinion suggested both by John Goodwin and by the Presbyterians. The *Theomachia* had allowed the Presbyterians to locate themselves at the center of Goodwin's concept of truth, and he merely appeals to the Presbyterians to tolerate related satellite opinions. By contrast, Milton turns imperfect and grotesque opinions into the only format of truth that can be legitimately obtained through the imperfect means available to human beings. This does not mean, of course, that Milton is a relativist, but he *does* seem to maintain that opinions, as earthly reflections of absolute, divine truth, are an inevitable result of that "mortall glasse wherein we contemplate." At the same time he rejects the Presbyterian view that "the utmost prospect of reformation"—and with it ultimate religious truth—is already attained, and provocatively turns their position into a mere "opinion" (compare 2:554, 566).

The passage reveals that for Milton, truth has a dualistic nature: on the one hand, it appears distorted, grotesque, subject to constant change and restricted by man's imprecise contemplative capabilities; on the other hand, it is an unobtainable, complete, and divine entity, which can only be revealed through a *"beatific* vision," and which in its completeness lies beyond the possibilities of purely human realization. Unlike Williams, however, Milton places a heavy emphasis on the grotesqueness and distortion of the earthly form of truth, and in this Milton comes much closer to the Platonic concept of the *daimon.* Both Plato's and Milton's concepts instill, because of their deficient natures, an inner longing to be at one with the fullness of the divine ideas, symbolized, for example, in *Areopagitica* by Isis's quest to perfect the mangled body of Osiris. The consequence of this dual understanding of the nature of truth is that it appears no longer as a purely divine entity, but like another Platonic *daimon,* earthly love, a grotesque, multifaceted, and ever-altering mediator between this world and the next (see *Symposium,* 202d–203a). It is important in this context that Plutarch, who in *Of Isis and Osiris* assembles a confounding abundance of potential interpretations for the Egyptian myth, agrees with those who consider Isis, Osiris, and Typhon to be Platonic *daimons* that hold a middling and mediating position between the human and the divine.[59]

Milton's new understanding of truth as a grotesque entity within a specifically Neoplatonic context is fundamental for an understanding of *Areopagitica* as a whole, and it provides the key for solving many of the problematic aspects of the tract, in particular the nature of the authorial persona, and the reason for the tract's incongruous position on press control.

THE POET-PROPHET

In the light of Milton's new concept of grotesque truth, a reassessment of the figure of the author becomes possible, and his vacillating stance becomes comprehensible. To place this persona more fully into this context, it is necessary to assess, briefly, the role poets, playwrights, and prophetic writers play in the social settings in *Areopagitica.* The portrayal of the prophet-poet's function in society is remarkably homogeneous, considering the tract's incongruities: poets work on and fashion society, refining its communal attitudes and preparing minds so that they become receptive to the process of civilization. Indeed, the existence of prophet-poets is a prerequisite for that process. Thus, Lycurgus the lawgiver introduces Homer's poetry to the Spartans in order to ennoble and prepare them to receive his laws. The Spartan

"Law-giver was so addicted to elegant learning, as to have been the first that brought out of *Ionia* the scatter'd workes of *Homer*, and sent the Poet *Thales* from *Creet* to prepare and mollifie the *Spartan* surlinesse with his smooth songs and odes, the better to plant among them law and civility" (2:496).

"Our sage and serious Poet *Spencer*" (2:516) is—despite the seventeenth-century decline in the estimation of Romance literature[60]—valued more highly as a teacher than Duns Scotus and Thomas Aquinas (2:516), and Milton goes to considerable lengths to explain that Plato was insincere and whimsical when he excluded the poet from his ideal republic (see YP 2:522). Instead, Milton points out that Plato himself recommended the usefulness of poetry and literature, even of the "malicious libeller" Aristophanes, for the education and fashioning of the ideal philosophical ruler (2:522–23).

One may ask why the poet plays such an important part in Milton's argument, especially as no pamphlet in the Toleration debate places such emphasis on literature and poetry. Milton's insistence on the traditional license of poets was not a crucial issue: the concept would probably have been approved of by many of Milton's contemporary readers, and indeed taking away this license was never a primary concern of the supporters of licensing (see YP 2:519). Of course, since Milton was just about to publish his first collection of poems (1645), he was naturally anxious about the role of the poet as far as licensing was concerned,[61] but the intrinsic reason for the unprecedented emphasis *Areopagitica* places on the function of the poet lies in the similarity that the poet, and especially the prophet-poet, has to the Platonic concept of truth. The poet-prophet is also, like truth itself (or like the Platonic concept of love), a mediator between the human and the divine. Thus, Milton points to the dangers of burning books that "might . . . be the dictat of a divine Spirit, yet not suiting with every low decrepit humor" (2:534), thus echoing the Platonic cave image (*Republic,* 517d; compare YP 2:565, 567–68). Like the Platonic concept of truth itself, the enlightened poet-orator is a mediator who transfers his divine visions to the populace at large.

The spiritual aspect of the poet-prophet (and of the Platonic mediator) also reflects on the figure of the orator of *Areopagitica,* and this becomes increasingly evident as the tract progresses through the more frequent incorporation of authorial visions. It is perhaps most evident when the authorial persona launches into an exhortation of the nation:

Methinks I see in my mind a noble and puissant Nation rousing herself like a strong man after sleep, and shaking her invincible locks: Methinks I see her as an Eagle muing her mighty youth, and kindling her undazl'd eyes at the full midday beam; purging and unscaling her long abused sight at the fountain it self of heav'nly radiance. (2:557–58)

Although the immediate application of Milton's allegory exhorts the English nation to act as enlightened prophet to others still in the dark, the image of reaching "the fountain it self of heav'nly radiance" has a finality about it that has apocalyptic undertones.[62] Final enlightenment, both in Plato and in Milton's simile of Osiris, is unobtainable in a temporally finite existence, and Milton's comment, "we have not yet found them all [that is, the limbs of Osiris, the particles of truth], Lords and Commons, *nor ever shall doe, till her Masters second comming*" (2:549; italics mine), suggests that the search for truth can never be completed until the end of time. However, in the vision of the nation as eagle, glancing directly at the sunlight, the attainment of full enlightenment is depicted as achievable. What appears as inconsistency, however, is justified through the opening: "Methinks I see in my mind," which marks the allegory as an inspired poetical vision, an image of ultimate perfection rather than of the indefinite toil of reality. This ability to relate visions also indicates, indirectly, the importance of the poet-prophet in a society: by relating visions of the ideal, the poet-prophet can encourage and exhort the Commonwealth (and its people) not to forbear in their search for truth, and to continue in their striving toward this ideal (see 2:550). The poet-prophet, then, is as much a half-creature, a Platonic *daimon*, as truth itself: on the one hand, he is a real person with physical existence and particular expressions; on the other hand, his prophetic vision links him to the realm of the divine.[63] At the same time, in creating a bridge between the real and the ideal, and in relating his inspired insights, the prophet-poet can instill a desire for perfection in others.

The author's similarity to the concept of truth also explains the deliberately incongruous poses he assumes throughout the tract. Like the metamorphosing and grotesque form of earthly truth, the figure of the author, his views and his positions, undergo metamorphoses and appear as incongruous and inconsistent. But by presenting himself in this way, Milton links himself to the imprecise, grotesque entity of earthly truth. At the same time, the concept of the poet-prophet-orator validates Milton's incongruous stance within the licensing debate: as poet-prophet, his function is not to suggest practical legislation, but to refine and civilize the minds of his readership. Milton pursues this process by complicating the readers' conception of the problems of press control, and of the meaning of truth.

Here lies the essential misunderstanding of Sirluck's and Hill's reading of *Areopagitica* as a political pamphlet with real political and strategic intentions, and here also lies the root of the sense of exasperation some modern critics have felt as a result of the tract's theoretical incongruity. *Areopagitica* is not a political or a philosophical text that aims to promote a particular policy in a methodical manner. In this context, Milton's call to abolish the

1643 Licensing Order and to reestablish the *status ante quo* is merely one aspect of a much less well-defined scheme. Milton intends to fashion his readers' minds, to raise the issues in their full and unsystematic complexity, and it is only from this point of view that the reader can perceive the author's offer of a limited and tentative guidance. Milton's intention is not to contribute an immediate scheme for press control—*Areopagitica* works, rather, as a precursor for a more appropriate and critical debate. Milton's intentions in *Areopagitica* are those of a poet, and not of a philosopher or politician. His role is that of Homer (or Thales) to Sparta, not that of Lycurgus. He prepares and civilizes society so that it can receive efficient and appropriate legislation; he does not produce immediate policies. This particular aim also indicates one of the reasons Milton cannot approve of the quasi-Catholic model of licensing: within such a model, pamphlets like *Areopagitica* are not permitted to appear, and the crucial civilizing process of society is prevented from taking place.

RIVALING GROTESQUE STRUCTURES

Although understanding Milton's concept of grotesque truth gives the reader a clue as to how the figure of the author is to be understood, it also raises a central question: if the author and truth are portrayed in a grotesque manner, and Milton's opponents, the anti-Tolerationists, are also associated with the grotesque, how does their grotesqueness differ?

The two major twentieth-century definitions of the grotesque are those of Wolfgang Kayser and Michael Bakhtin: Kayser focuses chiefly on Romanticism and sees the grotesque as "uncanny" and frightening, while Bakhtin sees it as a positive, amusing, and life-affirming bodily principle defined by the style of Rabelais.[64] Neither of these theories is critically sufficient, as they merely capture facets of the grotesque, valid only for specific literary periods or for particular types of work. A more discerning and flexible approach is needed.

Based on a study of canonical grotesque works in the visual arts, architecture, and literature, I have proposed a new definition, which envisions the grotesque as a structural composite.[65] In this structure, a grotesque entity is merely a minor, fringe component that interacts with a larger idea, norm, notion, or object. Grotesqueness is only perceived as a result of this interaction. For example, the fool is perceived as grotesque because he appears in conjunction with the king; Raphael's *grottesche* in the Vatican loggia are grotesque because they interact, on an aesthetic level, with the biblical paintings at the center of the vaults; Hieronymus Bosch's hellish nightmares in *The Last Judgment* interact with the image of Christ on the rainbow. The nature

of this interaction is characterized by a paradox: on the one hand, the grotesque challenges the norm/idea/entity to which it is attached; on the other
hand, it affirms this very norm/idea/entity because it is aesthetically subordinate, dependent, and even to some extent ornamental to it. This is the basic
and perhaps simplest form the grotesque can take: it is a grotesque structure
made up of what I propose to call a "principle" at the center and a "grotesque
agent" at its margins. A series of variations from this composition exists,[66] but
for a discussion of the grotesque in *Areopagitica* the basic structure of the
grotesque is of central importance.

To understand how the depiction of the anti-Tolerationists and the self-
presentation of the author differ, it is necessary to place Milton's grotesque
portrayals in the context of their overall structures and to locate the central
principle they share: this principle is the body of state. Within this section I
aim to show the difference between the two grotesque structures: it lies in
the nature in which the principle is influenced by its grotesque agent. In one
structure, grotesque truth attaches itself to the individual or to the body of
state, and by doing so it creates a system that is in its essence dynamic, as it
allows and encourages its principle to engage in a life-long quest for perfect
truth. Crucially, the principle of this structure is subject to change, and it may
either bring about improvement or, conversely, deterioration. The second
structure aims at stagnation and cessation of any development. Milton highlights the essential difference between the two juxtaposed types of principles
when he points out: "He that can apprehend and consider vice with all her
baits and seeming pleasures, and yet abstain, and yet distinguish, and yet
prefer that which is truly better, he is the true warfaring Christian. I cannot
praise a fugitive and cloister'd vertue" (2:514–15).

Throughout *Areopagitica* the notion of arrested development is a highly
significant, recurring theme, and it is evident, for example, in the motif of
monastic or quasi-monastic society—a society that refuses any new, unusual,
or grotesque influences, that is happy in its current state, and that rejects
the possibility of potential improvement. Types of this society are the pre-
Lycurgian Sparta, the Rome of Cato, the medieval monastery, and the regime
of the Counter-Reformation. It is also in the context of the monastic or
pseudomonastic society that Milton rejects states as those portrayed in
Thomas More's *Utopia,* Bacon's *New Atlantis,* and also in Plato's *Republic* (see
YP 2:526). A similarly repugnant Spartan or monastic society is painted in Milton's *reductio ad absurdum* of the Licensing Order of 1643. He demands that

No musick must be heard, no song be set or sung, but what is grave and *Dorick.* There
must be licencing dancers, that no gesture, motion, or deportment be taught our youth
but what by their allowance shall be thought honest. . . . The Windows also, and the

Balcone's must be thought on, there are shrewd books, with dangerous Frontispices set to sale . . . The villages also must have their visitors to enquire what lectures the bagpipe and the rebbeck reads . . . for these are the Countrymans *Arcadia's* . . . what shall be done to inhibit the multitudes that frequent those houses where drunk'nes is sold and harbour'd? Our garments also should be referr'd to the licencing of some more sober work-masters to see them cut into a lesse wanton garb. . . . These things [that is, mixed conversation, idle resort, evil company] will be, and must be. (2:523–26)

The end result of such a pseudomonastic society is a monolithic homogeneity, which, ironically, is much more grotesque, in a threatening and destructive sense, than a dynamic society, which permits the existence of grotesque influences on it. Milton illustrates the *real* and hidden grotesqueness of the pseudomonastic society in the image of the "cros-leg'd" Juno, and he heightens the grotesqueness of the image with a reference to the "mysterious iniquity," the whore of Babylon (that is, the papacy) and the monstrous beast of Revelations 17 (see YP 2:506 n. 70):

And thus ye have the Inventors and the originall of Book-licencing ript up. . . . We have it . . . from the most Antichristian Councel, and the most tyrannous Inquisition that ever inquir'd. Till then Books were ever as freely admitted into the World as any other birth; the issue of the brain was no more stifl'd then the issue of the womb: no envious *Juno* sate cros-leg'd over the nativity of any mans intellectuall off spring . . . But that a Book . . . should be to stand before a Jury ere it be borne to the World, and undergo yet in darknesse the judgement of *Radamanth* and his Collegues, ere it can passe the ferry backward into light, was never heard before, till that mysterious iniquity . . . sought out new limbo's and new hells wherein they might include our Books also within the number of their damned. (2:505–6)

The point Milton is making is that although licensing may succeed in suppressing what it considers to be grotesque influences on the state, the real grotesqueness of the system remains hidden. The licensing process occurs in the darkness of an inaccessible region, remains invisible, but colors all of society with a grotesqueness that is more fundamental than if there were no licensing at all. As such, the grotesqueness of this system remains concealed, and it becomes the (enlightened) author's task to make it visible: Milton depicts a world that has gone grotesquely topsy-turvy, in which birth and death have swapped places, and where the ferry that normally delivers the dead to the underworld must act as midwife, sailing backward toward the light in order to aid delivery. By using the image of the Realm of the Dead as a precursor for intellectual genesis, Milton also communicates that the Catholic and quasi-Catholic societies are marked by a certain finality and stasis.

It is here that Milton's central criticism of licensing—and indeed of society as a whole—is to be located: although the quasi-Catholic licensing model appears to remove vice from society, and ensures the appearance of a peaceful existence, it leads to stagnation, and to general decadence: "it will be primely to the discouragement of all learning, and the stop of Truth, . . . by disexercising and blunting our abilities in what we know already" (2:491–92).[67] In effect, it leads to the uncritical submission of many in the populace who

give themselvs up into your [i.e. Parliament's] hands, mak'em, & cut'em out what religion ye please; there be delights, there be recreations and jolly pastimes that will fetch the day about from sun to sun, and rock the tedious year as in a delightfull dream. What need they torture their heads with that which others have tak'n so strictly, and so unalterably into their own pourveying. These are the fruits which a dull ease and cessation of our knowledge will bring forth among the people. How goodly, and how to be wisht were such an obedient unanimity as this, what a fine conformity would it starch us all into? doubtles a stanch and solid peece of frame-work, as any January could freeze together. (2:545)

All three press control schemes that Milton (partially) approves in *Areopagitica* are fundamentally based on the idea of allowing social and intellectual development of individuals: thus, in Athens, "Books and Wits were ever busier then in any other part of *Greece*" (2:494), and the model of press control based on effect presupposes the awareness that "Books . . . contain a potencie of life in them" (2:492). Intellectual development is also essential in that system of press control in which readers act as their own licensors (see, for example, 2:521).

The two rival grotesque structures that Milton establishes in the course of his tract are essential for an understanding of some of the passages in *Areopagitica,* which at first glance seem to advocate the prosecution of books, and which have perturbed and angered some modern critics. Despite its implicit and at times unclear and metamorphosing viewpoints and proposals, *Areopagitica* provides a tentative guidance through the grotesque structures it establishes. My reinterpretation of the contentious passages is not based on a straightforward and instantly assessable reading process, but it involves a reassessment of seemingly disparate elements in the light of the greater intellectual architecture. The technique of presenting a fluid argumentative structure and a suspect authorial stance is not affected by these reinterpretations because they form in many ways a second stage in the reading experience.

REINTERPRETING

As the grotesque structures that make out Milton's models for the Commonwealth emerge, his earlier and seemingly conciliatory statement needs to be reassessed: "it is of greatest concernment . . . to have a vigilant eye how Bookes demeane themselves, as well as men; and thereafter to confine, imprison, and do sharpest justice on them as malefactors: . . . I know they are as lively, and as vigorously productive, as those fabulous Dragons teeth; and being sown up and down, may chance to spring up armed men" (2:492). If placed in the context of Milton's new concept of truth, it becomes clear that books have natural limitations in that they necessarily distort absolute and divine truth. Yet, like the poet himself and like grotesque truth, good books also possess the quality of a Platonic *daimon* in that they are half-creatures. To some extent they are earthly and like humans: they contain "in a violl" the essence of their authors, and, like a criminal, they can be subjected to earthly forms of punishment. However, at the same time, they are also part of the divine because they represent "the Image of God . . . in the eye," and hence they should be "imbalm'd and treasur'd up on purpose to a life beyond life" (2:492–93).

A failure to understand the essential (and paradoxical) role of books as *daimons,* akin to the poet-prophet and to truth itself, has led Stanley Fish into misinterpreting this passage: Fish claims that Milton depicts books with "papist idolatry," exalting them "above the living labors of faithful men" with the intention of creating an ironic and subversive effect, thereby illustrating the indifference of books (2001, 193–94). However, the point Milton is making is that books are incongruous composites, and as mediators contain elements both of the human and of the divine. The contradictory imagery he employs highlights this point. Far from being indifferent, books (as well as poets and earthly truth) in *Areopagitica* have an essential position as instruments of communication between the divine and the human.

The meaning of the above passage becomes more complicated if one understands the nature of books as *daimons:* if they are seen as mediators, books can never really "demeane themselves" like "malefactors" (2:492), even if they have potentially evil contents or effects. In this new context, books can only become criminal in the minds of the readers, and that through their interpretative choice. If a different interpretation is chosen, the effect can be wholly different: "bad books . . . to a discreet and judicious Reader serve in many respects to discover, to confute, to forwarn, and to illustrate" (2:512–13). Even potentially evil books, it seems, can inadvertently operate as good mediators and allow positive intellectual development. In this context, Milton's demand "to confine, imprison, and do sharpest justice on them," which had appeared as a simple and straightforward plea for the persecution of evil books, also becomes more difficult.

An element of absurdity in Milton's proposal to destroy books can already be felt later in the same passage when he explains that, in the destruction of an entire impression, "the execution ends not in the slaying of an elementall life, but strikes at that ethereall and fift essence, the breath of reason it selfe, slaies an immortality rather then a life" (2:493). On the surface, Milton seems to argue that caution must be used in censorship, as the destruction of an entire print run can be equated to the death of a living person. However, Milton's expressions indicate a certain absurdity in the very premise of censorship, which becomes particularly evident when the nature of the book as *daimon* is considered. If properly applied, press control is not really concerned with the earthly manifestation of a particular truth or untruth. It aims to eliminate the (Neoplatonic) idea that stands behind this manifestation, that is, the divine and eternal form of a particular truth (or untruth). The absurdity of this approach is debunked in Milton's paradoxical imagery that an "immortality" can be slain, or indeed the "breath of reason" assailed by purely physical means. If reinterpreted within the context of grotesque truth, what had seemed a relatively straightforward call for caution in the censorship process turns out to be a fundamental criticism of press control.

The conciliatory tone of the above passage is further undermined if the allusion to the Ovidian myth of Cadmus and the dragon's teeth is taken into consideration. It appears that Milton uses the myth to illustrate his proposal that seditious, divisive, and belligerent books should be banned; the grotesqueness of the image of teeth metamorphosing into soldiers seems to suggest that civil unrest and civil war are intrinsic and grotesque evils, which the magistrate must suppress at all costs. However, as the tract progresses, warfare is used increasingly in a metaphorical rather than literal sense.[68] The notion of the beneficial nature of warfare in the search for truth is communicated through the Spenserian model of the "true warfaring Christian" (2:515), through the allegory of Truth wrestling with Falsehood (2:561) and the image of the city under siege (2:554). Indeed, in this last image Milton arrives at the full anti-model to the monastic or pseudomonastic system he condemns throughout his tract. At the same time, he offers a reinterpretation of the Cadmus myth:

the shop of warre hath not there more anvils and hammers waking, to fashion out the plates and instruments of armed Justice in defence of beleaguer'd Truth, then there be pens and heads there, sitting by their studious lamps, musing, searching, revolving new notions and idea's wherewith to present, as with their homage and their fealty the approaching Reformation: others as fast reading, trying all things, assenting to the force of reason and convincement. What could a man require more from a Nation so pliant and so prone to seek after knowledge. What wants there to such a towardly and pregnant soile, but wise and faithfull labourers, to make a knowing people, a Nation of Prophets, of Sages, and of Worthies. (2:554)

An enclosed society, which parallels to some extent the monastic system, is contrasted by mental activity and constant improvement of ideas and the immense urgency that is communicated through the siege image. In the image of the "pregnant soile" of England, the Cadmus myth is finally reversed, and the notion of a grotesque human birth from the soil becomes the epitome of positive social development. At the heart of this concept of society stands intellectual competition, which is also expressed in the commercial images evident in *Areopagitica,* especially in its rejection of monopolies (see 2:535).[69]

Embedded in the idea of civil competition, which makes out the dynamic character at the heart of Milton's principles, there lies a new concept of peace. "Truth and peace" is one of the central battle cries of the Toleration debate. For Milton, finding *"the bond of peace"* (2:565) no longer implies a homogeneous or monolithic society, but instead a *modus vivendi* for a pluralistic society, which is in constant competition with itself and with others.

Under these fantastic terrors of sect and schism, we wrong the earnest and zealous thirst after knowledge and understanding which God hath stirr'd up in this City. What some lament of, we rather should rejoyce at. . . . A little generous prudence, a little forbearance of one another, and som grain of charity might win all these diligences to joyn, and unite into one generall and brotherly search after Truth. (2:554)

This bond is the concept of mutual toleration. More importantly, however, this mutual toleration is based on an understanding of the grotesqueness of earthly truth, and on the dynamic role its principle has to play. Milton does not criticize the degeneration of individuals or of states, but rather the grotesque system in which no development is possible at all. The difference between the two grotesque systems is exposed perhaps most powerfully through Adam and Eve's example:

many there be that complain of divin Providence for suffering *Adam* to transgresse, foolish tongues! when God gave him reason, he gave him freedom to choose, for reason is but choosing; he had bin else a meer artificiall *Adam,* such an *Adam* as he is in the motions. . . . God therefore left him free, set before him a provoking object, ever almost in his eyes; herein consisted his merit, herein the right of his reward, the praise of his abstinence. . . . Suppose we could expell sin by this means [that is, remove temptation]; look how much we thus expell of sin, so much we expell of vertue: for the matter of them both is the same; remove that, and ye remove them both alike. (2:527)

In the first system, the "provoking object" is the grotesque influence on Adam, which enables development. The second system, in which there is no object of temptation, is equated with the monastic system, where no choice is possible at all. Milton illustrates the danger of stagnation in this system by turning Adam into a grotesque puppet, "a meer artificiall *Adam,* such an

Adam as he is in the motions." The lack of outside grotesque stimuli dehumanize Adam, paradoxically, turning him into a grotesque. The implication of Milton's metaphor is even more far-reaching: it turns God into a licensor, and the implied consequence is a godhead that, absurdly, would have to be perceived as grotesque.

Ultimately, an understanding of the grotesque and of the two juxtaposed social systems of *Areopagitica* opens up tentative guidance for a reading that can serve as a final vindication of Milton's violence against evil or monstrous books. As it becomes clear that there is some good that can come from a contemplation of evil books, it appears that there is only one type of book that is "evil absolutely" (2:565): the sort that enforces complete social and intellectual stagnation. Milton points out at the end of his diatribe against the Roman Catholic system of licensing, "no envious *Juno* sate cros-leg'd over the nativity of any mans intellectuall off spring; but if it prov'd a Monster, who denies, but that it was justly burnt, or sunk into the Sea" (2:505).

Milton has thus far in *Areopagitica* only mentioned two books that correspond in imagery to the description of "monstrous": the *Index of Prohibited Books* and the *Index of Expurgations,* "brought forth" as the grotesque offspring from a grotesque act of copulation between "the Councell of Trent, and the Spanish Inquisition" (2:502–3).[70] This type of book is truly grotesque, in the parasitic and monstrous sense, and guaranteed to lead to a degeneration of the mental capacities of society as a whole. Milton's discussion of the quasi-Catholic licensing system leaves no doubt about its stifling effects, but even before he commences his analysis, he points out, "I am of those who beleeve, it will be a harder alchymy then *Lullius* ever knew, to *sublimat any good use* out of such an invention" (2:507; italics mine). Because Raymond Lully is the "patron saint" of alchemy (2:507 n. 74), the allusion heightens the impression that it is utterly impossible (both by fair and foul means) to derive any benefit from the Catholic system of licensing. Contrary to all potentially evil stimuli, for Milton licensing is the only entity from which even the most highly qualified person can derive no profit whatsoever. Books like the *Index of Prohibited Books* and the *Index of Expurgations* are the only type of books that can unequivocally be considered evil.

Another book equally fits the criteria of monstrous book, if only by implication: the *Licensing Order,* published in June 1643 by Parliament's order. Although not quite as objectionable as the *Index,* it equally denies development, and by inference it is on the *Licensing Order* that "sharpest justice" should be executed.

A closer understanding of Milton's method of providing tentative authorial guidance, of operating within the system of the grotesque, allows the reader a reassessment of many of the seemingly incongruous passages in

Areopagitica. This reassessment is, however, not forced, but tentative and left open for the reader to deduce once the larger context of Milton's grotesque structures is understood. The process is not necessarily conducted on a well-defined logically, philosophically, and politically cohesive level. However, the fact that for three hundred years, until the second half of the twentieth century, readers and critics praised Milton's tract as one of the central documents of tolerance and of the freedom of the press shows that, in practical reading experiences, Milton's indirect and tentative strategy transcended the tract's apparent logical flaws. Milton writes as poet and prepares minds indirectly: an intuitive understanding of the grotesque nature of truth as agent and of the state as grotesque principle are fundamental instruments in this indirect process of structuring minds and of providing tentative guidance. The fact that someone from the circle of Hartlib considered translating *Areopagitica* into German[71] in order to introduce the concepts of freedom of the press to a people unaware of English discussions on liberty, indicates that Hartlib's circle considered *Areopagitica* precisely in terms of a precursor with the ability to fashion minds and to initiate larger debates. The reemergence of *Areopagitica*'s arguments in 1679, 1681, and 1789 also illustrates that the tract was highly effective not as an immediate instrument of policy, but as preparation for a greater awareness of the issues of press control.

Royal Holloway University of London

NOTES

    This article grew out of my doctoral research, "Aspects of the Grotesque in Milton's Prose, 1641–1651" (University of London, 2002). I would like to thank John W. Creaser, Martin Dzelzainis, Gordon Campbell, and Warren Chernaik for their help and advice. The responsibility for the claims here made lies, of course, entirely with myself.

    1. William Haller, ed., *Tracts on Liberty in the Puritan Revolution, 1638–1647*, 3 vols. (New York, 1933–34), 75.

    2. Thomas Kranidas, "Polarity and Structure in Milton's *Areopagitica*," *ELR* 14 (1984): 189; Michael Wilding, "Milton's *Areopagitica*: Liberty for the Sects," in *The Literature of Controversy: Polemical Strategy from Milton to Junius*, ed. Thomas N. Corns (London, 1987), 31; see also Thomas N. Corns, *Uncloistered Virtue: English Political Literature, 1640–1660* (Oxford, 1992), 55; David Norbrook, *Writing the English Republic: Poetry, Rhetoric and Politics, 1627–1660* (Cambridge, 1999), 120.

    3. John Coffey, "Puritanism and Liberty Revisited: The Case for Toleration in the English Revolution," *The Historical Journal* 41 (1998): 969; John Coffey, *Persecution and Toleration in Protestant England, 1558–1689* (Harlow, 2000), 54; see William E. A. Axon, "Milton and the Liberty of the Press," in *Milton Memorial Lectures, 1908*, ed. Percy W. Ames (London, 1909), 46 n. 1; Arthur E. Barker, *Milton and the Puritan Dilemma, 1641–1660* (Toronto, 1942), 99.

    4. Fredrick Seaton Siebert, *Freedom of the Press in England, 1476–1776: The Rise and*

Decline of Government Control (1952; rpt. Urbana, IL, 1965), 197; Abbe Blum, "The Author's Authority: *Areopagitica* and the Labour of Licensing," in *Re-membering Milton,* ed. Mary Nyquist and Margaret W. Ferguson (New York, 1987), 74, 77; Stephen B. Dobranski, "Licensing Milton's Heresy," in *Milton and Heresy,* ed. Stephen B. Dobranski and John P. Rumrich (Cambridge, 1998), 146; Blair Worden, "Literature and Political Censorship in Early Modern England," in *Too Mighty to Be Free: Censorship and the Press in Britain and the Netherlands,* ed. A. C. Duke and C. A. Tamse (Zutphen, 1987), 45.

5. John Illo, "The Misreading of Milton," in *Radical Perspectives in the Arts,* ed. Lee Baxandall (Harmondsworth, 1972), 182–83; John Illo, "*Areopagiticas* Mythic and Real," *Prose Studies* 11 (1988): 6; Willmoore Kendall, "How to Read Milton's *Areopagitica,*" *Journal of Politics* 22 (1960): 448, 464.

6. Barker, *Milton and the Puritan Dilemma,* 95.

7. Ernest Sirluck, in John Milton, *The Complete Prose Works,* 8 vols., ed. Don M. Wolfe et al. (New Haven, 1953–82), 2:176. All references to Milton's prose are to this edition, hereafter cited as YP. Christopher Hill, *Milton and the English Revolution* (1977; rpt. London, 1997), 150–51; Stephen Burt, "'To the Unknown God': St. Paul and Athens in Milton's *Areopagitica,*" *MQ* 32 (1998): 26; Christopher Kendrick, *Milton: A Study in Ideology and Form* (New York, 1986), 20. See also Nigel Smith, "*Areopagitica:* Voicing Contexts, 1643–5," in *Politics, Poetics and Hermeneutics in Milton's Prose,* ed. David Loewenstein and James Grantham Turner (Cambridge, 1990), 103; Paul M. Dowling, *Polite Wisdom: Heathen Rhetoric in Milton's "Areopagitica"* (Lanham, MD, 1995), xi–xii; Mary Ann McGrail, "Milton and Political Correctness," *Diacritics* 27, no. 2 (1997): 98–105.

8. Joseph Anthony Wittreich, "Milton's *Areopagitica:* Its Isocratic and Ironic Contexts," in *Milton Studies* 4, ed. James D. Simmonds (Pittsburgh, 1972), 109–12; Henry S. Limouze, "'The Surest Suppressing': Writer and Censor in Milton's *Areopagitica,*" *Centennial Review* 24 (1980): 109–14; Harry R. Smallenburg, "Contiguities and Moving Limbs: Style as Argument in *Areopagitica,*" in *Milton Studies* 9, ed. James D. Simmonds (Pittsburgh, 1976), 179–80; Blum, "The Author's Authority," 87; Dobranski, "Licensing Milton's Heresy,"154; John D. Schaeffer, "Metonymies We Read By: Rhetoric, Truth and the Eucharist in Milton's *Areopagitica,*" *MQ* 34 (2000): 87.

9. Stanley E. Fish, *How Milton Works* (Cambridge, MA, 2001), 189, 201, 212; see also Lana Cable, *Carnal Rhetoric: Milton's Iconoclasm and the Poetics of Desire* (Durham, NC, 1995), 125; see also *Riverside Milton,* ed. Roy Flannagan (Boston, 1998), 990; Corns, *Uncloistered Virtue,* 57–58.

10. Martin Dzelzainis, "John Milton, *Areopagitica,*" in *A Companion to Literature from Milton to Blake,* ed. David Womersley (Oxford, 2000), 151–58.

11. Catherine Belsey, *John Milton: Language, Gender, Power* (Oxford, 1988), 77–78; Annabel Patterson, *Early Modern Liberalism* (Cambridge, 1997), 64; Barbara K. Lewalski, "How Radical Was the Young Milton?" in *Milton and Heresy,* ed. Stephen B. Dobranski and John P. Rumrich (Cambridge, 1998), 64; compare Dzelzainis, "John Milton, *Areopagitica,*" 153.

12. Illo, "*Areopagiticas* Mythic and Real," 19.

13. John T. Shawcross, *Milton: The Critical Heritage* (London, 1970), 13; E. M. Forster, "The Tercentenary of the *Areopagitica,*" in Forster, *Two Cheers for Democracy* (London, 1951), 64.

14. *Apologeticall Narration,* in Haller, *Tracts on Liberty,* 2:306; for Selden, see *A Reply of Two of the Brethren,* 2nd ed. (London, 1644), Thomason tracts E54(18), p. 14.

15. Roger Williams, *The Bloudy Tenent of Persecution, for Cause of Conscience, discussed, in A Conference betweene Truth and Peace* (London, 1644), Thomason tracts E1(2), "To every Courteous Reader," n.p.

16. Stephen B. Dobranski, *Milton, Authorship, and the Book Trade* (Cambridge, 1999), 105.

17. See William Riley Parker, *Milton: A Biography,* and *Milton: A Biographical Commentary,* 2 vols., 2nd ed., ed. Gordon Campbell (Oxford, 1996), 1:264; Haller, *Liberty and Reformation,* 135; William M. Clyde, *The Struggle for the Freedom of the Press from Caxton to Cromwell* (London, 1934), 77.

18. See William Riley Parker, *Milton's Contemporary Reputation* (Columbus, 1940), 73–76.

19. The persona of *Areopagitica* is determined by its genre, and a comparison with *Bucer* has to take note of this. However, even in *Bucer* the postscript's vehemence deviates from the detached overall stance and the reader senses genuinely felt anger. Hence, the moderate tone of *Areopagitica* seems all the more surprising.

20. Hill, *Milton and the English Revolution,* 151.

21. Blum, "The Author's Authority," 77; Kendrick, *Milton,* 24.

22. Leo Miller, "A German Critique of *Areopagitica* in 1647," *N&Q* n.s. 36 (1989): 29–30. I have supplied my own translation because Miller's misses out the crucial "ohne ursach" (without cause).

23. Aristotle, *The "Art" of Rhetoric,* 3.14.1415a; Cicero, *De Oratore,* 1.31.143; Quintilian, *Institutio Oratoria,* 4.1.5.

24. See also YP 2:488, where Milton describes himself generically as a "private" person, giving "publick advice."

25. See William Haller, "Before *Areopagitica,*" *PMLA* 22 (1927): 898.

26. Milton does mention two contemporary authorities on Toleration, John Selden and Lord Brooke (killed in action on 2 March 1643). However, these references are even more extraordinary in this context because both texts which Milton refers to predate the Toleration debate instigated by the *Apologeticall Narration.* By the end of 1644, the intellectual debate had moved on considerably from these early statements and was contested much more directly and heatedly. A reference to the fact that John Selden had publicly and successfully defended the *Apologeticall Narration* in Parliament on 13 March 1644 would have been more topical and indeed more polemically effective. *A Reply of Two of the Brethren to A. S.,* an anonymous defence of the *Apologeticall Narration,* contains such a reference (14).

27. This circumstance is particularly topical because all five Smectymnuans had publicly denounced the Independents by the time *Areopagitica* was published (compare Haller, *Liberty and Reformation,* 132).

28. Williams, *Bloudy Tenent,* 40–49; *John the Baptist, Forerunner of Christ Iesus; or, A Necessity for Liberty of Conscience* (London, 1644), Thomason tracts E9(13), pp. 87–89; William Walwyn, *The Compassionate Samaritane,* 2nd ed. (London, 1644), in Haller, *Tracts,* 3:77; Thomas Hill, *The Good Old Way, Gods Way, to Soule-Refreshing Rest* (London, 1644), Thomason tracts E48(4), p. 14; see also Coffey, *Persecution and Toleration,* 60.

29. See Alexander Forbes, *An Anatomy of Independency; or, A Brief Commentary, and Moderate Discourse upon the Apologeticall Narration* (London, 1644), Thomason tracts E50(36), p. 1; and Thomas Hill, *The Good Old Way, Gods Way,* 24.

30. William Prynne, *Independency Examined, Unmasked, Refuted, By twelve new particular Interrogatories* (London, 1644), Thomason tracts E257(3), p. 2.

31. The possibility that "new" involves the rediscovery of old, lost pieces of wisdom, as implied in the Isis-Osiris myth (2:549) is, of course, always an undercurrent. What is provocative, however, is the formulation, "new notions." In *Animadversions,* Milton had still insisted that "the good way is to be searcht with diligence among the old wayes" (1:698).

32. See Haller, *Tracts,* 1:50.

33. *Apologeticall Narration,* in Haller, *Tracts,* 2:306; for Selden, see *A Reply of Two of the Bretheren,* 14.

34. Walwyn, *Compassionate Samaritane,* in Haller, *Tracts,* 3:69; Hesikiah Woodward, *Inquiries into the Causes of our Miseries* (London, 1644), Thomason tracts E22(1), p. 20; Henry Robinson, *Liberty of Conscience* (1644), in Haller, *Tracts,* 3:148; [Goodwin, Thomas, and others], *A Coole Conference. Between the Scottish Commissioners* CLEARED REFORMATION, *and the Holland Ministers* APOLOGETICALL NARRATION, *brought together by a Well-Willer to both* (London, 1644), Thomason tracts E35(15), p. 9; *A Reply of Two of the Brethren to A. S.,* 19, 3.

35. Williams, *Bloudy Tenent,* 18.

36. See, for example, Walwyn, *Compassionate Samaritane,* in Haller, *Tracts,* 3:89.

37. For example, [Overton, Richard], *The Araignement of Mr. Persecution* ([London], 1645), in Haller, *Tracts,* 3:203–56; C. C., *The Covenanter Vindicated From Periurie: Wherin is fully cleared, that it's no Perjury, for him to yet doubt, whether the Classicall Coercive Presbyterian Government of Churches, be Jure Divino* (London, 1644), Thomason tracts E44(20).

38. Sidrach Simpson, *The Anatomist Anatomis'd; or, A Short Answer to Some Things in the Book, Intituled, An* ANATOMY OF INDEPENDENCIE (1644), Thomason tracts E52(22), p. 3.

39. Thomas Hill, *The Season for Englands Selfe-Reflection, and Advancing Temple-work* (London, 1644), Thomason tracts E6(7), epistle dedicatory, n.p. (sig. A3) and p. 34.

40. Kranidas's contention that the *Imprimatur* passage contains excursions into the Martinist style (183) cannot be fully sustained: the passage lacks the contentious mixture of mockery and serious religious contemplation, as well as the authorial figure of the fool.

41. As noticed, for example, by James Egan, *The Inward Teacher: Milton's Rhetoric of Christian Liberty* (University Park, PA, 1980), 14, and Keith W. Stavely, *The Politics of Milton's Prose Style* (New Haven, 1975), 67.

42. The licensor's spinelessness becomes even more evident if the three books Milton refers to are identified; see Leo Miller, "The Italian Imprimaturs in Milton's *Areopagitica,*" *Papers of the Bibliographical Society of America* 65 ([1971]): 345–55: the first two are Bernardo D'Avanzati Nostichi's *Scisma D'Inghilterra* (Florence, 1638) and George Conn's *De Duplici Statu Religionis Apud Scotos Libri Duo* (Rome, 1628). The licensor's cautious deference reflects the personal danger to themselves which authorizing a publication on English and Scottish Protestantism might imply, especially if higher approval is not secured. The third imprimatur is probably from Galileo Galilei's *Dialogo* (Florence, 1632; see Miller, "The Italian Imprimaturs," 355), initially approved for printing by Florentine and Roman Catholic Church authorities, but in 1633 famously banned by the Inquisition; see Maurice A. Finocchiaro, ed. and trans., *The Galileo Affair: A Documentary History* (Berkeley and Los Angeles, 1989), 291. Milton's examples illustrate the contentiousness of licensing, as all three books would have been widely approved by an English readership. The particular cautiousness of the licensors illustrates that the entire process is flawed by a inconsistent and self-contradictory system of authority.

43. The logical objective is more obvious: Milton shows Parliament the ill company it is keeping.

44. For example, Katherine Chidley, *The Justification of the Independant Churches of Christ* (London, 1641), Thomason tracts E174(7), "To the Christian Reader."

45. Illo, "*Areopagiticas* Mythic and Real," 14; see also Ann Baynes Coiro, "Milton and Class Identity: The Publication of *Areopagitica* and the 1645 *Poems,*" *Journal of Medieval and Renaissance Studies* 22 (1992): 262.

46. The formal model Milton upholds is the order of 29 January 1642. Implicitly, Milton agrees to the Licensing Orders of 26 August 1642 and 9 March 1643 (*Journal of the House of Commons* 2:739, 2:996).

47. Direct censorship by parliamentary process occurred, for example, in May 1643 (*Book*

of Sports) and in August 1644 (*Bloudy Tenent*). Neither book falls into the categories "Atheisticall" or "Libellous."

48. At the end of his life in 1484, Pulci was reputed to be a notorious heretic. See Ernst Walser, *Lebens- und Glaubensprobleme aus dem Zeitalter der Renaissance: Die Religion des Luigi Pulci, ihre Quellen und ihre Bedeutung* (Marburg, 1926), 19, and several of his poems were on the *Index of Prohibited Books;* see Heinrich Reusch, *Der Index der Verbotenen Bücher: Ein Beitrag zur Kirchen- und Literaturgeschichte,* 2 vols. (Bonn, 1883–85), 2:392. The notion that Pulci was fundamentally atheistic is, however, usually rejected by critics; compare, for example, Walser, 75–76; Lewis Einstein, *Luigi Pulci and the Morgante Maggiore* (Berlin, 1902), 40–41; Lord Byron, *The Complete Poetical Works,* 4 vols., ed. Jerome J. McGann (Oxford, 1980–86), 4:247–48. It is important to note, however, that a general feeling of suspiciousness in religious matters surrounds Pulci's work, and that he often teeters on the very edge of heresy. See, for example, Constance Jordan, *Pulci's Morgante: Poetry and History in Fifteenth-Century Florence* (Washington, 1986), 38–42, 188 n. 76; see also Mark Davie, *Half-Serious Rhymes: The Narrative Poetry of Luigi Pulci* (Dublin, 1998), 24–25. *Il Morgante* was one of the books destroyed by Savonarola's followers in the 1497 Florence "burning of vanities"; see Paul F. Grendler, *The Roman Inquisition and the Venetian Press, 1540–1605* (Princeton, 1977), 67. The 1574 and 1606 Florence editions of *Morgante* were expurgated and abridged (Reusch, 2:392 n. 2).

49. Aretino is relevant not only as a libeler but also as a heretic: his works were on the *Index* not because of their "gross indecencies," but because of their "suspected heresies." See Axon, "Milton and the Liberty of the Press," 51–52; compare George Haven Putnam, *The Censorship of the Church of Rome and Its Influence upon the Production and Distribution of Literature: A Study of the History of the Prohibitory and Expurgatory Indexes, together with some Consideration of the Effects of Protestant Censorship and of Censorship by the State,* 2 vols. (New York, 1906–7), 1:202.

50. See John Rushworth, *Historical Collections. The Third Part in two Volumes: Containing the Principal Matters which Happened from the Meeting of the Parliament, November the 3rd, 1640. To the End of the Year 1644* (London, 1721), 317; Haller, *Liberty and Reformation,* 130.

51. The parliamentary order of 29 January 1642 never suggests that licensing should be confined to a book's *effect:* it is an assertion of a text ownership, not an agreement to freedom of the press.

52. There is an element of overlap between the models of censorship based on content and on effect. In both, for example, censorship follows a legal process. It is also possible (in theory) to combine the two methods (for example, censorship for atheistical and libelous books that have a seditious effect). The models are distinguished, however, by a fundamentally different intellectual approach: indeed, if "effect" is selected as a primary benchmark for governmental interference, there is no more room for any particular categories for censorship (for example, scholarly publications in Latin that are unlikely to cause civil unrest face no further restrictions).

53. See Parker, *Milton: A Biography,* 1:266; Kendall, "How to Read Milton's *Areopagitica,*" 463.

54. Milton seems to advocate the free publication of Catholic books, even if he does not promote a toleration of Catholics in the Commonwealth: "I mean not tolerated Popery" (565) is followed two paragraphs later with "And as for regulating the Presse" (569), which suggests that the previous passages were not directly related to licensing, but to toleration only. Although these two paragraphs span several pages, they are connected by a continuous train of thought so that Milton's pointer, with which the discussion returns to licensing, marks the previous contemplations as a digression on toleration.

55. See, for example, Robinson, *Liberty of Conscience,* in Haller, *Tracts,* 3:107.

56. See, for example, Thomas Edwards, *Antapologia; or, A Full Answer to the APOLOGET-*

ICALL NARRATION (London, 1644), Thomason tracts E1(1), p. 1; Matthew Newcomen, *A Sermon Tending to Set Forth the Right Use of the Disasters that Befall our Armies* (London, 1644), Thomason tracts E16(1), p. 36; Haller, *Liberty and Reformation,* 130–32; Forbes, *Anatomy of Independency,* 3; compare *Apologeticall Narration,* in Haller, *Tracts,* 2:336.

57. John Goodwin, *Theomachia; or, The Grand Impudence of Men Running the Hazard of Fighting Against God* (London, 1644), rpt. in Haller, *Tracts,* 3:38–39.

58. Williams, *Bloudy Tenent,* 15.

59. Plutarch, *The Philosophie, Commonlie Called the Morals,* trans. Philemon Holland (London, 1603), British Library C.74.e.3, p. 1296; see also Holland's contemporary, Neoplatonic interpretation, pp. 1286–87.

60. See Gillian Beer, *The Romance* (London, 1970), 39, 47–55.

61. John Langley, headmaster of St. Paul's, and any of "the School-Masters of *Paul's*" were appointed licensers for poetry (see Rushworth, *Historical Collections,* 336). Milton must have imagined the indignity of taking his poems back to his old school for approval and licensing (compare YP 2:531).

62. See Egan, *The Inward Teacher,* 17.

63. The idea that Socrates is also a double-natured *daimon,* grotesque in appearance but full of divine wisdom, is current in seventeenth-century thought. See John Hales, *Golden Remains of the Ever Memorable Mr. John Hales, of Eaton College* (London, 1659), Thomason tracts E769, pp. 139–40.

64. Wolfgang Kayser, *The Grotesque in Art and Literature* (Bloomington, IN, 1963); Mikhail Bakhtin, *Rabelais and His World,* trans. Hélène Iswolsky (Bloomington, IN, 1984).

65. For a full discussion of my theory of the grotesque, see Markus Klinge, "Aspects of the Grotesque in Milton's Prose, 1641–1651" (Ph.D. thesis, University of London, 2002), 10–45.

66. For example, "grotesque agents" can appear without the immediate context of a "principle," as in Velasquez's portraits of court fools. In such structures, it is the beholder's task to locate and identify the appropriate principle (for example, in the Renaissance context the appropriate principle would be the implicit figure of the fool's owner/employer).

67. The reference to the Galileo affair highlights Milton's point (YP 2:538; see also the reference to the imprimatur of Galileo's *Dialogo;* Miller, "The Italian Imprimaturs," 355).

68. See Alan F. Price, "Incidental Imagery in *Areopagitica,*" *Modern Philology* 49 (1952): 217.

69. Compare Blair Hoxby, "The Trade of Truth Advanced: *Areopagitica,* Economic Discourse, and Libertarian Reform," in *Milton Studies* 36, edited by Albert C. Labriola (Pittsburgh, 1998), 177–202; Kevin Dunn, "Milton among the Monopolists: *Areopagitica,* Intellectual Property and the Hartlib Circle," in *Samuel Hartlib and Universal Reformation: Studies in Intellectual Communication,* ed. Mark Greengrass, Michael Leslie, and Timothy Raylor (Cambridge, 1994), 186–92.

70. Milton's direct source is Paolo Sarpi, *The Historie of the Councel of Trent,* trans. Nathaniel Brent (London, 1620), 472–73, which describes a sequence from the first (unsystematic) condemnation of heretical books by the papal bull *In Cœna;* the subsequent, systematic catalogs of the Spanish Inquisition; the first Spanish *Index* of 1558, printed by order of Philip II; to the first printed, general *Index,* sanctioned by Pope Paul IV in 1559. The grotesqueness of the Spanish Inquisition, in particular, is a common motif of Protestant propaganda. The anonymous *Clamor Sanguinis Martyrum* (London, 1656), Thomason tracts E1694(2), for example, points out: "all the monstrous shapes 'twixt *Affrica* and *India,* cannot frame a likeness to this savage Inquisition" ("To the Reader," [xxiii]). The reorganization of the Spanish and the Italian inquisitions in the sixteenth century is often seen as an illegitimate usurpation of secular authority; compare Pietro Sarpi, *History of the Inquisition,* trans. Robert Gentilis (London, 1639), 10; see

also Reginaldus Gonsaluius, *Full, Ample and Punctall Discovery* (London, 1625), "The Preface," [C2 recto and verso]). The illegitimate mixture of church and state is also a particular concern of the emerging Independent movement in England in the mid-1640s. By denouncing the Inquisition and the Council of Trent as progenitors of licensing, Milton may imply (to those aware of his sources) a wider political comment about the intermingling of secular and ecclesiastical power.

71. See Hartlib's correspondent, who intends to make *Areopagitica* available in "other languages . . . and other countries which are governed by a similar tyranny." Leo Miller, "A German Critique of *Areopagitica* in 1647," *N&Q* n.s. 36 (1989): 30; my translation.

"FIT THOUGH FEW": *EIKONOKLASTES* AND THE RHETORIC OF AUDIENCE

Daniel Shore

MILTON BEGINS HIS *First Prolusion* by acknowledging that the "first and chief duty of an orator" is "winning the good-will of his audience." But as he looks around at the "hostile glances" on the faces of his classmates, he realizes—or rather has decided in advance to realize—that he must disregard this duty in order to "say something contrary to all the rules of oratory." He cites the first rule only to break it:

> I see here and there, if I do not mistake, some who without a word show clearly by their looks how well they wish me. The approval of these, few though they be, is more precious to me than that of the countless hosts of the ignorant, who lack all intelligence, reasoning power, and sound judgment, and who pride themselves on the ridiculous effervescing froth of their verbiage.[1]

Rather than trying to win over his audience, Milton divides his classmates into two groups. On one side are those, "few though they be," whose approval is already assured; on the other are the "countless hosts of the ignorant" who are capable only of "animosity." To gain their goodwill would be, as Milton laments, to "placate the implacable." He acknowledges that treating the audience this way seems to be a poor strategic move: debates are rarely won by the approbation of the few, and the many are rarely seduced by abuse. Even if his audience were in fact largely composed of stubborn ignoramuses, it is hard to see what would be gained by addressing them as such. Every classical rhetorician, following Aristotle, recognized that it is precisely the job of oratory to appeal to "persons who cannot take in at a glance a complicated argument, or follow a long chain of reasoning."[2] In a notable turn, however, the second sentence of the passage, which begins by portraying the "countless hosts" as an ignorant mob of listeners, ends by insulting them as "proud" but "ridiculous" orators.

With this description of his divided audience Milton has not only violated a basic axiom of oratory and derided the "effervescing froth" of schoolboy rhetoric, he has also discounted the very possibility of persuasion. Stanley Fish offers the following explication of the problem: "If one-half of your audience is presumed to be incapable of being persuaded because it is made up of persons not fit to be taught, and the other half is already persuaded because it is made up of persons who, like you, are members incorporate of an indwelling truth, it is hard to see how your writing could possibly have any effect."[3] The world is, in short, composed only of those who will never agree with you and those who already do, rendering any attempt at persuasion useless. This portrayal of his classmates in the *First Prolusion* is only a proto-example of a trope that is nearly omnipresent in Milton's polemical works. The best-known example of this trope (in his poetry, no less) is the call to his muse to help him find a "fit audience . . . though few" in Book Seven of *Paradise Lost*—although in this instance Milton does not explicitly address the unfit and far too many (*PL* 7.31). At some point in nearly every polemical tract Milton represents his audience as divided into categories of believers and nonbelievers, and then claims that he cannot possibly convince the latter.

David Norbrook argues for a "significant expansion of the public sphere" in the years following 1620 and especially during "periods of parliamentary crisis." He suggests, with ample qualification, that we might see Milton—particularly in *Areopagitica*—as a Habermasian *avant la lettre*. The "public sphere" is, in Habermas's theory, a space of genuine communication and debate between members of the bourgeoisie educated in critical and informed interpretation.[4] But Milton's representations of an immutably divided audience seem to deny the possibility of an authentic public sphere. On any particular public question his descriptions group all private individuals into communities incapable of being persuaded through argument and debate. Every reader has, in Milton's construction, irrevocably decided on a set position, regardless of any communicative process. The drastic increase in political writing during the 1640s—pamphlets, religious tracts, reports of parliamentary debates, newsbooks, politically charged poetry and satire—all this is made a false pageant if the very possibility of persuasion is nonexistent.

The apparent contradiction between an emerging public sphere and an audience closed to genuine argument disappears, however, when we cease to consider Milton's descriptions as simply pictures of the world as it actually was or even as Milton believed it to be. They are not passive representations that mirror the world, but active, rhetorical, instrumental gestures that seek to shape the audience in the process of describing it. Although Milton presents himself in the *First Prolusion* as violating the basic rules of oratory and disclaiming the possibility of persuasion, we must understand this presentation as itself a reassertion of rhetoric, refashioned to the demands of his listeners. A fit audience is not, in the prose tracts, simply something Milton finds already constituted; rather, his descriptions are an attempt to create the proper readers and interpreters of his tracts. An instrumental reading of

Milton's descriptions does not claim that the composition of his audience is *necessarily* different from the way it is portrayed: Milton's biographers have convincingly suggested, for example, that he was not, in fact, well liked by his classmates, and many of his mature tracts were written against overwhelming public opinion.[5] The claim is, rather, that his descriptions have rhetorical designs on the very audience they represent as immune to rhetoric. Milton repeatedly constructs an inscribed readership in order to alter the disposition —and even more significantly, the mode of interpretation—of his actual readers.

Far from contradicting the possibility of genuine debate and political communication in early modern England, I shall argue that Milton's descriptions of his audience are pragmatic responses to the problems of a rapidly emerging public sphere. A full examination of the fit-though-few trope is thus an exploration of the way Milton's prose shapes and is shaped by contemporary interpretive practices, and by the changing conditions of political and religious debate. My discussion will focus largely on *Eikonoklastes* since it is the prime locus of Milton's concerns about the problems of reading and misreading, and concomitantly of being read and misread. Written in 1649, during one of the "periods of parliamentary crisis" that Norbrook sees as providing space for increased public debate, it is also, not coincidentally, the site of some of the most elaborate and vexed constructions of his readers. Previous studies of *Eikonoklastes* have not sufficiently explored the rhetorical mechanisms, particularly the treatment of audience, by which the tract attempts to reform contemporary interpretive practices and thereby brings into being a genuine public sphere composed of critical readers. In an effort to begin this exploration I will give an account of the fit-though-few trope (1) as it rhetorically shapes its readers, (2) as a response to contemporary reading practices, and (3) as a significant instance of a phenomenon called self-reading.

I

In the preface to the second edition of *Eikonoklastes* we find Milton doing in a more elaborate form what we witnessed in the exordium of the *First Prolusion*. He takes on the task of rebutting *Eikon Basilike*, Charles's posthumously published book, "as a work assign'd rather, than by me chos'n or affected." He is reluctant to weigh in on the subject because "it might have seem'd in vaine to write at all; considering the envy and almost infinite prejudice likely to be stirr'd up among the Common sort." He begins by portraying the part of his readers—the "Common sort"—that judges according to "almost infinite prejudice" and is moved only "by faction and the easy literature of custom and opinion." The "irksome labour" of writing seems a waste of time when he is certain that it will be "neither waigh'd, nor well read" by those who already disagree. His eventual decision to write is related through a miniature quest story:

[writing] shall be ventur'd yet, and the truth not smother'd, but sent abroad, in the native confidence of her single self, to earn, how she can, her entertainment in the world, and to finde out her own readers; few perhaps, but those few, such of value and substantial worth, as truth and wisdom, not respecting numbers and bigg names, have bin ever wont in all ages to be contented with. (YP 3:339–40)

Milton, perhaps remembering his own travels abroad, represents his argument as a young truth sent out in the world to find "those few" readers of "value and substantial worth." The split in audience—between the valued few and the common sort—allows for the two groups to be accorded separate treatment. Those who disagree with Milton are portrayed as near illiterates who judge according to custom and prejudice; those who entertain the truth of his argument fare much better. By distinguishing fit and unfit readers, Milton can exalt the former and denigrate the latter. This combination of praise and blame causes the fit-though-few trope to function as a kind of heuristic device for the reader: the choice made while reading is not so much who you are as who you want to be and how you want to be treated. The criterion for being one of Milton's ideal readers is laid out in the very beginning of the tract, and the decision is as simple as whether to be abused or glorified. Aristotle writes that for the orator, praise and blame are merely ways of "urging us to accept or reject proposals for action."[6] Milton uses praise or blame to urge us to take the action of becoming a certain kind of reader—the kind that will receive his arguments favorably.[7]

In some instances the formula of praise or blame is so direct as to become a kind of tautological equation. In *The Tenure of Kings and Magistrates,* Milton's tract in defense of killing tyrannous kings, he writes, "indeed none can love freedom heartilie, but good men; the rest love not freedom, but licence." Tyrants fear only those "in whom virtue and true worth most is eminent." The equation is drawn up fairly directly: to be good is to love freedom is to hate tyrants is to side with Milton. "Bad men," by contrast, are "naturally servile," love "license" and "indulgence," and are therefore willing to offer "base compliance" to tyrants. To take cover behind the "falsifi'd names of *Loyalty,* and *Obedience*" is only to place yourself on the wrong side of the equation with all the other "bad men." The first sentence of the tract presents a slightly more subtle persuasive effect, working through wordplay rather than explicitly asserted equivalences: "If men within themselves would be govern'd by reason, and not generally give up thir understanding to a double tyrannie, of Custom from without, and blind affections within, they would discerne better, what it is to favour and uphold the Tyrant of a Nation" (YP 3:190–91). The alignment of readers is described through two instances of zeugma: to be "govern'd by reason" is to be self-governed, while to be led by the "double tyrannie" of custom and blind affections is to submit to the "Tyrant of a Nation." The choice of governance is not simply between king and Parliament, but between reason and blindness as well; grasping the associative connections between the different categories—between reason and self-governance, blindness and Tyranny—is part of learning to "discerne better."

In *The Doctrine and Discipline of Divorce,* the associative links are necessarily more abstruse: through a set of extended metaphors Milton constructs a covert denigration of those who oppose him. In the tract's introduction, addressed "to the Parlament of England with the Assembly," Milton begins by speaking of Truth—and this is, remember, the truth that speaks in favor of divorce—as a fertile mother. Those who stand against more humane marriage laws "cry-down the industry of free reasoning . . . as if the womb of teeming Truth were to be clos'd up, if shee presume to bring forth ought, that sorts not with their unchew'd notions and suppositions" (YP 2:224). The maternal metaphor is altered at the end of the preface to the first book of the tract when Milton again turns to address—and thereby describe, and by describing shape—his audience:

This onely is desir'd of them who are minded to judge hardly of thus maintaining, that they would be still and heare all out, nor think it equall to answer deliberate reason with sudden heat and noise; remembering this, that many truths now of reverend esteem and credit, had their birth and beginning once from singular and private thoughts; while the most of men were otherwise possest; and had the fate at first to be generally exploded and exclaim'd on by many violent opposers. (YP 2:240–41)

Truth is no longer a pregnant mother, but a child who has received its "birth and beginning" from "private thoughts." If Milton seems to have no fit audience here—if his thoughts on divorce seem a bit too "singular and private" —then he is more than willing to praise himself as both the sole parent and lone nurturer of an infant truth. Those who support a more conservative understanding of marriage are metaphorically made to be anything but upholders of "family values": they are instead "violent opposers" by whom newborn truth is "exploded and exclaim'd on." And by describing their response to "deliberate reasoning" as "sudden heat and noise," Milton calls into question more than their argumentative demeanor. When, in the third chapter of the tract, he condemns marriage for the sake of "the prescrib'd satisfaction of an irrational heat," he speaks of intercourse motivated by pleasures of the flesh, not procreation (YP 2:249). Likewise, "heat and noise" are the products of unreasoned argument and—at least by implication—lustful intercourse. To overstate the case somewhat, Milton depicts the defenders of traditional marriage as lecherous child abusers, and those who advocate divorce as the parents and caretakers of children.

The fit-though-few trope trades on the crucial difference between an audience and a reader. Benjamin concisely states the distinction: the audience "always appears as a collective, and this differentiates it from the reader, who is alone with his text."[8] Milton blurs the two categories by collectivizing individual readers into a corporate audience, particularly in tracts like *Eikonoklastes,* where he is addressing a relatively broad public. The fit-though-few trope makes the individual reader acutely aware of herself as part of a readership, as making choices and decisions in conjunction with other readers. Put in Habermasian terms, Milton's constructions of his audience create in private individuals a sense of their own participation as critical readers in a sphere of public choice and political influence. This socialization has many implications for Milton's rhetoric and its relation to the public sphere. Most crucially, making readers aware of themselves as part of an audience allows him to employ a wide variety of social controls for his own rhetorical purposes. The tactic works especially well with the written word, as opposed to spoken orations, because readers encounter the text alone, and are consequently more susceptible to a sense of the larger audience constructed wholly by the author; they are not, as in an actual oratorical setting, able to readily gauge their responses against those of a crowd.[9]

Reading the fit-though-few trope is a diagnostic process of placing oneself into categories that Milton has preestablished—and he has gone to great lengths to make the choice anything but indifferent, since assent earns the reward of praise and avoids the bitterness of invective. Milton's portrayals of his fit audience are always pleasantly and appropriately vague, without distinctive social or cultural markers. Truth, remember, finds her proper audience "not respecting numbers and bigg names." The opening sentences of *An Apology* list the things for which Milton refuses to praise his audiences: birth, family, material advantages, upbringing, education, and example.[10] The characteristics that fit readers have in common are the invisible virtues of reason, intelligence, love of liberty, right-mindedness—or rather, virtues that become visible only through choice, action, and (again the manipulative dimension) assent to Milton's argument. The phrase "fit audience though few" illustrates the central requirement. "Fit" carries the sense of "superior in ability," but it also means "ready, prepared"—as in prepared to accept the given arguments. The implication is both subtle and effective: those who are fit (superior) are also fit (prepared) to side with Milton.

The unfit audience, by contrast, is concretely overdetermined, which is to say that its opinions are beholden to a range of things other than reason or truth: in *An Apology* to "the intrapping autority" of the prelates (YP 1:869); in the divorce tracts to custom; in *Eikonklastes,* perhaps most dramatically, to the image of a dead king. The unfit audience is frequently marked by negative associations of class and education. Think, for example, of the readers lined up at the bookstalls in *Sonnet XI* who are unable to pronounce the title *Tetrachordon,* much less understand the tract's argument.

When Milton does assign external cultural markers to his fit readers, he does so in a way that alters the definition of the marker itself. In one of the many descriptive divisions of his audience in *Eikonoklastes* he appears to use natural ancestry as the criterion for a fit reader:

except some few, who yet retain in them the old English fortitude and love of Freedom, and have testifi'd it by thir matchless deeds, the rest, imbastartiz'd from the ancient nobleness of thir Ancestors, are ready to fall flatt and give adoration to the Image and Memory of this Man. . . . Which low dejection and debasement of mind in the people, I must confess I cannot willingly ascribe to the natural disposition of an English-man.

The allusion is to the common ascription of republican virtue to the Saxons and of monarchical culture to Norman influence. And yet the criterion for true Englishness is anything but genetic. To be English is simply to possess those qualities—"fortitude and love of Freedom"—that would make "debasement" before an "image" impossible. The adoration of a tyrant's memory is so foreign to the "natural disposition of an Englishman" that Milton can only attribute it to the bastardization of "ancient nobleness." He subsequently attributes this negative influence to the "Prelats and thir fellow-teachers" who have bequeathed the "perpetual infusion of servility and wretchedness to all thir hearers" (YP 3:344). The fit audience is English through the possession of abstract virtues, while the unfit audience is foreign through their concrete servitude to vested interests.

II

If Milton's purpose in constructing his audience is to bring his readers out of servility into the virtue of assent, why does he always describe his fit audience as few? The elitist impulse is perhaps the most powerful social control he employs for rhetorical purposes. He brings readers to a consciousness of audience only so that they can immediately surpass and disassociate themselves from the many to join the elite few. Of course, the process of disassociation with the many (whom Milton would have be fewer) and the identification with the few (whom Milton would have be more) is exactly the point: his constructions of audience exclude so as to include exclusively. Self-evaluation and the resulting self-categorization are not just activities induced by Milton's rhetoric. They are, rather, already established habits of mind for Milton's potential audience. For a Calvinist believer, the question of personal election was a crucial and frequent subject of meditation and reflection. Since predestination denied the efficacy of works, people could no longer cause their salvation through good deeds. Calvin also denied that one could learn whether another is saved or damned through observing worldly activity: this remained one of God's secrets. But the relegation of election to the realm of inscrutability did not, in practice, keep believers from intensely searching themselves for signs of grace. Puritan readers were accustomed to examining their beliefs, desires, dispositions, and worldly activities as a means of placing themselves into the binary categories of elect and reprobate. This process of scrutiny and categorization was probably extended to other members of the community, although this practice is more difficult to establish.[11]

The fit-though-few trope exploits this already existing Puritan habit of thought by provoking a structured self-examination in the reader, except that within the confines of the text Milton is able to stipulate the terms of salvation. His rhetoric, in other words, makes assent something like the condition of election. It may well be the case that Milton, because of his Arminianism, did not participate in the same kind of self-scrutiny and anxiety over election as his Calvinist contemporaries, but this would by no means have prevented him from making rhetorical use of the habits of thought of his readership. To the contrary, Milton's Arminianism—his belief that God invested humans with genuine freedom of choice and moral responsibility—is the most general precondition for his investment in persuasion through reason, argument, and rhetoric.[12]

The doctrine of predestination did not in practice lead to the logical conclusion of fatalism but to a different kind of worldly activity; likewise, Milton's descriptions of his audience, although they represent static ontological and epistemological categories, aim to change the beliefs and activities of his readers through rhetoric. Responding to his audience's habits of thought, the display of predestinarian fatalism—manifest in the impossibility of persuasion—becomes an important tactic. The vehicle of Milton's rhetorical effectiveness within an emerging public sphere is the appearance of withdrawal to a private subjectivity. In the passage above from *The Doctrine and Discipline of Divorce,* for example, he portrays Truth as arising from "private thoughts"; he begins *Of Education* by remarking on his stubborn, but eventually discarded, intention to keep his pedagogical plans to himself; and nearly all of his tracts, like *Eikonoklastes,* address the question of whether it is "in vaine to write at all" (YP 3:339). He consistently refuses to portray the effect of his tracts as persuasion, insisting that their function is not to convince so much as discover his fit readers.

A kind of persuasive fatalism informs nearly all of Milton's descriptions of his audience, but it appears in especially grim form in the following passage:

> That they who from the first beginning, or but now of late, by what unhappines I know not, are so much affatuated, not with his person onley, but with his palpable faults, and dote upon his deformities, may have none to blame but thir own folly, if they live and dye in such a strook'n blindness, as next to that of *Sodom* hath not happ'nd to any sort of men more gross, or more misleading. (YP 3:341–42)

It is tempting to reduce the sentence above to something like, "You deserve to go blind if you are convinced by the king's book," but as is usually the case with Miltonic prose a paraphrase excludes much of what is said and, more importantly, all of what is done by a sentence. Remarkably, every phrase of this "sentence" is part of the initial subordinate clause; multiple phrases seem to hold the promise of the main clause but none, finally, delivers. The entire passage is implicitly concerned with the balancing of crime with punishment. Readers deserve "stricken blindness" (and the reference to Sodom marks this as figurative, spiritual blindness) because of "their own folly." Milton, avoiding theodicy, disclaims knowledge of what past "unhappiness" has caused this innate idiocy.

The present conditional statement, "if they live and die," poses the central problem: blindness is not a future punishment contingent upon present behavior, but a continuous condition of life, since those who "live . . . in stricken blindness" do not lose some prior state of spiritually correct vision, but are always unable to see clearly. There are essentially two types of blindness: the type that allows us to be "affatuated" with the king, to "dote upon his deformities," and to be misled by his writing; and the type that is a divine punishment precisely for not seeing the things that we are unable to see in the first place. The sentence proposes a supremely bleak equation: you will be punished for what you are, and for this your punishment is and always will be to remain what you are. Its incomplete structure further intensifies the fatalistic message: a main clause might hold the possibility of change or redemption, but the subordinate clause ("That they who . . .") only indicates a state of being that is static and inescapable.[13]

And yet the whole of *Eikonoklastes* is an attempt to restore these readers from blindness to sight, to make them—contingent on their own choosing—part of a fit audience. In Milton's polemical practice, the vaunted impossibility of the task is the rhetorical precursor to its undertaking. The condition of the fit-though-few trope's instrumental effectiveness is the repudiation of instrumental ends; the condition of effective persuasion within the public sphere is the repudiation of the very possibility of that sphere. Stanley Fish reads Milton's professions of fatalism as part of what he calls an "aesthetic of testimony." In this view Milton's tracts are not actual attempts to participate in public debate in a consequential way; they are, to quote Fish, "not so much an argument as a breaking out of what cannot be kept within."[14] But, finally, nothing is more convincing—especially for an interregnum audience—than the truth that "cannot be kept within." Milton manages to disclaim purpose, agency, eloquence, and rhetoric, with the ultimate effect of achieving his purpose through augmented agency, eloquence, and rhetoric. In a kind of Nietzschean reversal, renunciation of efficacious action results in increased oratorical power.[15] The "aesthetic of testimony" is, especially for Milton, a misnomer: a better term for what happens in his polemics would be a "rhetoric of testimony."

The "plain style" is, understood in these terms, ultimately the most rhetorical style—or at least the most instrumentally efficacious style—of all. It manipulates its audience and disclaims that manipulation with each display of simplicity. Its primary operation is a continual covering up of artifice by means of artifice, which, in its turn, is covered up as well. This is why Milton has such a difficult time responding to *Eikon Basilike:* it is prodigiously effective at appearing as self-presentation, without future political or personal goals. Its subtitle, "Portraiture," beyond referring to its visual depiction of the king, indicates that the book contains his private thoughts and prayers rather than polemical designs on his former subjects. Milton repeatedly bemoans the fact that he must refute a doubly privileged rhetorical position: not only a king, but a dead king (YP 3:341). Death has the significant benefit of freeing Charles from suspicion of self-interested designs, and the established relationship between a king and his subjects frees him from the need to elaborately construct his audience. *Eikon Basilike,* at least to its contemporary audience, probably read more like "a breaking out of what cannot be kept within" than any of Milton's polemical writing ever did. Whereas Milton sets out his persuasive goals and then repudiates the possibility of ever convincing his audience, Charles (or rather Gauden—who stays as hidden as the rhetorical simplicity he has engineered) never even needs to address the problems of rhetoric in the first place.

The status of *Eikon Basilike* as an idol is intimately related to its rhetorical effectiveness. An idol evokes what Milton calls a "servile" or uncritical response in its audience, appealing to "men whose judgement was not rationally evinc'd and perswaded, but fatally stupifi'd and bewitch'd" (YP 3:347). Essentially a falsely sanctified object, an idol allows not for reasoned opposition or critical response, but only the worship and subjection of the idolater.[16] It presents itself as unquestionable truth, obviating the need for interpretation. Lana Cable notes that the "habituated affective response to the icon" is "conceptual peace and rest": put in other terms, idolatry is fundamentally the suspension of critical reading.[17] The type of credulous seeing that an idol calls for is what Milton repeatedly refers to as blindness. One of his primary tasks in *Eikonoklastes*, therefore, is to reveal the self-presenting transparency of the king's book as itself a rhetorical ruse, to show its purposeful designs, and to unveil the continual covering up of artifice that generates its rhetorical power. He repeatedly works to disclose the theatricality of the book—to show that it consciously manipulates its own modes of presentation according to its effect on the audience. As David Loewenstein points out, "the numerous theatrical tropes in *Eikonoklastes*—including references to interludes, revels, comedies, and Sunday theater—suggest that the king's court and his activities have all been skillfully stage-managed."[18] In calling attention to the theatrical art of *Eikon Basilike,* Milton transforms Charles's "spectacle of martyrdom" (Loewenstein's apt phrase) into a nearly Brechtian production, with the mechanisms of performance laid bare before the reader. The tract, as Miltonic analysis reveals, is not self-presenting but self-performing. Richard Helgerson writes that Milton's enterprise is to "strip away the mystifying 'garnish' of 'portraiture [and] stage-work' and reveal the 'puny' book beneath"—a book, I might add, that has covert rhetorical designs on its readers, despite its puniness.[19] Milton's iconoclastic purpose is, in Cable's words, "the radical disruption of the familiar."[20] After pointing out, for example, that Charles has cribbed one of his prayers from Sir Philip Sidney's *Arcadia,* Milton disparages the king for the inability to find his own sincere address to God. But the borrowing is also a sign of the rhetorical construction of the book that shows it as something other than a "portraiture." That the borrowing is unacknowledged is a further sign of the artifice used in covering up the evidence of rhetorical construction to achieve a self-effacing style.[21]

Milton vents his iconoclastic wrath on the idolatrous reading public as much as on the idol they worship. The crucial problem, as he sees it, is not so much the king's book as it is the king's readers. He begins the tract by diagnosing the blindness of these readers and ends by describing the self-mutilation of their other relevantly interpretive sense, hearing. Ultimately the only power of *Eikon Basilike* is that it can

Catch the worthles approbation of an inconstant, irrational, and Image-doting rabble; that like a credulous and hapless herd, begott'n to servility, and inchanted with these popular institutes of Tyranny, subscrib'd with a new device of the Kings Picture at his praiers, hold out both thir ears with such delight and ravishment to be stigmatiz'd and boared through in witnes of thir own voluntary and beloved baseness. (YP 3:601)

If the king's book attempts to portray Charles as a martyr, Milton here transfers this role to the rabble of unfit readers who voluntarily and unnecessarily martyr their senses to the rhetorical tyranny of idolatry. Were readers at large well trained in intelligent and critical reading and free from "servility" to the idols of pictures, images, and texts, *Eikon Basilike* would not have needed refutation in the first place.[22] Good readers, as Milton points out in *Areopagitica,* are unassailable: "bad books . . . to a discrete and judicious Reader serve in many respects to discover, to confute, to forewarn, and to illustrate" (YP 2:512–13).

Eikonoklastes is thus part of a larger effort to retrain the audience as "discrete and judicious" readers. Sharon Achinstein has argued that Milton helped to define a "revolutionary public" by fashioning his readers as active participants in political debate. In her account, Milton constructs "a positive image for his public," and, although he frequently "scorns the rabble," he nonetheless explains "how any rank of citizen may become virtuous—by proper discipline, trial, and reading." While I think that Achinstein offers an excellent description of how Milton "postulates his public," I do want to qualify her argument in this respect: he fashions his audience "as a valuable participant in political discussion" precisely by representing it as an uneducable rabble. Indeed, his rhetorical manipulation achieves its ends by bequeathing the better part of the public with anything but a "positive image." Milton, with all of his elitist impulses, probably did have some variety of genuine disdain for "the rabble"; the claim advanced here is only that the *expression* of that scorn in his polemical tracts serves a substantial and efficacious rhetorical purpose. Although Milton's scorn should be understood as a strategic means of persuading his audience, this tactic by no means obviates "discipline, trial, and reading." The fit-though-few trope cannot in itself transform servile readers into active participants in public debate, but it can encourage them to choose a more rigorous course of training.[23]

In fact, reading Milton's own writing is part of the process of discipline, trial, and reading necessary to become a virtuous citizen. The bulk of *Eikonoklastes* is spent studying *Eikon Basilike,* chapter by chapter, with a closely critical eye. This sustained analysis allows Milton to "refute the missayings" throughout the book, to reveal its artifice, and, most significantly, to show his audience what type of skills and methods critical reading requires (YP 3:342). The tract is an attempt both to substitute his own critical interpretive responses for the public's idolatrous ones and, in the process, to train them in a particular mode of reading. If the greater part of his audience suffers from self-inflicted deafness and blindness, then the central purpose of the tract is to restore them to a critical perception more in line with his own. *Eikono-klastes* offers the special opportunity of following along with Milton as he exhibits the interpretive skills necessary for genuine debate within an emerging public sphere. A short passage should suffice as an example of his reading (Milton's italics indicate quotations from *Eikon Basilike*):

> *Hee hoped by his freedom, and their moderation to prevent misunderstandings.* And wherfore not by their freedom and his moderation? But freedom he thought too high a word for them; and moderation too mean a word for himself: this was not the way to prevent misunderstandings. He still *fear'd passion and prejudice in other men;* not in himself: *and doubted not by the weight of his* own *reason, to counterpoyse any Faction;* it being so easie for him, and so frequent, to call his obstinacy, Reason, and other mens reason, Faction. (YP 3:356)

Words are shown to be persuasive tools; their meaning need not correspond to the truth; their use is dependent on the limited perspective and self-interested intentions of the speaker. Critical reading requires an imaginative grasp of the author's purposes and designs on the reader coupled with the recognition that language is rhetorically constructed; it requires the ability to infer private motives and intentions from public expression. It also involves an aesthetic dimension, a sense of which words are "high" or "mean," and the ability to think subjunctively—to imagine what a sentence would signify had other, more correct word choices been made. John Staines writes that Milton "challenges his readers to learn to read such language skeptically, to become readers alert to how rhetoric is 'intended' to 'catch' them."[24] He trains his audience, in short, to be active readers, close readers, aesthetic readers, rhetorical readers, imaginative readers, skeptical readers. These, in conjunction with other interpretive skills that he brings to bear elsewhere in the tract, would presumably free his audience from the "servility" that had allowed them to become enthralled by the single, uncritical interpretation of the king and his book that Milton calls the "civil kinde of Idolatry" (YP 3:343). In the process of reading for his audience, he teaches his audience to read for itself.[25]

III

While a genuinely critical audience is Milton's polemical goal, it is also an impediment to his own project of rhetorical persuasion. He risks having his newly educated readers turn their critical arsenal back on his own tracts. Sharon Achinstein points out that although he "induces his audience to reinterpret the king's self-representations by a process of reading," he does not want to "threaten the stability of his position by admitting a plurality of readings."[26] Throughout the interregnum, but especially when Milton was writing *Eikonoklastes* as Secretary of Foreign Tongues in 1649, the overwhelming plurality of interpretation posed a daunting barrier to any attempt at generally efficacious persuasion. Following the execution of Charles in January of that year, England saw an enormous increase in the amount of open and vocal sectarianism.[27] Society was divided into Anglicans, Presbyterians, Puritans, and more radical sects such as Quakers, Ranters, Diggers, Fifth Monarchists, Seekers, Muggletonians, Grindletonians, and so on. The exceptional sectarianism of the period meant that Milton's public not only approached his writing with varying preconceptions, beliefs, and values, but also with significantly disparate interpretive practices. Nearly every literate member of society—and even those who were not literate—had been trained in biblical interpretation; for some this training came from sermons given in large community churches, while others learned to read and interpret texts in the smaller religious communities of conventicles. Interpretive practices were as diverse as the conservative confidence in canons of custom and church hierarchy, the Puritan reliance on the light of conscience, and, at the furthest extreme, the Ranter rejection of any scriptural (and, for that matter, textual) authority whatsoever. Especially in the years following Charles's execution Milton was faced with the challenge not only of creating a "revolutionary public," but of addressing, in a rhetorically effective and meaningful way, revolutionary *publics*.

Milton was well aware of the difficulties arising from the diversity of reading practices. In the preface to *Eikonoklastes* he establishes the following interpretive principle: "For in words which admitt of various sense, the libertie is ours to choose that interpretation which may best minde us of what our restless enemies endeavor, and what wee are timely to prevent" (YP 3:342). This kind of rule acknowledges that our own perspectives, interests, and personal choices always condition the way we read a text. In *An Apology* he writes that there are many who "notwithstanding what I can allege have yet decreed to mis-interpret the intents of my reply," although, had he not written, "they would have found as many causes to have misconceav'd the reasons of my silence" (YP 1:871). In *The Doctrine and Discipline of Divorce* he hopes that his readers' "experience of [their] owne uprightnesse mis-intepreted" will cause them to sympathize with his situation and to grant his tract "free audience and generous construction" (YP 2:225). One of his aims in the divorce tracts is to emancipate society from the oppression arising from "the strictnes of a literall interpreting" and to substitute a reading of Scripture based on mercy and "charitie, the interpreter and guide of our faith" (YP 2:242, 236). He most explicitly recognizes the inescapable plurality of interpretation in *A Treatise of Civil Power,* where he writes that it is not only the right, but also the "general dutie" of each Christian conscience to interpret Scripture with the aid of the "illumination of the Holy Spirit." The "final judge" of scriptural interpretation can only be each "Christian to himself." Matters of religion, he acknowledges, are "liable to be variously understood by humane reason," so that a divine precept "must needs appeer to everie man as the precept is understood." There are, at least potentially, as many interpretive responses as there are readers, and the way to create agreement and consensus is through persuasion and dialogue rather than the imposition of an "outward rule" (YP 7:241–45).

Milton uses his depictions of audience as a central strategy for coping with the plurality of interpretations—with the "Many-Headed Reader" that Achinstein sees as a prime source of "terror" for Dryden and his royalist contemporaries.[28] The fit-though-few trope reduces the diversity of readings to a manageable number of categories, making them treatable, assessable, addressable. Classical rhetoricians emphasized that an oration needed to "look both ways," adapting itself to both its subject matter and its audience. Quintilian stressed that the composition of the audience is crucial to the way an argument is presented; one must, in writing an oration, take into account the "sex, rank, age" and, most importantly, "character [*mores*]" of the audience.[29] The sheer multiplicity of Milton's readers would make this kind of accommodation impossible if he did not order them into groups by workable criteria. Once he has condensed the numerous readers and reader responses into a limited set of categories he is able to tailor his writing to meet the interpretive standards of each group and establish the types of evidence and reasoning by which they can be convinced. Much of the expository structure of *The Tenure of Kings and Magistrates,* for example, is geared toward providing the kinds of argumentative proof demanded by disparate factions. The tract addresses the concerns of different kinds of readers: those "govern'd by reason" (YP 3:190), "sincere and real men" (191), "Vulgar and irrational men" (192), "another sort" that has begun to "swerve" from the "noble deed" of regicide (194), "our Adversaries, Presbyterial" (198), and "malignant back-sliders" (222). Even when the tract has progressed deep into the exposition of its argument the concern with audience largely determines its structure. After giving a history and analysis of pre-Christian kingship, Milton writes, "But of these I name no more, lest it bee objected they were Heathen" (213). He responds to Presbyterian objections by stating that "the examples which follow shall be all Protestant and chiefly Presbyterian" (222). The argument, in short, develops as much through its relation to its plurality of audiences— successively addressing the concerns and standards of each constituency—as it does by any other internal logic.

Milton's use of the fit-though-few trope is a response to the interpretive diversity of the reading public in a more drastic and complex way. Harold Bloom has famously argued for viewing him as the Oedipal father against whom subsequent strong poets rebel, exhibiting the anxiety of influence.[30] But the fit-though-few trope can be better understood as a sign of the anxiety of influencing—as one way to cope with the overwhelming possibility that, considering the various interpretive practices in play, his tract would be violently misread. Just as the greater part of *Eikonoklastes* endeavors to substitute Milton's reading of *Eikon Basilike* for the idolatrous reading of his public, so also does the fit-though-few trope substitute prefabricated responses to Milton's own tract as a way of limiting misreadings. His various constructions of audience attempt to allow for only one possible misreading— disagreement—which is marked as the product of various deficiencies, such as blindness, deafness, servility, and illiteracy. In what might be understood as a kind of rhetorical prior restraint, Milton licenses a discrete number of possible responses to his argument before he makes it. The gesture of describing his audience is a kind of self-reading—an attempt not only to produce a text, but to generate and control its variant readings. Understood as a response to the plurality of interpretation, it is no wonder that Milton goes through the greatest pains to construct his readers (and thereby delimit their readings) in *Eikonoklastes*, a tract written during the height of sectarianism and concerned intensely with the problems of critical reading.

While many Miltonists, following William Kerrigan, have found in Milton evidence of a dominant Oedipal complex, this type of interpretive anxiety and its rhetorical manifestations might be better figured as part of a Saturn complex.[31] Fearing the power of his children, Saturn swallowed each one whole at birth, retaining them harmlessly within his own body. Like Saturn, Milton generates polemics only to confine them within the body of his own responses. In *A Treatise of Civil Power* he writes that a Protestant is one who "acknowledges none but the Scripture sole interpreter of it self to the conscience" (YP 7:243). At least in this model of the reading process (and it must be said that within the tract Milton forwards other very different models) Scripture is represented as a self-interpreting text. "Conscience" holds the grammatical position of indirect object: it is the passive recipient of a preinterpreted message. By delivering to the reader an already interpreted argument, a tract bypasses the dangers of willful and misguided reading. In an attempt to move toward this model of auto-interpretation, Milton's fit-though-few trope accounts for—which is to say that it constructs—the possible responses to his argument in advance.

So far I have looked at a substantial number of instances where Milton prereads his audience into two distinct and mutually exclusive groups as a means of overdetermining their possible interpretive responses, but it is necessary to note that this strategy is not quite universally employed. A sentence from *The Doctrine and Discipline of Divorce* begins with our familiar binary construction: "I seek not to seduce the simple and illiterat; my errand is to find out the choisest and the learnedest, who have this high gift of wisdom to answer solidly, or to be convinc't" (YP 2:233). "To seduce" is eschewed for another verb, "to find out," that merely discerns an already existing elect. But the last clause acknowledges the possibility of "choisest and learnedest" readers who may not already "be convinc't"—although even in this case the syntax slyly intimates that the ability to be convinced, along with the capacity to "answer solidly," is a "high gift of wisdom." At the end of *Eikonoklastes* Milton also relents from his habitual schematization. In addition to the "knowing Christians" that are impervious to the seductions of the king's book and the "Image-doting rabble" that is hopelessly enthralled, he makes room for a third response: "The rest, whom perhaps ignorance without malice, or some error, less then fatal, hath for the time misledd, on this side Sorcery or obduration, may find the grace and good guidance to bethink themselves, and recover" (YP 3:601).[32] For this third audience a radical change of mind seems genuinely possible. And yet this possibility, coming in the closing line of the tract, is deferred into the future. If "good guidance" can recover them from error, Milton is not—or at least not here—the one to dispense these curative arguments. The mention of "Sorcery" and "grace" also intimates that if persuasion is to take place it will occur through supernatural or divine, rather than merely human, agency. In any case, occasional inconsistencies in Milton's depictions of his audience do not undermine the claim that he uses the fit-though-few trope as a significant and pervasive rhetorical strategy. In fact, these exceptions suggest all the more strongly that the trope is not a sign of any sort of overarching theological or epistemological view about the impossibility of persuasion, but rather a strategic tool employed according to circumstance and context.

Despite acknowledging the manipulative, instrumental nature of Milton's representations, we must be cautious of understanding his rhetorical practice as overly authoritarian.[33] Susanne Woods has argued for what she calls an "elective poetics" in Milton's polemical writings, which is "an author's method for requiring and empowering reader choice, often to get the reader to enact the liberating and self-defining process of choosing."[34] Milton does allow his readers choices; the option of rejecting his arguments is never absent from the possible responses he offers, but it is always accompanied by the prospect of abuse. And it is difficult overall not to see his "elective poetics" as another kind of rhetorical manipulation: by offering his readers a choice—of who they want to be and what sort of virtues they want to exemplify—Milton gains the power to construct the circumstances under which choice occurs. Presenting the reader with options is, at least within the logic of the text, a way of rhetorically foreclosing on other possible choices.

The fit-though-few trope is one means of coping with two opposing problems of reading. In *Eikonoklastes,* especially, Milton must navigate between the Sin and Death of critical-rational interpretation, confronting the singular and uncritical response of idolatry on one side and the threat of being variously misread on the other. These opposing problems also threaten the existence of a genuine public sphere, which is predicated not only on unconstrained communication, but also on a shared set of assumptions, interpretive practices, and discursive boundaries within which rational communication can occur. As Habermas makes clear, participation in the public sphere is not simply a matter of social or material possibility without political constraint, but of substantial cultural training.[35] Milton's constructions of his audience mediate between these two poles: choice occurs within boundaries, and readers are instructed in a common but critical mode of reading and interpretation. The fit-though-few trope both signals the difficulties associated with participation in a nascent public sphere and, as part of Milton's larger project, aims to create the kinds of readers necessary for its emergence.

Harvard University

NOTES

1. John Milton, *First Prolusion,* in *The Complete Prose Works of John Milton,* 8 vols., ed. Don M. Wolfe et al. (New Haven, 1953–82), 1:220; hereafter designated YP and cited parenthetically by volume and page number in the text.

2. Aristotle, *Rhetoric,* trans. W. Rhys Roberts (Princeton, 1984), 1357a.

3. Stanley Fish, *How Milton Works* (Cambridge, MA, 2001), 123.

4. David Norbrook, "*Areopagitica,* Censorship, and the Early Modern Public Sphere," in *The Administration of Aesthetics: Censorship, Political Criticism, and the Public Sphere,* ed. Richard Burt (Minneapolis, 1994), 7, 4; Jurgen Habermas, *The Structural Transformation of the Public Sphere,* trans. Thomas Burger (Cambridge, MA, 1991). See esp. 27–51.

5. See Barbara K. Lewalski, *The Life of John Milton* (London, 2000), 29.

6. Aristotle, *Rhetoric,* 1358b.

7. Steven Zwicker, *Lines of Authority: Politics and English Literary Culture, 1649–1689* (Ithaca, NY, 1993), recognizes that "Milton attempts to control the affective power of the *Eikon Basilike* by embarrassing or, perhaps more accurately, humiliating and denouncing its audience"; he likewise acknowledges Milton's attempt to "conjur[e] a fit audience among the intellectual elite" (48–49). What Zwicker, like all previous critics, misses is the transformative, rather than simply descriptive, purpose of these categories.

8. Walter Benjamin, *Illuminations,* trans. Harry Zorn (London, 1999), 147.

9. There have been suggestions that in the seventeenth-century political pamphlets were

read aloud in small groups, which would obviously complicate the dynamics of response. See, for example, Richard Helgerson, "Milton Reads the King's Book," *Criticism* 29 (1987): 1–25: "Where *Eikon Basilike* could be read aloud (and no doubt often was) and still be understood by the listening audience (parts of it were even sung), Milton's book can only be apprehended by an individual reader who can *see* the difference between roman and italic type and thus know whether Milton is speaking in his own voice or quoting the king" (12).

10. Fish, *How Milton Works*, 112.

11. Max Weber, *The Protestant Ethic and the Spirit of Capitalism,* trans. Talcott Parsons (New York, 1930), 64–65. Weber's account of Puritan habits of self-examination is still the most insightful that I have encountered. Although his broader claims have been endlessly attacked and defended, his interpretation of election and self-examination has received relatively little critical attention. The closest and most thorough criticism can be found in M. H. MacKinnon, "Part I: Calvinism and the Infallible Assurance of Grace," *British Journal of Sociology* 39 (1988): 143–77. The obvious difficulty, for both Weber and MacKinnon, is that self-examination is a habit of thought, not a doctrine or belief, and is therefore unlikely to be registered in doctrinal texts. Nonetheless, Puritan autobiography (most dramatically that of Bunyan) gives an ample sense of the persistence, pervasiveness, and intensity of questioning one's own salvation. See also Barbara Lewalski, *Protestant Poetics and the Seventeenth-Century Religious Lyric* (Princeton, 1979), 158–62, for examples of tracts that advocate the practice of such systematic self-examination.

12. See Lewalski, *The Life of John Milton*, 420–24, for an exposition and defense of Milton's Arminianism.

13. The incomplete structure of the sentence is more readily apparent when greatly reduced: "That they . . . may have none to blame . . . if they live and dye in . . . blindness."

14. Fish, *How Milton Works*, 127.

15. Friedrich Nietzsche, *On the Genealogy of Morals*, trans. Walter Kaufmann (New York, 1967), 139–43. I read Nietzsche's invective against the ascetic priest as basically an argument against a certain kind of rhetoric. He acknowledges, however, the immense power wielded by the high priest through the mechanism of renunciation.

16. See Barbara K. Lewalski, "Milton and Idolatry," *SEL* 43, no. 1 (2003): 213–32.

17. Lana Cable, *Carnal Rhetoric: Milton's Iconoclasm and the Poetics of Desire* (Durham, NC, 1995), 146.

18. David Loewenstein, *Milton and the Drama of History: Historical Vision, Iconoclasm, and the Literary Imagination* (Cambridge, 1990), 57.

19. Helgerson, "Milton Reads the King's Book," 12. See also Bruce Boehrer, "Elementary Structures of Kingship: Milton, Regicide, and the Family," in *Milton Studies* 23, ed. James D. Simmonds (Pittsburgh, 1987): "In responding to the King's Book [Milton] was seeking to use traditional rhetoric against an adversary for whom the rules of rhetoric simply did not apply" (105). Although *Eikon Basilike* does not follow the "rules of rhetoric," we should not take this to mean that it is without rhetorical craft—a point *Eikonoklastes* is at constant pains to point out.

20. Cable, *Carnal Rhetoric*, 147.

21. As Achsah Guibbory comments in "Charles's Prayers, Idolatrous Images, and True Creation in Milton's *Eikonoklastes*," in *Of Poetry and Politics: New Essays on Milton and His World*, ed. P. G. Stanwood (Binghamton, NY, 1995), Milton "exposes" Charles not simply as an artist, but as a "bad artist, incapable of originality" (288).

22. Cable, *Carnal Rhetoric*, makes a similar point: "Ultimately for Milton . . . the call to reform meant restructuring not just icon-manipulating institutions and their agents, such as icon-exploiting kings and bishops and royalist propaganda. Even more than these it meant radical restructuring of the imaginative dynamics of individual faith" (147). For a scriptural

society, in which political discourse was increasingly tied up in the rapidly growing print culture, the "restructuring of the imaginative dynamics of individual faith" was simultaneously the restructuring of reading and interpretive practices.

23. Sharon Achinstein, *Milton and the Revolutionary Reader* (Princeton, 1994), 16.

24. John D. Staines, "Charles's Grandmother, Milton's Spenser, and the Rhetoric of Revolution," in *Milton Studies* 41, ed. Albert C. Labriola (Pittsburgh, 2002), 164.

25. See Achinstein, *Milton and the Revolutionary Reader,* 162–68.

26. Ibid, 155.

27. For a detailed account of the increased sectarianism of the 1640s and 1650s and its relation to Milton, see Christopher Hill, *Milton and the English Revolution* (London, 1977), esp. chapter 8. In my view we need not argue that Milton shared beliefs—much less a pipe or pint of ale—with contemporary radicals to accept that he viewed them as a significant part of his audience, one that needed to be strategically assessed and addressed in any public debate over religion or politics.

28. Sharon Achinstein, *Literature and Dissent in Milton's England* (New York, 2003), 14. See also Dryden, *Religio Laici,* esp. lines 400–422.

29. Quintilian, *Institutiones Oratoriae,* trans. Donald A. Russell (Cambridge, MA, 2001), 3.8.35–38.

30. Harold Bloom, *The Anxiety of Influence: A Theory of Poetry*, 2nd ed. (New York, 1997).

31. William Kerrigan, *The Sacred Complex: On the Psychogenesis of "Paradise Lost"* (Cambridge, MA, 1993).

32. For a similarly tripartite division of the audience, see the end of *The Reason of Church-Government*.

33. Although, as Helgerson, "Milton Reads the King's Book," 13, points out, the title of *Eikonoklastes* is recognized by Milton as the "famous surname of many Greek emperors" (YP 3:343).

34. Susanne Woods, "Elective Poetics and Milton's Prose," in *Politics, Poetics, and Hermeneutics in Milton's Prose,* ed. David Loewenstein and James Grantham Turner (New York, 1990), 196.

35. Habermas supposes that this training took place at coffeehouses, salons, and table societies, and that art criticism prepared private citizens for critical political discourse (*Structural Transformation,* 30–36). Following Norbrook, "*Areopagitica,* Censorship," I see no reason why the earlier stages of this training might not have occurred in the written political debates of the Interregnum.

"THAT REALLY TOO ANXIOUS PROTESTATION": CRISIS AND AUTOBIOGRAPHY IN MILTON'S PROSE

Brooke Conti

A LEXANDER MORE, WHOM Milton vilified in the *Second Defence of the English People,* is the first person known to have remarked on the autobiographical passages in Milton's prose.[1] "In this very *Second Defence* of yourself or the people," More writes of the tract with which he is particularly concerned, "as often as you speak for the people your language grows weak, becomes feeble, lies more frigid than Gallic snow; as often as you speak for yourself, which you do oftener than not, the whole thing swells up, ignites, burns."[2] More may have held a grudge against Milton, but these observations are hard to quarrel with. In the four political tracts in which Milton provides some kind of autobiography, once he starts talking about himself he seems hardly able to stop: the autobiographical material in *An Apology against a Pamphlet,* for example, amounts to fully a third of a work that otherwise argues for the elimination of bishops. More does not conclude from Milton's enthusiasm for himself that he believes his own press, however, and his suggestions about the psychological underpinnings of Milton's auto-biographies are shrewd:

> you picture yourself dear to God, but do not believe it. . . . How handsome you are, in your own opinion, when you imagine that you have painted those things for eternity which you have only painted for a while, and, as you are drawn by four white horses, imagine that all nations everywhere are transfixed with admiration for you, that all the centuries applaud you. This is a vain delusion. (YP 4:1109)

More implies that the versions of himself that Milton presents to his audience mask his fear that he is *not* in fact dear to God. "Hence," More will say later, rolling his eyes as Milton calls God as his witness, "that really too anxious protestation."[3]

Although Alexander More is far from a reputable character and his own self-defenses are often ludicrous, he is nevertheless a more astute reader of Milton's autobiographies than many twentieth-century literary critics. There

149

is no question that Milton's autobiographical excursions in the antiprelatical
tracts and the *Defences* are well known; few passages of his prose are more
familiar. But while these passages are continually trotted out to fill in Milton's
biography or to support biographical readings of his poems, the critical attention that they have received has been exceedingly limited. The central question would seem to be: what are Milton's autobiographies *doing* in the middle
of these four political tracts? Attempts have been made to answer this question, of course, but so far most such efforts have been confined to studies of
individual polemics. Such studies are necessarily invested in proving some
connection between their particular autobiographical passage and the work
as a whole, and thus the conventional explanation for these passages has long
been that Milton is "giving his credentials for speaking."[4] This argument has
dozens of variants, which come buttressed with details about classical and
Renaissance oratory and pagan and Christian notions of decorum, but while
such scholarship has been useful, it has rarely engaged in any meaningful way
with the content of a given autobiographical passage or considered it in
relation to other similar passages. In this essay, I will reevaluate both the
context and the effect of Milton's prose autobiographies. While these extraordinary passages are each dependent upon the circumstances surrounding the
tracts in which they appear, and each deserves careful individual attention,
none can be fully understood apart from the other three; their relationship to
one another is far stronger than their relationship to the nonautobiographical
material that surrounds them.

The continuities among Milton's autobiographical passages do not mean
that they form anything like a unified whole, however, and neither should we
make the mistake of believing them to be cut from the same cloth as Puritan
spiritual autobiography.[5] For one thing, in the early years of the civil war,
what we normally think of as spiritual autobiography did not yet exist. Those
works, which narrate an author's path from sinfulness to a conviction of
regeneracy, were not in wide circulation until after the Restoration, and thus
it would have been impossible for Milton to be imitating or adapting this
form for his own purposes. Although the tradition of Christian autobiography
that began with Augustine survived in some form throughout the Middle
Ages, until the sixteenth century it tended to manifest itself in brief flashes
rather than in any sustained way. According to Wayne Shumaker, "Before
1500 self-revelation tended . . . to be fragmentary, more or less accidental,
and, more often than not, in some degree allegorized or fictionalized."[6] Well
into the seventeenth century, prose autobiography of any sort was still quite
rare in England, and when Milton wrote his antiprelatical tracts in 1641 and
1642 the works most similar to Puritan spiritual autobiography were the
autobiographical accounts of John Lilburne.[7] Even these, however, focused

considerably more upon the punishments that Lilburne received for his non-conformist activities (the printing and distribution of banned books and his refusal to take the required oath in Star Chamber) than upon the nature of his beliefs, his relationship with God, or how he arrived at either.

Chronology is not the only problem with this purported parallel between Milton's autobiographies and those of his near contemporaries. As even proponents of the argument acknowledge, Milton's readers "are not told . . . the precise moment when he first felt the conviction of grace,"[8] and nearly all the other markers of the spiritual autobiography are likewise missing: in Milton's autobiographical writings there is no early sinning, no hearing the call, resisting the call, believing, doubting, and finally arriving at a full conviction of salvation. Indeed, although Milton's works may be autobiographical and written from a more or less recognizably "Puritan" perspective, they have almost nothing else in common with the later genre. Milton's autobiographies, written right in the messy middle of life, also lack the distance of the typical spiritual autobiography, in which the real story is always in the past and told retrospectively.[9] Instead, Milton's autobiographical passages show a man deeply anxious about both present and future, hoping for great things but half convinced that they will pass him by.

Milton only rarely admits to this uncertainty—as he does in the anti-prelatical tracts, where he confesses his sense of having little to show for his years—and acting to counter these few indications of insecurity is virtually everything else Milton says about himself, which promotes the popular image of him as a man of unparalleled self-confidence. No matter how thoroughly *in medias res* Milton finds himself, he always acts as though he were surveying his life from a remote distance. He admits no doubts and recognizes no setbacks, presenting himself as a man with an unshakable conviction in himself and his calling, and who has never altered in the least: it was not Milton who changed his mind about the ministry—it was the church that changed under the prelates; Milton has not abandoned poetry—he's just deferring it while his country calls. Christopher Hill has said that Milton himself is the worst enemy of Milton biographers, and often, too, he is the worst enemy of Milton critics: even readers with a healthy amount of skepticism are frequently taken in by Milton's self-presentation in these passages.[10] But while there is no disputing that Milton's works nearly always assume a tone of overwhelming self-confidence, if Milton were really so certain of his literary election (which is, to a large degree, inseparable from his spiritual election), it would seem that he would not need to declare it so insistently or at such length.

As the quotations from Alexander More suggest, and as I shall argue in the remainder of this essay, it is paradoxically a sense of unease and uncertainty about his mission that leads Milton to produce autobiographical passages that say nearly the opposite. Milton's autobiographies occur at what appear to be the two most pivotal moments in his life, when he is reassessing what he believes God wants from him and questioning the wisdom of the path he has taken so far. Sometimes his autobiographies are provoked, in part, by the attacks of other pamphleteers, but Milton never confines himself to answering specific insults, and there are several examples of published attacks that Milton fails to answer (or fails to answer in a personal vein).[11] I believe that Milton responds with autobiography when he feels most vulnerable and when his opponents' attacks hit closest to his own deepest fears. For this reason, the subject of a tract need not be "personal" (in the way we know the divorce tracts to have been personal) in order to prompt autobiography, but the subject matter is clearly not irrelevant. Milton produces his first autobiographies as he reluctantly sets aside his poetic ambitions in order to serve God with his prose, and he produces his later ones as he confronts the possibility that, having allowed him to go blind while defending the republic, God may not actually *want* the epic work that Milton always thought would be both his greatest achievement and his greatest gift to the deity. Milton's stridency in his autobiographies masks a deep anxiety, and the passages seem intended less to convince his audience of his literary-spiritual destiny than to convince himself. Despite Milton's best efforts, this strange handful of passages periodically lets a reader behind the public mask that he strives to hold in place; or at least they do if one knows how to read them—and between their lines.

The Antiprelatical Tracts, 1641–1642

Milton's first published prose works are a series of five antiprelatical tracts, the last two of which, *The Reason of Church-Government* and *An Apology against a Pamphlet,* contain half of Milton's total autobiographical output; they also represent the first time that Milton publicly attempted to describe or justify himself in print.[12] With these pamphlets Milton was joining a debate about the proper form for Protestant ecclesiastical government that extended back as far as the English Reformation, but which had gained new momentum since the 1633 appointment of the imperious William Laud as archbishop of Canterbury. Those who opposed episcopacy found the hierarchical structure of the English church dangerously close to papacy, prone to corruption, and indifferent to the spiritual needs of the common worshipper. In the 1620s and 1630s the kind of outspoken opposition to prelacy found in Milton's tracts inspired swift and brutal punishment: for Alexander Leighton's 1628 *An Appeal to the Parliament; or, Sions Plea Against the*

Prelacie (a work that was to inspire more than a few aspects of Milton's *Of Reformation*, including the arresting image of the bishops as a poisonous wen on the head of the state[13]), Laud had Leighton arrested and whipped, his face branded, his nose slit, and one ear cut off.[14]

If never without risk, by 1641 the political climate was safer for pamphlet writers. In November 1640 the Long Parliament met, beginning a session that was to last through the following September and include a concerted assault upon the bishops. In December 1640 the Root and Branch Petition, signed by 15,000 Londoners asking for the destruction of episcopal government and "all its dependencies, roots and branches," was delivered to the House of Commons, and the following February Archbishop Laud was charged with treason, impeached, and eventually imprisoned. At the same time, the Long Parliament had significantly loosened the restrictions on the press, and a flood of pamphlets on issues of church and state washed over London. While Bishop Joseph Hall was chosen by the Church of England to defend episcopacy in this war of polemics, one of his principal opponents was a group of reform-minded ministers whose initials spelled their pseudonym, Smectymnuus. The two sides had been exchanging ever-longer and more tediously entitled pamphlets for several months when Milton decided to enter the fray with *Of Reformation* (1641), siding with his former tutor, Timothy Young (he who put the "TY" in Smectymnuus) and Young's associates.[15]

Over the next year Milton would contribute four more antiprelatical tracts to the debate. These differ from those of the other contestants in the controversy in a number of ways—including their disinclination to rely upon church fathers or to delve too deeply into historical disputes—but perhaps their most striking difference lies in the strange autobiographical passages that occur in the last two of the series. Scholars have sometimes "explained" these autobiographical passages by pointing out that *The Reason of Church-Government* is the first of Milton's tracts to bear his name, and thus might have seemed to Milton to mandate a public proffering of credentials.[16] However, while a relationship surely exists between the presence of Milton's autobiography in *The Reason of Church-Government* and his decision to sign his name to the work, there is no more reason to think that putting his name on the title page prompted Milton to provide some autobiographical background than that writing an autobiography inspired him to stake an authorial claim. (Moreover, the notion of any easy connection between name and autobiography is immediately thrown into question by *An Apology*—a work that does not bear Milton's name.) Simply put, the autobiographical passage in *The Reason of Church-Government* is too long and inconsistent to be explained away as easily as it often is, whether as an ethical proof, a proto-spiritual autobiography, or Milton's attempt to model himself on the prophets of the Hebrew Bible. Although there are moments in which Milton is indeed writing within one or another recognizable tradition, the design as a whole is ad hoc, with Milton taking models for his autobiography wherever he can find them. The fact that Milton supplies a lengthy autobiographical account in this work, and not in his three previous ones (or in the many polemics of the 1640s that will follow *An Apology*) suggests that something other than ad-herence to literary convention is at work. The very inconsistency of Milton's autobiography betrays the anxiety behind it, which I believe has its roots not simply in his feelings of unpreparedness or reluctance to take the public stage, but rather in a deeper uncertainty about God's plans for Milton's life—and whether or not Milton's own ambitions coincide with the divine design.

Milton's autobiographical passage in *The Reason of Church-Govern-ment* appears at the work's halfway mark, in what is commonly referred to as the preface to its second book (although it bears no title). He begins by lamenting the burden of knowing spiritual truths and the lack of welcome that the bearer of disagreeable information often experiences. But, he writes,

[I]f the Prelats have leav to say the worst that can be said, and doe the worst that can be don . . . no man can be justly offended with him that shall endeavour to impart and bestow without any gain to himselfe those sharp, but saving words which would be a terror, and a torment in him to keep back. For me I have determin'd to lay up as the best treasure, and solace of a good old age, if God voutsafe it me, the honest liberty of free speech from my youth, where I shall think it available in so dear a concernment as the Churches good. (YP 1:804)

Milton's autobiography thus begins on a relatively impersonal note, but it swiftly takes a turn to the particular. *Any* man might be justified in writing tracts that others find unseemly, so long as his conscience impels him and he is doing so without hope for gain. However, as Milton turns to his own situation he seems to discard the image of terror and torment for a more pragmatic motive: he is speaking boldly now so that in his senescence—when perhaps he will be unable to do so—he might look back on his life with contentment. The language Milton uses certainly makes it sound as though he is seeking "gain to himselfe" (at least of a sort), and the picture he paints of himself as a shrewd, long-term planner does not seem to have much in common with that of the man whose writing is motivated by holy terror. Although the proximity of those two images suggests that both motives might be Milton's, with the shift from third to first person Milton willfully distances himself from that first, anxious writer, as if determined to emphasize the control he has over both himself and his work.

This same pattern is repeated throughout the tract's autobiographical section: a half-formed expression of uncertainty is quickly followed by an assertion of confidence. Even when, as with his next lines, Milton seems on the verge of self-scrutiny—"For if I be either by disposition, or what other cause too inquisitive or suspitious of my self and mine own doings, who can help it?"—he rushes on:

> but this I foresee, that should the Church be brought under heavy oppression, and God have given me ability the while to reason against that man that should be the author of so foul a deed, or should she by blessing from above on the industry and courage of faithfull men change this her distracted estate into better daies without the lest furtherance or contribution of those few talents which God at that present had lent me, I foresee what stories I should heare within my selfe, all my life after, of discourage and reproach. (YP 1:804)

Milton sandwiches his brief admission to some feelings of self-doubt between two strong declarations of what he is "determin'd" to do, and he has hardly begun to consider the reasons for his uncertainty (is it his natural disposition? or something else?) before he dismisses the entire discussion with a shrugging "who can help it?"

No one may be able to help Milton's tendency to overanalyze himself and his actions, but he quickly transforms the habit from a possible weakness into a strength: with an extraordinary act of projection he abruptly casts his narrative into the future, imagining a scenario in which he has chosen *not* to pen his antiprelatical tracts. Some critics have argued that, with his insistence upon his own foresight, Milton is styling himself as a Hebrew prophet.[17] However, while Milton does occasionally ventriloquize those voices crying out in the wilderness, this analysis is not wholly accurate: for one, the only thing that he "foresees" is his own spiritual and emotional state, and Milton makes no bets as to whether the church will be brought out of danger by the work of faithful men or whether their absence and neglect will lead to its oppression.[18] Whatever concern Milton may have for the church's welfare, in this passage his focus is less upon the institution's fate than upon his own. Thus, in reproducing for his reader the voice of his conscience (as he imagines it speaking to the version of himself who has declined to write pamphlets in God's service), Milton supplies a rebuke for both possible outcomes. First, envisioning a church imperiled, he has his conscience scold,

> Timorous and ingratefull, the Church of God is now again at the foot of her insulting enemies: and thou bewailst, what matters it thee for thy bewailing? . . . when the cause of God and his Church was to be pleaded, for which purpose that tongue was given thee which thou hast, God listen'd if he could heare thy voice among his zealous servants, but thou wert domb as a beast; from hence forward be that which thine own brutish silence hath made thee. (YP 1:804–5)

Then Milton considers the other possibility:

Or else I should have heard on the other eare, slothfull, and ever to be set light by, the Church hath now overcom her late distresses after the unwearied labours of many her true servants that stood up in her defence; thou also wouldst take upon thee to share amongst them of their joy: but wherefore thou? where canst thou shew any word or deed of thine which might have hasten'd her peace; what ever thou dost now talke, or write, or look is the almes of other mens active prudence and zeale. Dare not now to say, or doe any thing better then thy former sloth and infancy . . . what before was thy sin, is now thy duty to be, abject, and worthlesse. (YP 1:805)

Far from conceiving of himself as a voice crying out in the wilderness, Milton is anxious about all the *other* voices that might be raised without his joining the chorus. In recounting this period of his life in the *Second Defence,* he will say, similarly, that the bishops "had become a target for the weapons of all men," and "all mouths were opened against them" (YP 4:623, 621). Whether or not the church recovers from her enfeeblement, there is glory to be won, and Milton, terribly aware that he is a latecomer to this particular vineyard, seems oppressed by the fear of missing out on it entirely. (And indeed, the very same month that Milton published *The Reason of Church-Government* the bishops were ousted from the House of Lords.)

But although Milton appears genuinely concerned about his belatedness, and speaks slightingly of his own effort and courage—describing his actions as "this litle diligence" and only "something more than wish[ing] [the church's] welfare" (YP 1:805–6)—soon a new explanation for his uneasiness emerges: *this* sort of writing is really not what he has prepared himself for. He hopes, however, that he will meet with an understanding reader:

To [the reader] it will be no new thing though I tell him that if I hunted after praise by the ostentation of wit and learning, I should not write thus out of mine own season, when I have neither yet compleated to my minde the full circle of my private studies, although I complain not of any insufficiency to the matter in hand, or were I ready to my wishes, it were a folly to commit any thing elaborately compos'd to the carelesse and interrupted listening of these tumultuous times. Next if I were wise only to mine own ends, I would certainly take such a subject as of it self might catch applause, whereas this hath all the disadvantages on the contrary. . . . Lastly, I should not chuse this manner of writing wherin knowing my self inferior to my self, led by the genial power of nature to another task, I have the use, as I may account it, but of my left hand. (YP 1:807–8)

Milton never makes a claim but he deletes or emends it, seemingly torn between asserting the value of his current work and denying its artistic pretensions. The subject of Milton's tract may be "no new thing" to the learned reader, but if Milton were seeking praise for his work—which he could gain if he wanted to!—he would not be writing while his studies are still incomplete. On the other hand, if he were better able to produce something that he felt was a true work of both learning and art, that, too, would be unseasonable:, the age is too restless and distractible for such a thing. The upshot of all of this seems to be that Milton's work should be taken as evidence of his sincerity and selfless intentions: since it cannot redound to the glory of his craftsmanship or talent, it must speak only to his sense of duty.

However, as earlier, Milton seems eager to leave the muddle of the present behind. Rather than dwelling on what he might or might not be able to do right now, he quickly turns first to his past and then to his future:

And though I shall be foolish in saying more to this purpose, yet since it will be such a folly, as wisest men going about to commit, have only confest and so committed, I may trust with more reason, because with more folly to have courteous pardon. For although a Poet soaring in the high region of his fancies with his garland and singing robes about him might without apology speak more of himself then I mean to do, yet for me sitting here below in the cool element of prose, a mortall thing among many readers of no Empyreall conceit, to venture and divulge unusual things of my selfe, I shall petition to the gentler sort, it may not be envy to me. I must say therefore that after I had from my first yeeres . . . bin exercis'd to the tongues . . . it was found that . . . [whether] in English, or other tongue, prosing or versing, but chiefly this latter, the stile by certain vital signes it had, was likely to live. (YP 1:808–9)

Although Milton acknowledges the oddity of focusing so much of his writing upon himself, he excuses it with the vague assertion that "wisest men" have done the same. Unusually for Milton, he does not name any of these men, although he does suggest that he surpasses them by divulging yet more autobiography than they; a moment later he claims that he is still not going as far as he might if he were writing verse. This first part of the passage shows the same uncertain back-and-forth motion as the previous one, but it soon disappears in the second half. Once Milton begins his account of his early years, his narrative suddenly has a shape, with all its events tending toward one end: the emergence of Milton as a great poet. It is precisely because he is a poet—though he has shown few signs of it to the outside world—that Milton claims indulgence for his prose autobiography.

Milton now gets to what most readers would regard as the meat of his autobiography, what Louis Martz has called "that surprising and rather embarrassing revelation of Milton's poetical hopes and dreams."[19] Fueled equally by the encouragement of his friends and his own "inward prompting," Milton came to believe that, "by labour and intent study . . . joyn'd with the strong propensity of nature, I might perhaps leave something so written to aftertimes, as they should not willingly let it die" (YP 1:810). Skipping over

the uncertainty of the present, Milton imagines his future as a linear continuation of his past—or at least the version of his past that he gives here; as
John Shawcross and Richard Helgerson note, there is little evidence that
Milton envisioned a poetic future for himself until he was nearly twenty, and
he here conveniently omits any mention of his early intention to enter the
ministry.[20] For all Milton's confident, prophetic language, what he actually
predicts is quite vague: at some undetermined point in the future his literary
talent will manifest itself in some undetermined way. He asserts that he will
write in his native tongue for "God's glory by the honour and instruction of
my country" (YP 1:810–12), but otherwise he does not know what form his
great work will take; instead (and despite his protestation that "time servs not
now" to discuss the specifics of his literary ambitions), Milton devotes several
dozen lines to considering, by turns, suitable subjects for an epic, tragic, or
lyric celebration of his nation and its God.

After this discussion Milton apologizes again for coming before the
public eye before he can do justice to his talent: "The thing which I had to say,
and those intentions which have liv'd within me ever since I could conceiv my
self any thing worth to my Countrie, I return to crave excuse that urgent
reason hath pluckt from me by an abortive and foredated discovery" (YP
1:820). This time Milton is excusing himself not simply for coming forward as
a writer before being ready, or even for doing so in a format that he believes
to be inferior, but rather for having been *forced* to tell his audience of his
long-term literary ambitions before he is able to deliver on them. With this
Milton sets aside the matter of church government: no longer is he simply
providing evidence of his reluctance to enter the polemic fray; now he makes
plain what seems really to have been bothering him: his lack of poetic progress. He continues,

the accomplishment of [these ambitions] lies not but in a power above mans to
promise; but that none hath by more studious ways endeavour'd, and with more
unwearied spirit that none shall, that I dare almost averre of my self. . . . Neither doe I
think it shame to covnant with any knowing reader, that for some few yeers yet I may
go on trust with him toward the payment of what I am now indebted, as being a work
not to be rays'd from the heat of youth, or the vapours of wine . . . but by devout prayer
to that eternall Spirit who can enrich with all utterance and knowledge . . . to this must
be added industrious and select reading, steddy observation, insight into all seemly
and generous arts and affaires, till which in some measure be compast, at mine own
peril and cost I refuse not to sustain this expectation from as many as are not loath to
hazard so much credulity upon the best pledges that I can give them. (YP 1:820–21)

While early Milton criticism regarded Milton's "covenant" as proof of the
poet's unswerving sense of his life's mission (if not an outright demonstration

of his prophetic powers), more contemporary scholarship has tended to doubt this. However, although recent critics are correct in pointing out that Milton could not possibly have known what he would do in twenty-five years, and that, moreover, the audience for his polemics probably could not have cared less about his poetic ambitions, they have not arrived at a satisfactory answer as to why Milton makes this contract with his reader. One suggestion, advanced in different ways by John Guillory and Kevin Dunn, has been that Milton is not so much promising to deliver a specific work as he is demonstrating that he possesses sufficient literary and moral authority for his antiprelatical arguments to be taken seriously: not only does Milton, as a poet, have the right to act as a spokesman for his party, but by sacrificing something of great personal value he has proven his fitness to serve that party.[21] Whatever the merits of this argument, it seems inadequate in light of the sheer volume of information that Milton provides about his literary plans. Even if his audience does not care about his poetic dreams, Milton does, very much —to the point that they are almost all he can talk about.

More than his readers, Milton seems to be trying to convince himself. He claims that his literary talent is God-given, "a power above mans to promise," and elsewhere he equates the power of poetry with that of the priesthood (YP 1:820, 817). Despite his years of study, his abilities have borne only occasional fruit, and now that he feels compelled to serve God in polemic warfare Milton may be doubting whether he will ever have the opportunity to return to his poetic studies; more crucially, Milton may be doubting whether God even wants him to continue those studies, and whether God values the offering Milton vaguely hopes someday to make. In Milton's impassioned defense of poets and poetry, one can hear him trying to justify the value of a literary life (to himself? to God?) in much the same way that he once attempted to justify it to his father in *Ad Patrem*. The covenant with his readers, then, is really a covenant with himself, made in the public eye to give it more weight and make it that much harder to renege on.

Milton's final antiprelatical tract appeared two or three months later. As its title suggests, *An Apology against a Pamphlet Call'd A Modest Confutation of the Animadversions upon the Remonstrant against Smectymnuus* is a direct response to the pamphlets of Joseph Hall and the Smectymnuans (as well as a participant in their tradition of unwieldy titles), but it is also a defense of Milton himself. In an earlier tract, *Animadversions upon the Remonstrants Defense against Smectymnuus*, Milton had mocked Bishop Hall for everything from his opinions on church government to his writing style; moreover, Milton strongly implied that there was a relationship between Hall's pro-prelatical position and his weak transitions, infelicitous metaphors, and faulty logic.[22] Such taunts, in turn, provoked a new work from an unknown pen: *A Modest Confutation of a Slanderous and Scurrilous Libell, Entituled, Animadversions.*[23] Although most of the *Modest Confutation* is devoted to vindicating Hall and advancing his episcopal arguments, its author also rebukes the anonymous Milton for his unseemly language and allegedly equally unseemly behavior. Milton's *Apology* is thus a response to a response, and as such does not cover a great deal of new ground with its ecclesiastical arguments. However, in its refutation of the Confuter's personal attacks and the autobiography that this refutation seems to have inspired, Milton's work reveals his developing sense of himself as a writer and outlines the relationship he believes to exist between an author and his work.

Even taking into account the Modest Confuter's attacks upon Milton, *An Apology* contains an astonishing amount of self-disclosure: the first twenty pages of the original fifty-nine-page tract may be regarded as autobiography of a greater or lesser degree. Although there are no records of what Milton's original audience thought of this extraordinary feat of self-contemplation, it certainly is not typical of writers of the period. Among the hundreds of other tracts on the subject of church government published from 1640 to 1642, virtually none contains more than an autobiographical sentence or two.[24] By the mid-1650s, when Milton writes his Latin *Defences,* his opponents return autobiography for autobiography and one personal defense for one personal attack, but in the antiprelatical debates this does not happen: when maligned by Milton, neither Joseph Hall nor the Modest Confuter speaks up in his own defense.

Despite the personal nature of so many of the tract's pages, Milton left the work anonymous. It would not have been unusually difficult to track him down as its author—and Milton provides so much information about himself that he can hardly be too concerned with keeping his identity a secret—but in leaving his name off the title page Milton appears reluctant to take the same kind of credit for it as he did for *The Reason of Church-Government.*[25] Perhaps Milton felt it unwise to go on the record maligning a bishop as prominent as Hall, or perhaps he was faintly embarrassed by the nastiness of some of his own rhetoric. I suspect, however, that part of the explanation may lie in Milton's uneasy sense that his belief in the close relationship between a work and its author may not reflect entirely well upon *him.* As Milton attacks the Modest Confuter and his writing, he posits a direct correspondence between a writer and his work, insisting that he knows everything he needs to know about the Confuter (not to mention Joseph Hall) based upon his book. However, not only has the Confuter painted a very unflattering portrait of Milton based—he says—solely upon what he has found in the *Animadversions,* but, in the immensely long autobiographical portion of *An Apology,* Milton proves that he is far from willing to let his works speak entirely for themselves.

Although Milton's autobiographical passage in *An Apology* comes at the very beginning of the work rather than in the middle, as it does in *The Reason of Church-Government,* the two sections begin in much the same manner: after a general statement about the burden of knowledge and the difficulty of acting morally upon that knowledge, Milton enters into his autobiography by way of discussing the duty he feels toward God and his church—a duty that requires him to take on the somewhat uncomfortable task of writing in his own defense: "now against the rancor of an evill tongue . . . I must be forc't to proceed from the unfained and diligent inquiry of mine owne conscience at home (for better way I know not, Readers) to give a more true account of my selfe abroad then this modest Confuter, as he calls himselfe, hath given of me" (YP 1:869–70). Even though Milton has already freely given an account of himself in *The Reason of Church-Government,* he now depicts the task as one to which he has been driven only reluctantly, and only in self-defense. As in *Church-Government,* however, Milton again seems less interested in external reality—vindicating himself with proofs of his virtuous deeds and lifestyle—than with the internal: the results of an "unfained and diligent inquiry of [his] owne conscience." In the earlier pamphlet Milton focused on the future rather than the present, the speculative or desired rather than the verifiable, and a similar pattern is evident here: Milton privileges what he thinks and feels over whatever actions his antagonist may have alleged him to have taken—without first bothering to prove those allegations false.

Milton acknowledges that he might have followed the examples of many illustrious men by suffering in silence, but

when I discern'd [the Confuter's] intent was not so much to smite at me, as through me to render odious the truth which I had written, and to staine with ignominy that Evangelick doctrine which opposes the tradition of Prelaty, I conceav'd my selfe to be now not as mine own person, but as a member incorporate into that truth whereof I was perswaded, and whereof I had declar'd openly to be a partaker. Whereupon I thought it my duty, if not to my selfe, yet to the religious cause I had in hand, not to leave on my garment the least spot, or blemish in good name. (YP 1:871)

Milton's argument is that his self-defense is not really a self-defense since the Modest Confuter's target is not really Milton, but the antiprelatical faction as a whole. This is a reasonable enough claim, but it is one the *Modest Confutation* does not quite bear out. In the letter to the reader that prefaces the work, the Confuter writes,

If thou hast any generall or particular concernment in the affairs of these times, or but naturall curiosity, thou art acquainted with the late and hot bickering between the *Prelates* and *Smectymnuans:* To make up the breaches of whose solemn Scenes, (it were too ominous to say Tragicall) there is thrust forth upon the Stage, as also to take the eare of the lesse intelligent, a scurrilous *Mime*, a personated, and (as himself thinks) a grim, lowring, bitter fool.[26]

Although Milton is attacked as a scurrilous fool, it is the style and method of Milton's writing, not the substance of his views, that the Confuter decries. Indeed, he gives the opinions of the Smectymnuans exactly as much respect as those of the prelatical faction, using the same images for the works of both sides: they are (somehow simultaneously) "hot bickerings" and "solemn scenes." Later, the Confuter will say that Milton's greatest concern in *Anim-adversions* is not the proper form of church government, but rather private and personal spleen: "the other businesse being handled but by the by, or not at all: and where it is, in such a wretched, loathsome manner, as once I did almost doubt me, whether or no you did not jeer at both sides, at Religion, and God, and all."[27] While the Confuter makes no bones about his own political and religious sympathies and will spend the last third of the work arguing for episcopacy and a set liturgy, his personal attacks on Milton occur only in the first part of his tract, and only have to do with Milton's lack of decorum (and perceived related lack of virtue). He does not malign the other Presbyterians, and while he may indeed intend for his readers to extrapolate from Milton's character to the validity of his cause, it is Milton, not the Confuter, who appears to hold most tenaciously to the belief that the character of an individual man—as evidenced in his writing—tells the observer everything he needs to know about the cause he champions; these are the very grounds for his vitriol against both Joseph Hall and the Confuter.

Given his belief in the strong correlation between a man's character and his literary ability—"how he should be truly eloquent who is not withall a good man, I see not" (YP 1:874)—Milton spends the next several pages alternately defending his earlier work and disparaging the *Modest Confutation* by focusing upon the method and style of both. He devotes a full page to considering his opponent's title page, ridiculing nearly every word for its inappropriateness. A representative example is his treatment of the title's first word, "modest": "Whereas a modest title should only informe the buyer what the book containes," Milton writes, "this officious epithet so hastily assuming the modesty w[hi]ch others are to judge of by reading, not the author to anticipate to himselfe by forestalling, is a strong presumption that his modesty set there to sale in the frontispice, is not much addicted to blush" (YP 1:876). But although Milton subjects this and other parts of the Confuter's work to what might be considered an extremely close reading (and manages to mock, along the way, a number of unrelated works by Bishop Hall on the grounds that they show his ignorance of both literary and moral decorum), the Confuter's comments on Milton himself are what really preoccupy Milton.[28] The Confuter's attacks are an apparent combination of conjecture and falsehood based upon a few scattered and unilluminating passages in *Animadversions* (typical is the accusation that, because Milton uses a few theatrical metaphors, he must haunt playhouses), but, as nasty and haphazard as these attacks are, they amount to only a few charges, most of them recognizable as speculation rather than promoted as documented fact. At first Milton jumps on this weakness, noting that the Confuter "confesses, he has *no furder notice of mee then his owne conjecture*," adding snidely, "it had been honest to have inquir'd, before he utter'd such infamous words" (YP 1:882). A moment later, however, Milton reverses himself, saying, "I am credibly inform'd he did inquire, but finding small comfort from the intelligence which he receav'd, whereon to ground the falsities which he had provided, thought it his likeliest course under a pretended ignorance to let drive at randome" (1:882). The Confuter may or may not have known Milton's identity or made inquiries into his history and habits, but even if he had—and even if Milton somehow knew as much—it is curious that Milton should announce this fact.[29] If Milton's aim were only to vindicate himself of his opponent's charges, the easiest way would surely be to point to the Confuter's statement that he knows nothing of Milton apart from his writing, and thereby dismiss his attacks as groundless.

There seem to be two likely reasons that Milton emphasizes the Confuter's inquiries: first, to assert that he *has* some kind of a public reputation, and that it is a positive one; otherwise, the Confuter's statement that he "has no notice" of Milton might be taken as evidence of Milton's obscurity, which is one of the things that Milton's autobiographies seem meant to dispel. Second, if Milton were to argue too vehemently that the portrait the Confuter has assembled from reading Milton's text is flawed, Milton would have to revise his own notions about the relationship between authors and their works. So Milton harps on the supposed duplicitousness of the Confuter, with the perhaps inadvertent consequence that his antagonist appears fiendishly clever. Where some writers might be content with slandering their enemy with whatever weapons came to hand, the Confuter, in Milton's analysis, "burden[s] me with those vices, whereof, among whom my conversation hath been, I have been ever least suspected; perhaps not without some suttlety to cast me into envie, by bringing on me a necessity to enter into mine owne praises" (YP 1:883). That is, the Confuter has purposely made the picture so bad that he intends for Milton to embarrass himself by making an immodest self-defense—but Milton is not about to fall into his trap:

I know every wise man is more unwillingly drawne to speak [of himself], then the most repining eare can be averse to heare. Nevertheless since I dare not wish to passe this life unpersecuted of slanderous tongues, for God hath told us that to be generally prais'd is wofull, I shall relye on his promise to free the innocent from causelesse aspersions: whereof nothing sooner can assure me, then if I shall feele him now assisting me in the just vindication of my selfe, which yet I could deferre, it being more meet that to those other matters of publick debatement in this book I should give attendance first, but that I feare it would but harme the truth, for me to reason in her behalfe, so long as I should suffer my honest estimation to lye unpurg'd from these insolent suspicions. (YP 1:883)

Milton's conclusion in the second part of this passage—that God wishes for him to defend himself—does not seem to follow from the preceding state-ments that (1) wise men are reluctant to speak of themselves, and (2) being slandered is not uncommon, and being praised by all men would be worse. If Milton is alluding to the passage in the Sermon on the Mount in which Jesus says "blessed are you when they revile and persecute you, and say all kinds of evil against you falsely for my sake," he ought certainly to remember that the passage concludes, "Rejoice and be exceedingly glad, for great is your reward in heaven" (Matt. 5:11–12). Milton, however, seems unwilling to wait for vindication in the next world—he seems, in fact, to be challenging God to prove that he aids the innocent by doing so, right now, by helping Milton to vindicate himself. But as in *The Reason of Church-Government,* Milton again hesitates: even with God's promise, he could still put off this self-defense and get to the important matter of reforming church government—except that no one would heed what he had to say if they thought the Confuter's portrait of him were true.

As he has done earlier, Milton registers anxiety about being unknown, as well as an almost equal anxiety about not being able to control how he is known or how his works are read. In his essay on *The Reason of Church-Government,* Stanley Fish has argued that there is, in effect, no "reason" in *Church-Government*—that the point of Milton's work is to show the inade-quacy of human reason when it comes to a matter of religious faith: either one gets it, or one does not.[30] A similar attitude appears to be at work in *An Apology,* where Milton's excuse for his otherwise outrageous self-focus seems to be that who he *is* is more important than what he has done—or even what he has written. According to what he writes elsewhere, most notably in his statement that "he who would not be frustrate of his hope to write well hereafter in laudable things, ought him selfe to bee a true Poem, that is, a composition, and patterne of the best and honourablest things" (YP 1:890), Milton claims that writer and work should correspond perfectly, but his convulsive, overly explanatory autobiographies suggest that the Confuter's attacks on Milton's manner and method of writing have struck deeply at these beliefs.

Taking the Confuter's taunts as a starting point, Milton now enters into his autobiography proper. He summarizes his university career and the esteem in which he was held to counter the claim that he was "vomited out thence" (YP 1:884), and, to his antagonist's depiction of Milton's present life—"Where his morning haunts are I wist not; but he that would find him after dinner, must search the *Play-Houses,* or the *Bordelli,* for there I have traced him"[31]—Milton responds with an account of the early hours of his typical day:

> Those morning haunts are where they should be, at home, not sleeping, or concocting the surfets of an irregular feast, but up, and stirring, in winter often ere the sound of any bell awake men to labour, or to devotion; in Summer as oft with the Bird that first rouses, or not much tardier, to reade good Authors, or cause them to be read, till the attention bee weary, or memory have his full fraught. Then with usefull and generous labours preserving the bodies health, and hardinesse; to render lightsome, cleare, and not lumpish obedience to the minde, to the cause of religion, and our Countries liberty, when it shall require firme hearts in sound bodies to stand and cover their stations, rather then to see the ruine of our Protestation, and the inforcement of a slavish life. (YP 1:885–86)

As Hugh Richmond notes, Milton's detailed description of his morning is actually deeply indebted to a passage from Pierre de Ronsard's long poem, *Reply to the insults and calumnies of various unrecognizable preachers and ministers of Geneva* (1563).[32] Richmond's prose translation follows.

> You complain moreover that my life is licentious, over-burdened with luxury, sport, and vice. You lie maliciously: if you had followed me for two months you would know well the state of my life and now I intend to spell it out for you so that everyone will know you are a liar. When I wake each morning before I do anything I say a prayer to the Eternal Father of all Good. . . . When I get out of bed and am clothed I devote myself to study and learn virtue, writing and reading as my vocation requires since I have been inclined to the Muses since my childhood. I stay closeted for four or five hours; then when too much reading wearies my spirit I drop my book and go to church. Returning I devote an hour to recreation; then dine soberly, saying grace.[33]

In alluding to a great poet of the French Renaissance—and one who was also engaged in public polemic warfare—Milton surely intends to emphasize his own literary aspirations and to remind his audience (and himself) that poetry is not necessarily incompatible with political and religious engagement. However, in omitting Ronsard's name and in transforming his scenario into prose, Milton may be registering his discomfort with this autobiographical exemplar, whose own pious devotions were Catholic and whose poetic fury was directed at Protestants.

Milton's description of his morning, whether or not it is precisely accu-

rate or precisely original, is nevertheless nearly the only part of his autobiography that he places in the potentially verifiable present. The Confuter's
charge that Milton haunts playhouses provokes a discussion of Milton's reluctant theater-going at Cambridge (as well as the counteraccusation that the
Confuter himself must know the inside of a playhouse in order to have
recognized Milton's theatrical allusions), but Milton neither denies the accusation nor admits to it; he simply talks about something else. And when the
Confuter charges that Milton frequents bordellos, Milton leaves the realm of
facts entirely behind. Since, he writes, the Confuter

> would seem privily to point me out to his Readers, as one whose custome of life were
> not honest, but licentious; I shall intreat to be born with though I digresse: & in a way
> not often trod acquaint ye with the summe of my thoughts in this matter through the
> course of my yeares and studies. Although I am not ignorant how hazardous it will be
> to do this under the nose of the envious, as it were in skirmish to change the compact
> order, and instead of outward actions to bring inmost thoughts into front. (YP 1:888)

Where most men might deny their opponent's accusations or provide testimonials to their abstemious behavior, Milton declines to do so. Instead, he
declares that he will let the reader into his *thoughts* on the subject of sexual
morality, and their development over the years. He continues:

> With me it fares now, as with him whose outward garment hath bin injur'd and ill
> bedighted; for having no other shift, what helpe but to turn the inside outwards,
> especially if the lining be of the same, or, as it is sometimes, much better. So if my
> name and outward demeanour be not evident anough to defend me, I must make
> tryall, if the discovery of my inmost thoughts can. Wherein of two purposes both
> honest, and both sincere, the one perhaps I shall not misse; although I fail to gaine
> beliefe with others of being such as my perpetuall thoughts shall heere disclose me, I
> may yet not faile of successe in perswading some, to be such really themselves, as they
> cannot believe me to be more then what I fain. (YP 1:888–89)

Milton continues to be preoccupied with what is internal and unseen. Indeed, beyond simply asserting the value of the internal, Milton's language
hints at some actual dissatisfaction with his "outer garment," whose lining is
so "much better." This, coupled with the strange negative construction in the
last part of the passage, where Milton appears to be presuming failure from
the start—no one will believe him, and his only hope is *not* to fail in persuading some of his readers to be what they cannot believe that he is—makes him
sound like a man with something to hide.

Even when Milton goes out of his way to show how above-board he is
being with his audience, he still comes across as protesting too much. At the
end of his digression on chastity, he gives a new reason for having expanded
on the subject at such length:

Thus large I have purposely bin, that if I have bin justly taxt with this crime, it may come upon me after all this my confession, with a tenne-fold shame. But if I have hitherto deserv'd no such opprobrious word, or suspicion, I may hereby ingage my selfe now openly to the faithfull observation of what I have profest. I go on to shew you the unbridl'd impudence of this loose rayler . . . who from the single notice of the animadversions, as he protests, will undertake to tell ye the very cloaths I weare, though he be much mistaken in my wardrobe. (YP 1:893)

After again denying that the "single notice" of his previous text is sufficient to show the character of its author, Milton invites a public investigation of his prepared statements on matters of virtue, as well as public scrutiny of his actions—from this time forward (an "observation," anyway, which can hardly be made by those who do not know the anonymous author's identity). Milton seems to be asking for a second chance, saying, in effect, "judge me not on *that* work, but on my others; not on what you *think* my words say about my morals, but on what I *tell* you about my morals." As in *The Reason of Church-Government,* here he also offers his audience a deal, and the contractual language in both passages is notable for its combination of boldness and anxiety: "Neither do I think it shame to covnant with any knowing reader"; "it may come upon me with a tenne-fold shame"; "I may hereby ingage my selfe now openly." Just as in the previous passage we examined, Milton is acting quite as though he has a guilty conscience. There is no reason to think that this is the case when it comes to Milton's sexual morality, although at the time of writing this tract he does appear to have been contemplating marriage and may have worried about how this ambition reflected upon his earlier ideals.[34]

More likely, Milton's literary career is concerning him. We know from *The Reason of Church-Government* that Milton felt anxious about presenting himself to the public before he believed himself ready to do so, and in a mode that he considered second best. Milton does not explicitly voice this concern in his *Apology,* but it seems to lie not far below the surface, provoked by the Confuter's criticism of the *Animadversions.* There is no evidence that Milton regrets or is ashamed of the earlier tract, but he seems vexed that his opponent should have loaded it with so much significance that he proposed deducing Milton's character from it. If Milton hardly felt ready to go public as a writer in *The Reason of Church-Government*—despite controlling every aspect of his self-presentation—he must have felt that, in the *Animadversions,* the Confuter had caught him practically defenseless. Whatever satisfaction Milton may have derived from his early antiprelatical tracts, he appears not to have taken them quite seriously as literature; for the Confuter to deride one of these immature efforts, then, is to strike too close to Milton's own feelings of literary uncertainty.

It is essential to emphasize, however, that Milton's touchiness on the subject is not just the thin skin of a would-be literary luminary. His intellect and his facility with language are, he believes, gifts from God that demand some return—and, so far, he is not quite sure that he has made one. Moreover, as he repeatedly insists in *An Apology*, an author's poetic and prosaic styles are direct reflections on his moral character (and, it may be, his salvational status). I believe that Milton's fierce defenses of himself and his writing and his equally fierce attacks upon his opponents are impelled by a fundamental insecurity about how well he is measuring up in God's eyes. The Confuter's specific claims about Milton's loose morals may be ridiculous, but his sneering dismissal of Milton's writing and his assertion that Milton has done an injustice to the gravity of his subject seem harder for Milton to reject. If Milton were an inept or merely mediocre writer, how could he possibly be an upright person? According to his own arguments, he could not be. Milton's early autobiographies thus show him struggling to reconcile his belief in his literary-spiritual promise with the fact that this conviction has yet to manifest itself in a work with which Milton himself is satisfied—much less his Creator.

THE *DEFENCES*, 1651–1655

There is a gap of twelve years between Milton's antiprelatical tracts and his next prose autobiographies, which appear in *Pro Populo Anglicano Defensio Secunda* (*A Second Defence of the English People*) and *Pro Se Defensio* (*A Defence of Himself*). In the intervening years the English church had been disestablished, the civil war fought and won, and Charles executed. By 1654 Milton was famous (or in some quarters infamous) for his defenses of the republican cause and his attacks on tyranny in general and Charles in particular. This fame was a long time coming: although Milton produced numerous prose works during the civil war, it was not until 1649, after Charles's execution, that he took up the subject of divine right, and not until the 1651 publication of *Pro Populo Anglicano Defensio* (the first *Defence of the English People*) that he truly achieved a name for himself. With the exception of his four divorce tracts, which brought plenty of attention of exactly the wrong sort, none of Milton's polemics appears to have received much notice, and the publication of a volume of his verse went equally unremarked.[35] In virtually every one of these works Milton expends considerable effort on his self-presentation, and scholarly analyses of these efforts have greatly assisted biographical readings of Milton.[36] Nevertheless, not one of these publications contains anything like the autobiographical passages to be found in *The Reason of Church-Government* or *An Apology against a Pamphlet*, and this is true even when, as in the responses to *The Doctrine and Discipline of Divorce,* Milton was personally attacked for his views.[37]

Although Milton's prose works from the 1640s may not have made him a household name, apparently they attracted the notice of a sufficient number of leading parliamentarians to get him appointed as the Commonwealth's Latin secretary, a job that entailed composing the state's official papers and correspondence. Upon satisfactory service in this position, and probably because of his earlier spirited defenses of the revolutionaries in *The Tenure of Kings and Magistrates* and *Eikonoklastes,* Milton appears to have been asked to vindicate the regicides against some of the recently published accusations and expressions of horror from abroad.[38] He obliged with the *Defence of the English People,* writing in Latin to reach an international audience and following the format of the work he was most immediately refuting: *Defensio Regia pro Carole I* (1649), by the famous French Protestant Salmasius. Among its many other features and techniques, the *First Defence* employs the same sort of personal attack familiar from Milton's earlier controversial works, and it seems in part to have been these ad hominem attacks that inspired a new champion to enter the fray (Salmasius died before composing a response). The anonymous *Regii Sanguinis Clamor ad Coelum adversus Parricidas Anglicanos* (1652), which Milton mistakenly attributed to Alexander More, vigorously defended Salmasius while denouncing Milton; this work, in turn, provoked Milton's *Second Defence* (1654).

Although the immediate circumstances surrounding the autobiography in the *Second Defence* seem similar to those attending *An Apology*—Milton had been personally attacked and his party had been implicated in that attack—some differences are readily apparent. In the later work, Milton focuses much more upon the past than the future, and there are virtually none of the invitations to his innermost thoughts (on a poetic career, on chastity) that periodically punctuated the antiprelatical tracts. Another striking difference is the placement of Milton's autobiography. In *The Reason of Church-Government* and *An Apology* his autobiographical passages form a discrete unit, while in the *Second Defence* such material is scattered throughout. However, while many of these passages may seem individually to be confident and controlled, when taken together the picture changes. Milton will end one passage abruptly only to resume in an autobiographical vein several pages later, and the portraits he paints of himself in different places are often remarkably dissimilar. Thus, despite some superficial differences between Milton's late autobiographies and his earlier ones, their effect—and, I believe, their impetus—is quite similar. As in the antiprelatical tracts, Milton is again wrestling with feelings of extreme doubt, trying to convince himself that he has made the right decisions and that God and the world will remember him with satisfaction. The difference is that here the blind Milton is anxious not about the future, but about the past; believing his career to be over, Milton is desperate for a sign that what he has done has been worthwhile, and that it has been enough.

Milton begins his tract by proclaiming the favors God has shown him. He celebrates the threefold blessing of having been alive "when [England's] citizens, with pre-eminent virtue and a nobility and steadfastness surpassing all the glory of their ancestors . . . accomplish[ed] the most heroic and exemplary achievements since the foundation of the world"; of his having been selected "spontaneously with universal consent [for] the task of publicly defending . . . the cause of the English people"; and, finally, of having done so in a way that "satisf[ied] a host of foreigners . . . [and] so routed my audacious foe that he fled, broken in spirit and reputation" (YP 4:548–49).[39] However, only a few pages later Milton loses this confident tone and grows defensive:

Although I claim for myself no share in [England's] glory, yet it is easy to defend myself from the charge of timidity or cowardice, should such a charge be leveled. For I did not avoid the toils and dangers of military service without rendering to my fellow citizens another kind of service that was much more useful and no less perilous. (YP 4:552)

Not only has Milton spent the opening pages of the tract doing just what he here disavows—claiming his right to a share in England's glory[40]—but there is no evidence that anyone has accused him of cowardice. No such accusation appears in the *Clamor,* and, as Milton was a middle-aged man with failing eyesight for much of the civil war, it is unlikely that anyone would have looked upon him askance for not having fought. On the other hand, his claim that his pamphleteering was as dangerous as battlefield service might well have resulted in some raised eyebrows: not only did all of Milton's pamphlets prior to the *First Defence* have relatively low circulation, but, by the time the more inflammatory of these were published, Charles had already been executed.[41]

Nevertheless, despite the perilousness that Milton claims for his service, he assures his reader,

In time of trial I was neither cast down in spirit nor unduly fearful of envy or death itself. Having from early youth been especially devoted to the liberal arts, with greater strength of mind than of body, I exchanged the toils of war, in which any stout trooper might outdo me, for those labors which I better understood, that with such wisdom as I owned I might add as much weight as possible to the counsels of my country and to this excellent cause, using not my lower but my higher and stronger powers. And so I concluded that if God wished those men to achieve such noble deeds, He also wished that there be other men by whom these deeds, once done, might be worthily praised and extolled, and that truth defended by arms be also defended by reason—the only defence truly appropriate to man. Hence it is that while I admire the heroes victorious in battle, I nevertheless do not complain about my own role. Indeed I congratulate myself and once again offer most fervent thanks to the heavenly bestower of gifts that such a lot has befallen me—a lot that seems much more a source of envy to others than of regret to myself. (YP 4:552–53)

Milton's description of the service he *has* rendered his country provides at least one hint as to why he might be so touchy about his lack of military participation: his contribution to the war effort was praising "those deeds, once done."[42] As he acknowledges through his choice of tense, Milton was not publishing works championing the parliamentarians or challenging divine right while the civil war was actually raging; indeed, in 1646–1648 he published nothing at all. Just as he did with the antiprelatical faction, Milton publicly sided with the regicides only rather belatedly. He may well believe that he has since made up for his initial inaction, but surely part of Milton's grandiose claims for himself and his penchant for military metaphors (of his dispute with Salmasius he says, "I met him in single combat and . . . I bore off the spoils of honor" [YP 4:556])—can be attributed to an uneasy awareness that he had no good answer to the question, "What did you do in the war, daddy?"

Milton's next autobiographical passage is provoked by the description of him given in the *Clamor*'s dedicatory epistle, which is addressed to the exiled Charles II. Toward the end of this letter the author takes Virgil's characterization of Polyphemus as a starting point: "'A monster horrible, deformed, huge, and sightless.' Though to be sure, [Milton] is not huge; nothing is more weak, more bloodless, more shrivelled than little animals such as he, who the harder they fight, the less harmful they are."[43] Although Milton has already paid back the author of those lines with a long, nasty, and frequently hilarious biographical account of Alexander More's escapades, he seems unable to overlook this passing insult and replies,

Although it ill befits a man to speak of his own appearance, yet speak I shall, since here too there is reason for me to thank God and refute liars, lest anyone think me to be perhaps a dog-headed ape or a rhinoceros, as the rabble in Spain, too credulous of their priests, believe to be true of heretics, as they call them. Ugly I have never been thought by anyone, to my knowledge, who has laid eyes on me. Whether I am handsome or not, I am less concerned. I admit that I am not tall, but my stature is closer to the medium than to the small. . . . But neither am I especially feeble, having indeed such spirit and such strength that when my age and manner of life required it, I was not ignorant of how to handle or unsheathe a sword, nor unpractised in using it each day. Girded with my sword, as I generally was, I thought myself equal to anyone, though he was far more sturdy, and I was fearless of any injury that one man could inflict on another. (YP 4:582–83)

Milton does not precisely contradict the earlier explanation he has given for avoiding military service—that his physical condition makes him less useful on the field than in the study—but the two self-portraits certainly differ. Whereas here Milton describes himself as having been a fearless swordsman in his youth, and claims that he is still spirited and strong, in his earlier passage excusing his absence on the field of battle he protests that "any stout trooper might outdo [him]," since, "from early youth," he has had "greater strength of mind than of body" (YP 4:553). These previous lines imply a physical delicacy that is repudiated by the passage above, in which Milton asserts that he is neither small nor feeble; indeed, in the next line he adds, "Today I possess the same spirit, the same strength, but not the same eyes" (YP 4:583). Of course, the context of Milton's self-description has changed— he is no longer defending himself from (possibly imaginary) charges of avoiding military service, but rather attempting to ensure that his audience does not dismiss him as a useless, frail, blind old man. All the same, his concern with his physical appearance has struck many as curious. Some of it may be simple vanity on Milton's part, but as his aside about the supposed deformities of heretics suggests, to Milton calling someone a monstrosity is more than a hyperbolic way of saying that he is ugly. To Milton, for whom outsides and insides have such a fraught relationship, we may well suppose that physical defects strongly imply moral ones.

Milton's eyes soon become the locus for his anxieties about both kinds of defects. He maintains that his eyes "have as much the appearance of being uninjured . . . as the eyes of men who see most keenly," and this feature— which he mentions also in his sonnet to Cyriack Skinner—appears to have great significance for Milton (YP 4:583).[44] In the context of the ensuing discussion of his blindness and God's role in that affliction, Milton may be suggesting that his unclouded eyes are a sign that he is not hateful to God. The *Clamor* has not raised the possibility that God has blinded Milton for defending regicide, but Milton seems deeply afraid that *something* he has done might have precipitated his blindness.[45] To preempt such an argument from anyone else, he calls God himself as a witness:

For my part, I call upon Thee, my God, who knowest my inmost mind and all my thoughts, to witness that (although I have repeatedly examined myself on this point as earnestly as I could, and have searched all the corners of my life) I am conscious of nothing, or of no deed, either recent or remote, whose wickedness could justly occasion or invite upon me this supreme misfortune. (YP 4:587)

In fact, God appears not so much to be a character witness as Milton's most important audience, and in Milton's direct address of the deity there is a note of apprehension: "this is so—isn't it?" These are the lines that Alexander More will describe as "really too anxious," and, although Milton does not permit his reader very far inside his head (he does not, for example, reproduce the voices that he hears, as he has in *The Reason of Church-Government*), his obsessive return to the subjects of his blindness, his appearance, and his service to the state strongly supports More's reading—and suggests, moreover, the precise source of that anxiety.

Some pages pass before Milton abandons the subject of his blindness. Far from being blinded as a punishment, he maintains, he *chose* blindness rather than reject God's demands:

As for what I have at any time written (since the royalists think that I am now undergoing this suffering as a penance, and they accordingly rejoice), I likewise call God to witness that I have written nothing of such kind that I was not then and am not now convinced that it was right and true and pleasing to God. And I swear that my conduct was not influenced by ambition, gain, or glory, but solely by considerations of duty, honor, and devotion to my country. I did my utmost not only to free my country, but also to free the church. Hence, when the business of replying to the royal defense had been officially assigned to me, and at that same time I was afflicted at once by ill health and the virtual loss of my remaining eye, and the doctors were making learned predictions that if I should undertake this task, I would shortly lose both eyes, I was not in the least deterred by the warning. I seemed to hear, not the voice of the doctor . . . but the sound of a certain more divine monitor within. And I thought that two lots had now been set before me by a certain command of fate: the one, blindness, the other, duty. Either I must necessarily endure the loss of my eyes, or I must abandon my most solemn duty. (YP 4:587–88)

In this version of events, God has designed the writing of the *First Defence* as a test of Milton's obedience—but Milton, unlike Abraham with Isaac, actually loses what he has agreed to sacrifice. Although Milton has switched from directly addressing God to talking about him in the third person, this account of his actions and motives reads as much like a petition as the previous lines. Milton seems to be seeking reassurance from God, as well as trying to convince himself that this version of events is accurate. God may have allowed Milton to go blind, but Milton insists that God has not deserted him, and never will:

Then let those who slander the judgments of God cease to speak evil and invent empty tales about me. Let them be sure that I feel neither regret nor shame for my lot, that I stand unmoved and steady in my resolution, that I neither discern nor endure the anger of God, that in fact I know and recognize in the most momentous affairs his fatherly mercy and kindness towards me, and especially in this fact, that with his consolation strengthening my spirit I bow to his divine will, dwelling more often on what he has bestowed on me than on what he has denied. (YP 4:589)

Over the course of these lines Milton moves from a more tentative to a more confident position, from *feeling* and *discerning* to *knowing* and *recognizing* God's will, taking strength from his own continued strength in the belief that, if God were punishing him, he would not be bearing up as well as he is. He concludes,

> So long as I find in God and man such consolation for my blindness, let no one mourn for my eyes, which were lost in the cause of honor. Far be it from me either to mourn. Far be it from me to have so little spirit that I cannot easily despise the revilers of my blindness, or so little charity that I cannot even more easily pardon them. (YP 4:591)

Even more than the earlier parts of this passage on Milton's blindness, these last lines read like a prayer; Milton appears to be talking to himself—and to God—more than to his readers. (It is also worth bearing in mind that, blinded as he was, Milton would have had to compose his tracts orally, a process necessarily closer to prayer than writing.) As far as we know, Milton did not keep a diary, and the account of his blindness that occupies these many pages may well be the first time that he has written out his thoughts about the darkness that befell him a few years earlier.[46] In this tract, Milton appears to be working through and laying to rest some of the more distressing fears surrounding his blindness, hoping to find, in the process, strength enough to endure.

Milton's next autobiographical section is prompted by the biography that his antagonist supplies for him. After filling more than five quarto pages with a refutation of the version of his life given in the *Clamor,* Milton suddenly decides to start over and tell the story of his life from the very beginning—ancestry, boyhood, and all, for a total of thirteen additional pages—as if unwilling to limit his autobiography to the issues raised by his opponent. He describes his decision to enter the field of political polemic in much the same way that he described it in *The Reason of Church-Government,* but he now makes his antiprelatical tracts and all his subsequent writings out to be part of a single, coherent strategy:

> I . . . ask[ed] myself whether I could in any way advance the cause of true and substantial liberty, which must be sought, not without, but within, and which is best achieved, not by the sword, but by a life rightly undertaken and rightly conducted. Since, then, I observed that there are, in all, three varieties of liberty without which civilized life is scarcely possible, namely ecclesiastical liberty, domestic or personal liberty, and civil liberty, and since I had already written about the first, while I saw that the magistrates were vigorously attending to the third, I took as my province the remaining one, the second or domestic kind. (YP 4:624)

Milton then summarizes his arguments in the divorce tracts, *Of Education,* and *Areopagitica,* moves on to the regicide treatises, and brings himself up to

the present with the *Defences*. He excuses the great length of this autobiographical account on the grounds that, as he tells More, he had "to stop
your mouth . . . and refute your lies, chiefly for the sake of those good men
who otherwise would know me not" (YP 4:629). This is a familiar argument, a
version of which appeared in *The Reason of Church-Government*. However,
while Milton is now well known enough that some readers might actually
care about the details of his life, the person with the most to gain from such a
narrative is now, as it always has been, Milton himself. These seamless, tele-
ological life narratives seem to appear whenever Milton is facing his most
serious crises of faith and self-confidence, as if his ability to project such a
shape upon his life means that his life actually *has* a coherent design—and
that that design, moreover, is a function of God's providence.

After concluding this longest autobiographical section, Milton devotes
considerable ink to the biographies of various parliamentarian heroes. He
does so, most immediately, to counter the aspersions cast upon these figures
by his opponent, but in doing so he focuses not only on his subjects' external
lives, but also on the presumed events of their inner lives. These speculations
seem to be a continuation of his autobiography, for they reveal more about
Milton than they do about their ostensible subjects. As Milton describes
Cromwell,

he soon surpassed well-nigh the greatest generals both in the magnitude of his accom-
plishments and in the speed with which he achieved them. Nor was this remarkable,
for he was a soldier well-versed in self-knowledge, and whatever enemy lay within—
vain hopes, fears, desires—he had either previously destroyed within himself or had
long since reduced to subjection. Commander first over himself, victor over himself,
he had learned to achieve over himself the most effective triumph, and so, on the very
first day that he took service against an external foe, he entered camp a veteran and
past-master in all that concerned the soldier's life. (YP 4:667–68)

Milton does not go so far as to speculate on the details of this self-mastery—
what Cromwell's specific fears and desires may have been and how and when
he overcame them—but he takes it for granted that this would have been as
much a part of the narrative of Cromwell's life as it is of his own. In *The Reason
of Church-Government*, Milton had to struggle against his desire for delay and
development, and in the *Second Defence* he has to struggle against the fear
that God has blinded him out of displeasure. In his account of Cromwell's
victory over his "enemy within," one may read both the story of Milton's own
life, as he would like it to be told, and its hoped-for outcome: true self-mastery.

Later, in apostrophizing Cromwell, Milton pauses to gives him advice
that likewise emphasizes the importance of inner strength for effective lead-
ership:

You have taken upon yourself by far the heaviest burden, one that will put to the test your inmost capacities, that will search you out wholly and intimately, and reveal what spirit, what strength, what authority are in you, whether there truly live in you that piety, faith, justice, and moderation of soul which convince us that you have been raised by the power of God beyond all other men to this most exalted rank. . . . These trials will buffet you and shake you; they require a man supported by divine help, advised and instructed by all-but-divine inspiration.

Such matters and still others I have no doubt that you consider and reflect upon, times without number. (YP 4:673–74)

Milton's advice has come under fire for its presumptuous tone by critics beginning with Alexander More, and more than one reader has found veiled criticisms of Cromwell's policies in these lines and those that follow.[47] What no one seems to have noticed is the striking applicability of this advice to Milton's own circumstances, or the similarity of the description of Cromwell and his deeds to Milton's self-descriptions; compare, for example, the above passage with the opening paragraphs of the *Second Defence* and the *Defence of Himself*. Milton surely has both advice and criticism for Cromwell, which he hopes very much will be heeded, but at the same time he seems to be thinking of his own situation and hoping that his writings have indeed "reveal[ed] what spirit, what strength, what authority are in" him.

After Cromwell, Milton administers advice to his fellow citizens, but he seems to have, at best, only a passing interest in them. "If the most recent deeds of my fellow countrymen should not correspond sufficiently to their earliest," he writes, "let them look to it themselves" (YP 4:685). For his part,

I have borne witness, I might almost say I have erected a monument that will not soon pass away, to those deeds that were illustrious, that were glorious, that were almost beyond any praise, and if I have done nothing else, I have surely redeemed my pledge. Moreover, just as the epic poet, if he is scrupulous and disinclined to break the rules, undertakes to extol, not the whole life of the hero whom he proposes to celebrate in his verse, but usually one event of his life . . . and passes over the rest, so let it suffice me too, as my duty or my excuse, to have celebrated at least one heroic achievement of my countrymen. (YP 4:685)

The pledge that Milton speaks of having redeemed appears to be the obligation he has long felt to use his literary and intellectual talents in the service of God and England. Moreover, the fact that he compares his tracts to the epic poems of Homer and Virgil strongly suggests that Milton is remembering, specifically, the pledge he made in *The Reason of Church-Government* to produce a poem "so written to aftertimes, as they should not willingly let it die" (YP 1:810). However, there is sadness in the comparison: Milton's literary monument is not the work of epic or lyric or tragic verse that he once envisioned, but a succession of prose pamphlets on events already receding into the past: deeds that *were* illustrious, that *were* glorious, that *were* almost beyond any praise.[48] As good a face as Milton puts on his achievements, he himself seems to believe that he has "done nothing else"—where "else" represents whatever other ambitions he once held. Perhaps as vexing as the sense of things left undone is Milton's awareness that the success of his current work depends, in part, on the success of others in maintaining their new society. He concludes the work by addressing his fellow citizens:

> If after such brave deeds you ignobly fail, if you do aught unworthy of yourselves, be sure that posterity will speak out and pass judgment: the foundations were soundly laid, the beginnings, in fact more than the beginnings, were splendid, but posterity will look in vain, not without a certain distress, for those who were to complete the work. . . . It will seem to posterity that a mighty harvest of glory was at hand, together with the opportunity for doing the greatest deeds, but that to this opportunity men were wanting. Yet there was not wanting one who could rightly counsel, encourage, and inspire, who could honor both the noble deeds and those who had done them, and make both deeds and doers illustrious with praises that will never die. (YP 4:685–86)

Although Milton is still projecting his narratives into the future, this particular future is one in which he plays no active role; it is up to others to carry on the work begun by the revolutionaries, and he can only hope that they will. These are the words of a man who sees his life as essentially over, and whose seemingly arrogant assessments of his past importance only barely disguise a deep sense of loss.

Milton's final lines in the *Second Defence* sound like a valedictory to this particular debate—if not to his entire career as a public writer—but Alexander More's 1654 response, *Fides Publica*, provoked yet another pamphlet, Milton's *Pro Se Defensio* (*Defence of Himself*). Despite its title, the *Defence of Himself* is the least directly autobiographical of the four tracts considered in this essay, being devoted primarily to defending and justifying Milton's identification of Alexander More as the author of the *Clamor*. Since More had not, in fact, written that work (although he does appear to have written its dedicatory epistle and to have conveyed the work to the printer), he reacted with indignation to Milton's ad hominem attacks and to the airing of his religious and sexual dirty laundry. In the *Fides* More both returns Milton's personal attacks, making particular fun of his adversary's autobiographical excesses in the *Second Defence*, and attempts to defend his own honor with a great show of piety and false humility. By way of response, Milton provides an angry mishmash of a work that first refuses to admit that he could have been wrong about More's authorship, and then finally declares that More's delivering the work to its printer constitutes authorship every bit as much as actually writing it. He provides yet more evidence of More's unsavory life, attacks More's self-defense, and—to a surprisingly limited degree—defends himself against More's accusations. Milton does rebut More's specific charges one by one, but he rarely elaborates and he includes no extended auto-biographical passages of the sort his readers have grown accustomed to.

The abrupt change in both the quality of Milton's writing and the nature of his self-presentation has been noted by several critics, who identify Alex-ander More as the reason for this shift. Annabel Patterson has suggested that when Milton finally faced his error in assigning More the authorship of the *Clamor*, he began to lose faith in his own moral uprightness, and thus his voice of unswerving self-confidence; more recently Stephen Fallon has ar-gued that More's expert reading of Milton's *Second Defence*, and the skilled way his tract skewered Milton for his self-importance, provoked the incoher-ent and contradictory claims Milton makes for himself in this final *Defence*.[49] As we have seen, anxiety, contradiction, and even incoherence are not new features of Milton's autobiographies, but Patterson and Fallon are correct in noting that something in Milton's self-presentation *has* changed, and they are surely also right that a sense of shame is at the root of it. I would point out, however, that the most notable feature of the *Fides* is not its attacks on Milton, but rather its own extraordinary passages of autobiography.

More's detailed accounts of his life and habits, which are interspersed with letters from others testifying to his virtue, represent the first time that one of Milton's opponents has attempted an autobiographical defense similar to Milton's. (In fact, the *Fides* contains two such autobiographies, including one by the printer, who, having likewise felt smeared by Milton, gives a surprisingly detailed account of his own life in the work's prefatory letter.)[50] Milton repeatedly takes issue with More's testimonial letters, accusing him of hiding behind the words of others and not giving the full story, but he seems to have a more difficult time criticizing More's autobiographical passages. Rather than denounce the personal account as inherently untrustworthy, Milton generally prefers to give his own account of More's inner state, as though he has unlimited access to More's thoughts: "as soon as [More] learned . . . that I had published a reply to his *Cry of the Royal Blood*, the man's guilty conscience began to rage and his mind to thrash about in every direction" (YP 4:719). More's supposedly guilty conscience makes several more appearances in Milton's pamphlet, with Milton often telling More just what he is feeling: "Your dissention with yourself has long been most grave. Nothing is more offensive to you than to live with yourself, to be in your own company; no one do you avoid more willingly than yourself" (YP 4:776). Later, of More's laudatory letters, Milton asks,

Why do you foist upon us these matters which are utterly irrelevant—nay, why have you collected for yourself this huge heap of letters and testimonies at all? Was it that you were not sufficiently approved of in the sight of your own conscience? Or was it that you dared believe about yourself neither your own words nor the spontaneous remarks of mankind, unless a multitude of collected testimonies confirmed and attested to you that which you had never otherwise believed: that you could appear to anyone a good man or a tolerable one? (4:816)

As he has in *The Reason of Church-Government* and *An Apology,* Milton tries to focus on the internal and unseen, but when the inner life in question is someone else's, this is clearly a losing game. Milton has always appeared to value autobiography because he believes that it gives a reader access to the "real" inner self of a writer—but in this case, More's mendacity means that Milton has to step in and let the reader know the content of More's heart himself. This is a potentially damning comment on the reliability of autobiography, and I think Milton knows it; I suspect that one of the reasons he limits the autobiographical portion of the *Defence of Himself* is that he could hardly challenge the veracity of self-revelation in More (most notably in the confessional prayer which concludes the *Fides*) while insisting on it so strongly in himself.[51] As he has in his biographical description of Cromwell, however, in the above passage Milton seems to be projecting himself upon his subject, imagining how he would feel if he were More and perhaps even admitting obliquely to one motive behind his own autobiographies: the lack of approval he felt from his own conscience.

There are probably reasons other than More's use of autobiography that account for how little autobiography there is in Milton's final *Defence,* and my argument certainly does not preclude the explanations advanced by Patterson and Fallon. It may also be that Milton had already given voice in the *Second Defence* to the deepest of the fears he experienced after going blind, and so simply did not feel the same compulsion toward autobiography that I have identified in his other pamphlets. However, I wish to tread carefully here, for I am not suggesting that because Milton's autobiography is absent from a work, he therefore felt less passionately about the circumstances surrounding it—that, for example, Charles's execution must have "meant" less to Milton than the exclusion of bishops from the House of Lords since his antiprelatical pamphlets contain autobiographical passages but the regicide tracts do not. Given the vastly greater number of nonautobiographical tracts than autobiographical ones, it would be futile to try to account for the absence of autobiography in Milton's works. I can speak only to what I have observed in the pamphlets that do contain these astonishing self-declarations: in them Milton appears to be under extraordinary stress, doubting his own talents, sense of mission, and dearness to God. One can certainly hope that the last time he felt this way was in the 1650s, while writing the *Defences*, but there is no reason to be sure of it.

Temple University

NOTES

1. Under the misapprehension that Alexander More had authored an attack on his *Defence of the English People*, Milton spent large parts of the *Second Defence of the English People* accusing More of everything from impiety to the seduction of his friends' serving-women. While the substance of Milton's charges appears to have been true, the amount of time and venom he spends on his attacks against More is surprising, and the details of his often elaborate accounts of More's misdeeds would have been unlikely to stand up to scrutiny.

2. Alexander More, *Fides Publica* (1654), translated from the Latin by Paul W. Blackford and excerpted in *Complete Prose Works of John Milton*, 8 vols., ed. Don M. Wolfe et al. (New Haven, 1953–1982), 4:1106. Unless otherwise noted, all quotations from Milton's prose are from this edition, hereafter designated YP and cited parenthetically by volume and page number.

3. Quoted by Milton in *Pro Se Defensio*, trans. Paul W. Blackford, in YP 4:772. The original can be found at *Fides Publica*, 66.

4. Among the studies that make such a case are Stanley Fish, "Reason in *The Reason of Church Government*," in Fish, *Self-Consuming Artifacts: The Experience of Seventeenth-Century Literature* (Berkeley and Los Angeles, 1972); Joseph Anthony Wittreich Jr., " 'The Crown of Eloquence': The Figure of the Orator in Milton's Prose Works," in *Achievements of the Left Hand: Essays on the Prose of John Milton*, edited by Michael Lieb and John T. Shawcross, 3–54 (Amherst, MA, 1974); David Loewenstein, "Milton and the Poetics of Defense," in *Politics, Poetics, and Hermeneutics in Milton's Prose*, edited by David Loewenstein and James Grantham Turner, 171–92 (Cambridge, MA, 1990); Kevin Dunn, "Humanist Individualism and the Puritan Polity in Milton's Antiprelatical Tracts," *Pretexts of Authority: The Rhetoric of Authorship in the Renaissance Preface* (Stanford, 1994), chap. 3; Joseph Shub, "Milton's Prose Exordia and the Persuasion through Character," *Prose Studies* 21 (April 1998): 1–31. Quite a bit of scholarship is devoted to the somewhat different project of analyzing Milton's "authorial persona" or his "self-presentation," which considers Milton's explicitly autobiographical writings along with and in light of a broad range of rhetorical techniques and stylistic quirks. In addition to some of the above studies, others include Thomas Kranidas, *The Fierce Equation: A Study of Milton's Decorum* (The Hague, 1965); Peter Auksi, "Milton's 'Sanctif'd Bitternesse': Polemical Technique in the Early Prose," *TSLL* 19 (1976): 363–81; Reuben Sánchez Jr., *Persona and Decorum in Milton's Prose* (Madison, NJ, 1997); and Joseph Wittreich, " 'Reading' Milton: The Death (and Survival) of the Author," in *Milton Studies* 38, *John Milton: The Author in His Works*, ed. Albert C. Labriola and Michael Lieb (Pittsburgh, 2000), 10–46.

5. William Haller, *The Rise of Puritanism; or, The way to the New Jerusalem as set forth in pulpit and press from Thomas Cartwright to John Lilburne and John Milton, 1570–1643* (New York, 1938), refers to Milton's autobiographical passages, collectively, as Milton's "spiritual auto-biography," and he sees little difference between Milton's narrative and those of his near-contemporaries (296). Joan Webber, *The Eloquent 'I': Style and Self in Seventeenth-Century Prose* (Madison, WI, 1968), on the other hand, believes that Milton has adapted the conventions

of the spiritual autobiography for his own literary purposes (217). Other scholars have likewise looked for echoes of the spiritual autobiography in Milton's poetry and prose, beginning as early as his Nativity ode. See, for example, Arthur E. Barker, "The Pattern of Milton's Nativity Ode," *UTQ* 10 (1941): 167–81; but, for a persuasive refutation of Barker, see J. Martin Evans, "A Poem of Absences," *MQ* 27 (March 1993), 31–35. See also Sharon Desmond Paradiso, " 'Now Hear Mee Relate': Narrative Emplotment and Autobiography in *Paradise Lost*," *ELN* 35 (December 1997): 9–17; and Alinda Sumers-Ingraham, "John Milton's *Paradise Regained* and the Genre of the Puritan Spiritual Biography" (Ph.D. diss., George Washington University, 1984).

The contrary view is taken by many of the critics cited in note 4, above, although most do not dismiss the autobiographical component of Milton's prose as readily as Thomas Corns, *John Milton: The Prose Works* (New York, 1998), who claims that Milton's autobiographies serve only "some immediate exigency of his polemic," and that, moreover, Milton seems to have been drawn to literary works that "generally precluded the personal, confessional mode" (1).

6. Wayne Shumaker, *English Autobiography: Its Emergence, Materials, and Form* (Berkeley and Los Angeles, 1954), 16. Among the other works that trace the development of early English autobiography are Paul Delany, *British Autobiography in the Seventeenth Century* (London, 1969); Margaret Bottrall, *Every Man a Phoenix: Studies in Seventeenth-Century Autobiography* (London, 1958); and G. A. Starr, *Defoe and Spiritual Autobiography* (Princeton, 1965).

While the *Confessions* was well-known in Latin (and later in the two English translations of 1620 and 1631), before the second half of the seventeenth century it seems to have had little influence as a literary model in England; its Continental progeny, such as the self-consciously Augustinian *Life* of Teresa of Avila (published in Spanish in 1588 and translated into English in 1611) arrived much earlier. In England the earliest autobiographical religious works are transcripts of first-person examinations and confessions, the most famous of which are surely the *Examinations* of Anne Askew (1545 and 1546), who was burned at the stake for denying the doctrine of transubstantiation.

7. Lilburne's first autobiographical accounts were *A Worke of the Beast* (1638) and *The Poore Mans Cry* (1639). Many more followed over the next two decades, especially after Lilburne took up the Leveller cause.

Poetic autobiography is a tricky subject during this period. Although one would expect lyric poetry to contain some degree of autobiography, the subject of a lyric poem and the persona adopted (for example, the scorned lover) are often quite conventional; in the absence of detailed biographical information, it can thus be extremely difficult to determine the true autobiographical content of a given work. In any case, as poetic autobiography is of an entirely different genre and line of descent from Puritan or other prose autobiographies, my subsequent references to "autobiography" should be understood to refer to prose works in that mode.

8. Haller, *Rise of Puritanism*, 297.

9. Likewise, the secular autobiographies that appeared in manuscript in this period—usually in the context of a family history written by a nobleman for posterity—tended to be written relatively late in the author's life, or at least after he had accomplished something of note. See Delany, *British Autobiography*, 1–2, 109, 112–13. For the same reason, Milton's autobiographies have little in common with the autobiographical writings that began to appear on the Continent in the late sixteenth century.

10. Christopher Hill, *Milton and the English Revolution* (New York, 1978), 9, 451–58.

11. The divorce pamphlets—which inspired attacks both in Parliament and the press—are the most obvious case, but *Eikonoklastes* and *A Defence of the English People* also provoked attacks of a more or less personal nature. For published criticisms of the divorce tracts and of Milton himself, see *An Answer to a Book, Intituled, The Doctrine and Discipline of Divorce*

(1644), 15–16, 31–32, 33, 42–43; Herbert Palmer, *The Glasse of Gods Providence towards His Faithful Ones* (1644), 57; Robert Baillie, *A Dissuasive from the Errours Of the Time* (1645), 116; and Joseph Hall, *Resolutions and Decisions of Divers Practicall Cases of Conscience* (1649), 388–92. In *Anarchia Anglicana* the pseudonymous Theodorus Verax, like many other royalists, managed to combine an attack on Milton's views on marriage with an attack on his Independency; see 199–200. All the above works are cited in William Riley Parker, *Milton's Contemporary Reputation* (Columbus, OH, 1940). The personal attacks in these works are, by and large, incidental, but when added up they amount to a condemnation that is certainly more considerable than that in a single work such as the *Modest Confutation*.

12. *Lycidas* is sometimes considered Milton's first published "autobiographical" work, but that description is obviously problematic. Among Milton's Latin *Prolusions* are a few short, scattered autobiographical passages, but, although written during his years at Cambridge, none of these were published until 1674.

13. See *An Appeal to the Parliament; or, Sions Plea Against the Prelacie* (Holland, 1628), 11: "as a knob, a wen, or any superfluous bonch of flesh, being no member doth not onely overburthen the body, but also disfigureth the feature, yea killeth the body at length except it be cut; so these Bishops be the knobs & wens and bunchie popish flesh which beareth down, deformeth & deadeth the bodie of the Church, that there is no cure (as we conceive) but cutting off."

14. *Dictionary of National Biography* (*DNB*). For a brief summary of Leighton's career, see also YP 1:36–39. Laud also assigned similar punishments to radicals such as William Prynne and John Lilburne.

15. It is widely assumed that Milton wrote the postscript to the Smectymnuans's first pamphlet, *An Answer to a Booke Entitled an Humble Remonstrance* (ca. March 1641), but *Of Reformation* represents his first solo effort. See Barbara K. Lewalski, *The Life of John Milton* (Oxford, 2000), 128.

16. See, for example, Thomas Corns, *Uncloistered Virtue: English Political Literature, 1640–1660* (Oxford, 1992), 30–32.

17. See, for example, William Kerrigan, *The Prophetic Milton* (Charlottesville, VA, 1974), 176–77, 183–84; Louis Martz, "Milton's Prophetic Voice: Moving Toward Paradise," in *Of Poetry and Politics: New Essays on Milton and His World,* edited by P. G. Stanwood, 1–16 (Binghamton, NY, 1995), 3–5; Sánchez, *Persona and Decorum,* esp. 60–66; Dunn, *Pretexts of Authority,* 52, 58; Paul Stevens, "Discontinuities in Milton's Early Public Self-Representation," *Huntington Library Quarterly* 51, no. 4 (1988): 269. On the other hand, Richard Helgerson, *Self-Crowned Laureates: Spenser, Jonson, Milton and the Literary System* (Berkeley and Los Angeles, 1983), noting that Milton was a member of the establishment for most of his prose-writing career, agrees that Milton "may have felt" some kinship with the Hebrew prophets, but he maintains that Milton saw himself as "a figure neither of exile nor of opposition" (242).

18. This is not to say that Milton is indifferent to the state of the church, but in the great scheme of things it does not matter whether the church is saved or destroyed, since whatever transpires will be as God wills it. What matters is that Milton gives God his all by acting in the church's behalf. It is undeniable that Milton periodically casts himself in a prophetic role, both after the fact and before (the headnote appended to *Lycidas* for its publication in Milton's 1645 *Poems*—claiming that in the 1637 work the author "foresaw" the corruption of the bishops—is a perfect example of the former), and I would not disagree that elements of the role are present in the narrator of *The Reason of Church-Government;* however, Milton does not adopt the role wholeheartedly and neither does he have the sense of conviction that scholars advancing this argument tend to attribute to him.

19. Martz, "Milton's Prophetic Voice," 12.

20. See John T. Shawcross, *John Milton: The Self and the World* (Lexington, KY, 1993), 93,

and Helgerson, *Self-Crowned Laureates,* 249, 274. Milton does, of course, mention his ministerial ambitions in his later declaration that he was "destin'd of a child" to the ministry, until he was "Church-outed by the Prelats" (YP 1:822, 823), but this admission is deferred for many pages, until he has concluded his discussion of his poetic training and abilities.

21. See Dunn, *Pretexts of Authority,* 53–54, 59, and John Guillory, *Poetic Authority: Spenser, Milton, and Literary History* (New York, 1983), 95–98.

22. Both Milton and Hall, in fact, appear to have felt that there was a strong correlation between good style and good morals, but Milton's attacks are the fiercer and more constant. For specific instances of Milton's objections to Hall's word choice or argumentative strategy in *Animadversions,* see, for example, YP 1:686, 690, 692, 694, 697. In his footnotes to two of these passages, Don M. Wolfe writes, "Milton objects to Hall's use of language. He implies that bad language is an outward sign of bad thinking, even of error," and "both Hall and Milton looked upon a good style as an outward manifestation of virtue and wisdom. The objection to bad style was therefore a serious objection and not mere carping" (YP 1:686 n. 41, 692 n. 2). Later, in *An Apology,* explaining the grounds of his outrage at Hall and the reasons for the style he chose in *Animadversions,* Milton writes, "I took it as my part the lesse to endure that my respected friends through their own unnecessary patience should thus lye at the mercy of a coy flurting stile; to be girded with frumps and curtall gibes, by one who makes sentences by the Statute, as if all above three inches long were confiscat" (YP 1:872–73). For a more detailed consideration of Milton's and Hall's stylistic differences, and the possible moral valences that these differences may have suggested to Milton, see Henry S. Limouze, "Joseph Hall and the Prose Style of John Milton," in *Milton Studies* 15, ed. James D. Simmonds (Pittsburgh, 1981), 121–42.

23. Although Milton sometimes implies that this work was written by Hall, most scholars believe that his role was, at most, only a minor collaborative one. Milton's second candidate for authorship, Hall's son, seems much more likely. See Parker, *Contemporary Reputation,* 15–16; Lewalski, *Life of John Milton,* 136.

24. See Corns, *Uncloistered Virtue,* 33. The dedicatory epistle to Thomas Edwards's *Gangraena* (London, 1646) provides a representative example of both the length and degree of personal detail found in other controversial works of the period. Addressing Parliament, Edwards writes, "I am one who out of choise and judgement have imbarked my selfe with wife, children, estate and all thats dear to me in the same ship with you to sinke and perish, or to come safe to land with you" (A2v). Neither Hall nor the Smectymnuans become even this personal in their tracts, although both do use the first person periodically.

25. John Guillory, *Poetic Authority,* 95–96, suggests that Milton's anonymity in this tract is simply a practical acknowledgment of the fact that his name lacks sufficient reputation or recognition to advance his argument. Although Guillory provides a convincing reading of Milton's unwilling suppression of his name at various points throughout *An Apology,* I do not find his argument for the absence of Milton's name from the work's title page persuasive; as the counterexample of *The Reason of Church-Government* demonstrates, the presence or absence of Milton's name on the title page of his early pamphlets is extremely inconsistent.

26. *A Modest Confutation of a Slanderous and Scurrilous Libell, Entituled, Animadversions upon the Remonstrants Defense against Smectymnuus* (1642), A3 1r.

27. Ibid., 5–6.

28. Milton objects, among other works, to Hall's *The Passion Sermon Preached at Paule's Crosse on Good-Friday, Apr. 14. 1609,* which Hall dedicates "in great letters to our Saviour. Although I know that all we do ought to begin and end to his praise and glory, yet to inscribe to him in a void place with flourishes, as a man in complement uses to trick up the name of some Esquire, Gentleman, or Lord Paramont at Common Law, to be his book patron with the appendant form of a ceremonious presentment, wil ever appeare among the judicious to be but an an

[*sic*] insuls and frigid affectation" (YP 1:877). Milton also repeatedly refers to Hall's *Tooth-lesse Satyrs,* which he exhibits as proof that Hall and his defender have no idea what true satire consists of (see, for example, YP 1:916). For some of Milton's numerous other jabs at Hall's (nonprelatical) works, see also YP 1:880–81, 887, 914, 920, 930.

29. Other than Milton's own contradictory statements on the matter, there is no evidence that the Confuter inquired into his identity or habits. It has been suggested that the Confuter's description of the author's being "vomited out" of "the brest of the University" (*Modest Confutation,* A3 1v) may refer to Milton's rustication from Cambridge, but such a vague statement is a poor basis for building an argument one way or the other. As Parker, *Contemporary Reputation,* 268–69, notes, the very randomness of the Confuter's attacks on Milton suggests that he either did not make inquiries or that he was unable to discover much about him.

30. Fish, *Self-Consuming Artifacts,* 265–302.

31. *Modest Confutation,* A3 1v.

32. Hugh M. Richmond, "Personal Identity and Literary Personae: A Study in Historical Psychology," *PMLA* 90 (March 1975): 212–13.

33. The relevant passage reads in the original as follows:

> Tu te plains d'autre-part que ma vie est lascive,
> En delices, en jeux, en vices excessive;
> Tu mens meschantement: si tu m'avois suivy
> Deux mois, tu sçaurois bien en quel estat je vy;
> Or je veux que ma vie en escrit apparoisse,
> Afin que pour menteur un chacun te cognoisse.
> M'esveillant au matin, devant que faire rien,
> J'invoque l'Eternel, le pere de tout bien,
> Le priant humblement de me donner sa grace
> Et que le jour naissant sans l'offenser se passe;
> Qu'il chasse toute secte et toute erreur de moy,
> Qu'il me vueille garder en ma premiere foy,
> Sans entreprendre rien qui blesse ma province,
> Tres-humble observateur des loix et de mon Prince.
> Apres je sors du lict, et quand je suis vestu,
> Je me range à l'estude et apprens la vertu,
> Composant et lisant suivant ma destinée,
> Qui s'est dès mon enfance aux Muses enclinée;
> Quatre ou cinq heures seul je m'arreste enfermé;
> Puis, sentant mon esprit de trop lire assommé,
> J'abandonne le livre et m'en vais à l'église.

Pierre de Ronsard, *Oeuvres Complêtes,* 2 vols., ed. Gustave Cohen (Paris: Gallimard, 1950), 2:606.

34. Earlier in his digression Milton goes out of his way to include wedded intercourse under the rubric of chastity, quoting Saint Paul: "marriage must not be call'd a defilement" (1:892–93; 1 Cor. 7:1–2). Toward the end of the tract Milton describes his ideal wife as "a virgin of mean fortunes honestly bred," countering the Confuter's claim that he is on the lookout for a rich widow. Some scholars have taken this as an allusion to Mary Powell, whom Milton surprised his friends and family by marrying approximately two months after penning *An Apology.* Regardless of whether Milton even had Powell in his sights at the time that he wrote *An Apology,* his thoughts vis-à-vis marriage had manifestly altered since his youth.

35. According to Parker, *Contemporary Reputation,* 23, copies of the first printing of Milton's 1645 *Poems* were still available twelve years later.

36. Annabel Patterson, Stephen M. Fallon, and J. Michael Vinovich have each promoted different arguments for autobiographical readings of the divorce tracts, all interested in what they consider the significant suppression of autobiography in those works. See Patterson, "No Meer Amatorious Novel?" in Loewenstein and Turner, *Politics, Poetics and Hermeneutics,* 85–101; Fallon, "The Spur of Self-Concernment: Milton in His Divorce Tracts," in Labriola and Lieb, *John Milton: The Writer in His Works,* 220–42; and Vinovich, "Protocols of Reading: Milton and Biography," *Early Modern Literary Studies* 1 (December 1995): 1–15. The textual features of Milton's 1645 *Poems* have also inspired biographical readings from a number of scholars, among them Louis L. Martz, *Poet of Exile: A Study of Milton's Poetry* (New Haven, 1980), 31–59; John K. Hale, "Milton's Self-Presentation in *Poems . . . 1645,*" *MQ* 25 (1991): 37–48; and Leah Marcus, "John Milton's Voice," *Unediting the Renaissance: Shakespeare, Marlowe, Milton* (London, 1996), 208–24.

37. Milton was attacked both in Parliament and in print for *The Doctrine and Discipline of Divorce.* Admittedly, however, the "personal" attacks in, for example, *An Answer to the Doctrine and Discipline of Divorce* (1644) are less vicious than they are in the *Modest Confutation* or *Clamor.* See 15–16, 31–32, 33, and 42–43 of *An Answer.* As Parker suggests, Milton's attackers appear to have been unaware of his marital circumstances, for no contemporary criticism of the divorce tracts contains any reference to them.

38. This is, at any rate, the version of events given by Milton himself and his early biographers. See the *Second Defence,* YP 4:548–49, and "An Anonymous Life of Milton" (possibly by John Phillips or Cyriack Skinner), reproduced in *John Milton: Complete Poems and Major Prose,* ed. Merritt Y. Hughes (New York, 1957), 1041–42. Unfortunately, there is no other evidence either way.

39. Unless otherwise indicated, the English translation used for both *Defences* is from YP. For the Latin I have consulted the bilingual Columbia University Press edition of the work, located in volume 8 of *The Works of John Milton,* 18 vols., ed. Frank Allen Patterson et al. (New York, 1931–38), hereafter designated CM.

40. Indeed, he even asks, rhetorically, "who does not consider the glorious achievements of his country as his own?" (YP 4:550).

41. The exception is *The Doctrine and Discipline of Divorce,* which went through four editions in three years. None of Milton's other works from the 1640s received more than a single printing in that decade, and some left enough unsold copies that they were repackaged for sale in the 1650s, after Milton had achieved notoriety. See Parker, *Milton's Contemporary Reputation,* 18, 15–16. *The Tenure of Kings and Magistrates* was not published until February 1649, while Charles was executed on January 30; *Eikonoklastes* was published in October of that same year. Although *Eikonoklastes* later gained some renown, according to Parker it did not do so until after the *First Defence* made its author famous (30–31).

42. The full sentence reads, "Sic itaque existimabam, si illos Deus res gerere tam praeclaras voluit, esse itidem alios à quibus gestas dici pro dignitate atque ornari, & defensam armis veritatem, ratione etiam, (quod unicum est praesidium verè ac propriè humanum) defendi voluerit" (CM 8:10).

43. Blackford translation, excerpted in YP 4:1045. To confuse an already vexed issue, the epistle is believed to have been written by Alexander More and prefaced to Du Moulin's work. The quotation from the *Aeneid* comes from Book Three.

44. In his 1655 sonnet Milton writes, "Cyriack, this three years' day, these eyes, though clear / To outward view of blemish or of spot, / Bereft of light thir seeing have forgot." Hughes, *Complete Poems and Major Prose,* 170.

45. That Milton's blindness was a punishment from God was asserted by later royalists, most famously by Roger L'Estrange, *No Blinde Guides* (1660), and it may well have been whispered in Milton's presence before then, but no such accusation is made in the *Clamor* or any other published works of the mid-1650s.

46. Milton's other known discussions of his blindness from this period include the sonnet to Skinner, written in 1655, the sonnet on the death of one of his wives, written no earlier than 1652 and quite possibly after 1658, and his letter to Leonard Philaras in 1654.

47. More writes, "you would even appear more lofty than the very exalted Cromwell, whom you address familiarly, without any preface of honor, whom you advise under the guise of praising, for whom you dictate laws, set aside titles, and prescribe duties, and to whom you suggest counsels and even present threats if he should act in any other fashion." *Fides Publica*, quoted in YP 4:1109. For more contemporary responses, see, among others, Austin Woolrych, "Milton and Cromwell: 'A Short but Scandalous Night of Interruption'?" in Lieb and Shawcross, *Achievements of the Left Hand*, 192–97; Hill, *Milton and the English Revolution*, 193. Robert Thomas Fallon, "A Second Defence: Milton's Critique of Cromwell?" in *Milton Studies* 39, ed. Albert C. Labriola (Pittsburgh, 2000), 167–83, dissents. Fallon argues, in essence, that twentieth-century critics are overreading the text, creating subversive subtexts where none exists.

48. The relevant part of the passage reads as follows, "Si postrema primis non satis responderint, ipsi viderint; ego quae eximia, quae excelsa, quae omni laude propè majora fuere, iis testimonium, prope dixerim monumentum, perhibui, haud citò interiturum; & si aliud nihil, certè fidem meam liberavi" (CM 8:252).

49. Annabel Patterson, "The Civic Hero in Milton's Prose," in *Milton Studies* 8, ed. James D. Simmonds (Pittsburgh, 1975), esp. 95–98; Stephen Fallon, "Alexander More Reads Milton: Self-Representation and Anxiety in Milton's *Defences*," in *Milton and the Terms of Liberty*, ed. Graham Parry and Joad Raymond (Cambridge, 2002), 111–24.

50. In the *Modest Confutation*, the Confuter provides a very brief, general description of his background and qualifications for speaking—he is a man entirely contented with his station in life, is not speaking out of envy, and so on—before proceeding to defend Bishop Hall (6).

51. For the confessional prayer, see YP 4:1127–28. For Milton's reaction to it, see 4:823–25.

MILTON'S *ART OF LOGIC* AND THE FORCE OF CONVICTION

John T. Connor

INTRODUCTION

MILTON'S *ART OF LOGIC* has often been overlooked by Milton-ists. While various attempts have been made to associate the logician and the poet, these studies have not gone far enough to explain what I believe to be the intimate connection between the poet's logic and his structures of pure and practical reason.[1] Milton was preoccupied with the nature of logic, especially in the years following the Restoration, and I will seek to link his concern for logical method to notions of religious and political conviction that resonate in his later work. Central to my argument is that one should not read the *Art of Logic* with regard to its probable composition date (the 1640s), but, rather, that one should understand it in the context of the 1660s and 1670s when Milton revised and published the *Artis Logicae Plenior Institutio* in its 1672 and 1673 editions.[2] Thus situated, I will read the *Art of Logic* as basic both to Milton's account of Creation in the *Christian Doctrine* and to his understanding of subjectivity as modeled in *Paradise Regained.*

In his biography of Milton, William Riley Parker provides an example of the kind of critical reception that the *Art of Logic* seems often to have encountered when he dismisses it as "dull" and "derivative." "When Milton was not in the mood for poetry, he was sometimes capable of the most arid pedantry. Perhaps, for scholar-poets, if not for others, heights necessitate depths." Scratching his head to explain why Milton should ever have thought to acknowledge a work so "exceptionally pedestrian," Parker sees its publication as the product of a regrettable compromise between economic necessity and commonplace vanity—the desire to present "to the world the labours of a lifetime." Strapped for cash, Milton is forced to exploit his poetic notoriety, publishing unworthy castoffs and hand-me-downs, mixing "undistinguished schoolbooks with volumes of highly distinctive verse."[3]

In privileging Milton's poetic commitment over the pedestrian pedantries of a trivial textbook, Parker's treatment of the *Art of Logic* is perfectly consistent with Milton's own early opinion on the matter. When, in June

1644, Milton "set down in writing" his "voluntary *Idea* . . . of a better Education, in extent and comprehension farre more large, and yet of time farre shorter, and of attainment farre more certain, then hath yet been in practice" (YP 2:364), it was rhetoric, not logic, that he envisaged repairing "the ruins of our first Parents by regaining to know God aright" (YP 2:366–67). Milton's treatise *Of Education* holds logic in check: only so much should be taught "as is useful," and "her well couch't Heads and Topics" should serve only as a preliminary exercise toward the opening of "her contracted palm into a gracefull and ornate Rhetorick" (YP 2:402).

This relative neglect of reason and logical argumentation accords with what Stanley Fish regards as the absence of sustained expository argument in Milton's controversial prose of the 1640s. Fish detects a "basic 'ratiocinative emptiness'" beneath the "amplificatory rhetoric that characterises his prose" and suggests that Milton rests the strength of his argument on the associative power of words rather than in the force of logical conclusion.[4] Although this indeed characterizes Milton's prose at around the same time that he is supposed to have written and been teaching the *Art of Logic*, it does not hold true of the works that follow the Restoration. Compare *Areopagitica* (1644) with Milton's last published pamphlet, *Of True Religion* (1673), and one encounters radically different approaches to what are similar arguments concerning liberty of conscience and freedom from censorship; where the one expands rhetorically, the other expounds logically. *Of True Religion,* closely contemporary with the second edition of the *Art of Logic,* makes full use of logical method and fully reflects the later Milton's logical turn.

"*QUID SIT LOGICA?*"

Milton's *Art of Logic* is arranged specifically according to the method of Peter Ramus (1515–1572), whose drastic revision and simplification of the Scholastic syllabus had occurred roughly a century earlier.[5] Almost as much controversy surrounds the figure of Pierre de la Ramée now as it did in the sixteenth and seventeenth centuries. Now as then, Ramus is praised for his academic reforms or is damned as an intellectual delinquent. Milton, while committed to expounding the Ramist method and to expanding on the precepts of the *Scholae Dialecticae,* is by no means uncritical.[6] Milton promises dissent from the start and advertises his points of departure:

Peter Ramus is believed the best writer on the art [of logic] . . . but our author in seeking too earnestly for brevity seems to have fallen short not exactly of clarity but yet of copiousness of clarity. . . . So I have decided that it is better to transfer to the body of the treatise and weave into it, *except where I disagree,* those aids to a more complete understanding of the precepts of the art. (3; emphasis added)

Milton's various deviations from the Ramist system represent important declarations of his investment in the art of logic. These interventions reflect the
personal character of his logical predilection and emphasize virtues of constancy and conviction that draw from an experience of "solitude" and "evil
days."

Milton's *Art of Logic* responds to what he and others have regarded as the
central problem in Ramist methodology, namely its apparent "confusion" of
dialectic and rhetoric.[7] When Zeno first compared dialectic to the clenched
fist and rhetoric to the open palm he had been seeking not only to illustrate the
distinct virtues of the two disciplines but also to emphasize their shared and
inalienable implication in discourse. Both arts originated in a communicative
and social paradigm, the one born of disputation, the other rooted in oration,
but despite their close relation, the question of which art had preeminence
was a hotly disputed issue. I contend that Milton came to privilege the self-
contained, emphatic, and unmovable properties of logic over the previously
preferred palm of "a gracefull and ornate Rhetorick." In affirming logic's
formal fist as the secure parameter of an inviolable interiority, Milton refused
rhetoric's social and subtle capacity to move recalcitrance and to whisper
transgression.

Ramus had defined logic as the art of discoursing well, a time-honored
definition that recalled dialectic's Socratic heritage and found confirmation in
Cicero. Yet to the question posed at the outset of chapter 1—"What Is Logic?"
—Milton counters that "Logic is the art of reasoning well" (19). This is his chief
departure from Ramus.[8] Milton's "Logica est ars bene ratiocinandi" explicitly
rejects Ramus's definition of logic as an art of disputation:

In the definition I say reasoning rather than debating because to reason, not less
extensive in meaning than the reason itself, means the same as to use the reason, while
debating, in addition to being a word not obviously fitting but having a transferred
meaning, would not commonly have any wider significance than that of disputing. (21)

Milton's assertion of reason in lieu of disputation returns us to Aristotle at
exactly the point from which Ramus had taken his departure.[9] Milton defines
logic as the art of thinking with the assumption that thinking is (and indeed
needs to be) independent from discourse. Moreover, "in order to distinguish
the perfection of the art from the imperfection of the natural faculty, the
word *well,* that is rightly, skilfully, promptly, is added to the definition" (19).
Milton's dissociation of logic from discourse intimates the crucial contention
that thought need not commit itself to language and the talk of the public
sphere to argue and enjoy the strength of its truth claim. This is to assert that
logic's formal self-certainty is adequate to withstand rhetorical dissuasion and
the pressures of circumstance.

Logic may rightly be "first of all the arts" (7), but that is no reason, Milton argues, for logic to overreach herself; there must be moderation in her "empire." Milton inveighs against the "unbridled licence" (3) of those dialecticians who, "in their zeal for increasing the scope of their art contend that the doctrine of place as well as that of motion should be treated in logic" (83). Milton considers the doctrines of place and motion pernicious to the profession of logic on two accounts. Place and motion are extraneous to the logical properties of argument, as indeed is all that might be termed content.[10] But while he thus refers the concrete properties of place and motion, as better befitting geography and physics, to their "appropriate arts" (27), Milton's more radical objection to the inclusion of these doctrines directs us again to his definition of logic as an art, not of disputation, but of reasoning.

Milton finally rejects these terms because of what he believes they wrongly imply about the basic nature of logical practice. To a logician of Milton's persuasion, the doctrines of place and motion carried unpalatable connotations of elenctic dialectic; it is precisely this model of logical procedure, with its rhetorical inflections of dubitable argument, that Milton is seeking to leave behind. In disputation one learned to take a place or position and sought to move or persuade one's opponent. In logico-historical terms, talk of *loci* recalled Peter of Spain's elaborate treatment (expanding on Boethius and Cicero) that imagined place as "the seat of an argument" or "that place whence a *convenient* argument is drawn toward the question proposed." An argument was thus a means of "inferring" a conclusion in order to "create conviction in a doubtful matter."[11] Peter of Spain's suppositional theory of logic and its emphases on convenience and the manipulation of credible conviction were echoed in the teaching of Rudolph Agricola, whose *De inventione dialectica* (1480) had revived the dubitable (Aristotelian) inflection of dialectic.

Agricola defined dialectic as "the art of discoursing convincingly (*probabiliter*) on any given matter, so far as its nature can be found capable of conviction." Limiting rhetoric to "embellishments and elegance of language and all the baits for capturing ears," Agricola asserted a close connection between dialectic and real language: "for us the probable will be what can be said suitably and fittingly about the subject proposed." "Dialectic will be concerned with speaking convincingly, and probable will mean whatever can be said as suitably as possible for creating belief."[12] Agricola delimited dialectic to all cases involving doubt wherein we try to create belief and concluded that "the question is the subject matter of dialectic."[13] Milton's definition of logic as treating of reason rather than disputation seeks to disengage logic from the enthymematic and to stake its claim on certitude. Doubt, convenience, and verbal dexterity distress a Milton for whom the conviction born of labor underwrites faith.

"Since place is an external affection of some nature or other, whether corporeal or incorporeal," Milton is hard put to explain "what has come into the mind of the logicians, especially the disciples of Ramus, that although they teach that arguments, that is not things but reasons, are the natural subject of logic, yet they decree that things or affections of natural things, motion, place, and time, should be treated in logic" (81–83). With a deliberate formalism, Milton's *Art of Logic* "considers not what place is, whether a limited space or the surface of an encompassing body, but merely in what way place argues a thing located, just as the subject argues the adjunct" (83). Movement falls likewise beyond the logical pale:

> In this matter most interpreters of Ramus are of the opinion that the doctrine of motion . . . pertains to logic, but not rightly. For what can logic teach about motion that is not natural and according to physics. "Things known" they say from Aristotle (*Physics* 8.3) "and opinions, all use motion." Surely they use it, but, as physics teaches, taken from nature. Thus logic uses reason, yet does not teach the nature of reason but the art of reason. Every cause moves, an effect is moved, but the logician considers not what moves or is moved, but what argues or is argued. But *arguing or being argued* in itself, so far as it is motion or a thing made by motion, does not pertain to logic, but only so far as by some presentation of arguing it aids the power of reasoning or teaches the art. (75)

Begotten, not made, Milton's "power of reasoning" eschews elaboration; it is not the topical *vis inferentiae* of Abelard but something innately conceded in the formal confirmation of apodictic argument. Logic's animate action traces no movement of conditional illation; rather, it finds itself already inherent in every necessary conclusion. Dislocated and immobile, Milton's *Art of Logic* presents absolute complexion in place of probative inference.

What inspires logical reasoning is the power of its artificial "bent for arguing" (22). This "natural bent" or "affect or ratio for arguing" describes "a certain condition of terms proportional to each other" (27). When thus "affected," arguments combine together with the "innate and peculiar force" (27) that proves the "proper and primary potency" of artificial logic. Milton emphasizes throughout the fact that an argument is not a particular truth content but rather a quality of its "affect," for "in the proper sense of the word," an argument "is not a word or a thing, but a certain fitness of something for arguing" (25). Fitness depends not on a power of the word but on a strength of connection, an internal bond between argument and what is argued. This quality of "fitness" defines "ratio" or reason (25).

Take the example of the axiom, which is defined as "the disposition of one argument with another." This complex mode of reasoning depends on the strength of its "band" for its enunciation and truth claim. "An axiom is affirmed when its band is affirmed, and is denied when its band is denied. For the band is the form of the axiom; by the force of the band the matter of the axiom is disposed and as though animated" (*quasi animatur*) (305). Milton invokes the copulative power of artificial disposition in describing the "band" of the axiom as *quasi anima,* or "as it were the soul" (325). Artificial logic is invigorated by proximity between predicates and weakened by distance; closeness "argues with the greatest strength" (53). Logic in its formal aspiration to ever more intimate communion between distributed parts is understood as the supreme manifestation of inclination and association between subject and predicate, an interior alliance that might be called "as it were, the soul."

This logical animation upholds the "general end" of logic, the aim, "not merely [of] judging well, as Ramus holds, for that is too narrow, but [of] thinking well" (295). In thinking well, the universal aim of artificial logic intimates the absolute, for "to absolve is to make perfect" (27).[14] Agreement between logical parts is the highest demonstration of perfection in Milton's logical order, being "prior not by nature alone but also in use and dignity. For from affirmation and consent all art and teaching, like all knowledge, are deduced" (99). "*A consentany argument agrees with what it argues.* That is, it establishes or affirms the being of the thing which it argues" (27).

Milton's *Art of Logic* describes two modes of consent or degrees of intimate affection. The first order of "consentany" argument agrees "*absolutely*" or essentially; "of things which absolutely agree one is known to exist by force of the other; and thus cause and effect agree" (27–29). The second order of consentany argument agrees only "*after a fashion.*" This secondary relation exists between the subject and adjunct; fallen from absolute privilege, such arguments enjoy only an extrinsic (less proximate) relation to what they argue. The "difference in affect" (29) between arguments "consentany *absolutely*" and "consentany *after a fashion*" inscribes the difference between perfection and imperfection that structures Milton's pure and practical reason. This essay will treat each in turn.

"*EVIGILENT HIC THEOLOGI*"—THE LOGIC OF GOD

Milton admits but one argument that "absolutely" and alone enjoys the full felicity of logic's artificial "bent." God is Milton's single and supreme artificial intelligence and it is from God that all things proceed. "For the Father is not only he *by* whom, but also he *from* whom, *in* whom, *through* whom, and *on account of* whom all things are" (YP 6:302). In acknowledging God to be all causes conjoined, Milton asserts that God "argued" Creation. God gave being to Creation in the same way, "as causes give being to the effect," since "a cause is that by the force of which a thing is," "has been and will be" (31). The "primitive" precept of cause and effect is "eternal and of eternal truth" (31); the procreation of effect from efficient cause is therefore irrefragable and Milton dares the theologians to think otherwise (59).

"Since God is the first, absolute and sole cause of all things" (YP 6:307), it follows that he is the "principal cause, that is the efficient" cause of Creation. Only one cause can properly be called *"first"* and the only "absolutely" first efficient or "solitary cause" is God (37). The absolute primacy of efficient cause is the foundation on which Milton's "dearest and best possession" (YP 6:121), his *De Doctrina Christiana,* arrives at its narrative of Creation and its attendant anti-Trinitarianism. The privilege of "logic, that is, reason" (YP 6:159) alongside Scripture is not to be overlooked in Milton's "two books of investigations into Christian Doctrine."

Milton's logical understanding of the single particularity of efficient cause grounds his account of Creation. Since there can be but one absolute first cause, that cause must obey the logic of number and form. It is a contradiction in terms to assert that the solitary first cause of Creation be also triune; Creation cannot therefore be the work of three equal persons:[15]

Single things . . . have form singular and proper to themselves; certainly they differ in number among themselves . . . [b]ut what is differing in number among themselves except differing in single forms. For number, as Scaliger rightly says, is an affection following an essence. Therefore things which differ in number also differ in essence; and never do they differ in number if not in essence.—*Here let the Theologians awake.* (59)

Rather than admit the "tri-personall" Godhead of *Of Reformation* (1641), Milton asserts in *De Doctrina Christiana* and thereafter his own version of God the Father: supreme, self-existent, eternal, and *one* "in the numerical sense in which human reason always understands it" (YP 6:216). In addition, Milton adduces two temporal subordinate creatures: the Son—"of all creation first" (*PL* 3.383)—and Holy Spirit.

Milton intends his chapter "Of the Creation" in *Christian Doctrine* to protect God from disparagement of his creation. This he attempts logically by exploring the remit of material cause. That matter should have existed from eternity and independently from God Milton finds inconceivable, and that all things were created from nothing Milton thinks contradicts both Scripture and the logic of material cause, "for nothing is no cause at all" (YP 6:306–7),[16] and for anything to be, it has already to have been caused into being. Milton argues instead that God, as solitary first cause, created matter out of himself, thus conjoining material and efficient cause. "There remains only one solution . . . that all things came from God" (YP 6:307) and that God's "active efficacy" has always already encompassed all things. Insofar as matter succeeds cause, "*Matter is the cause from which a thing is*" (51), and God is the sum total of efficient and subaltern causes, all matter not only follows from God, but indeed is God: "I am who fill / Infinitude" (*PL* 7.168–69). "[I]t is, I say, a demonstration of God's supreme power and goodness that he should not shut up this heterogeneous and substantial matter within himself, but should disperse, propagate and extend it as far as, and in whatever way he wills" (YP 6:308). Such dispersal, propagation, and extension are readily recognizable as logical disposition in figurative guise; but a theory of *Creatio ex Deo*, while safeguarding God's infinity and omnipotence, yet threatens to account God as the author of evil. Milton counters this implication with the assertion that evil results only from the individual exercise of subordinate free will. "Those causes . . . which act according to reason and thought, as angels and men, act freely *ex hypothesi*—on the hypothesis of the divine will, which in the beginning gave them the power of acting freely. For liberty is the power of doing or not doing this or that, except, to be sure, God wished otherwise, or force from some other quarter assailed them" (43). Come what may of "will though free / Yet mutable" (*PL* 5.236–37), logic guarantees that evil not contaminate original essence; "heterogeneous and substantial matter," however much it may vary in form, and however much it may fall prey, fallen from God, to infection and pollution, remains in essence incorruptible. All matter simultaneously argues divinity as its efficient cause and recalls divinity in its impeccable essence.

The tautological autoreferentiality of Milton's monist universe proves "God's supremely powerful active efficacy" (YP 6:307) with the "innate and peculiar force" of artificial argument. Since there is no essential difference between God and the matter of Creation, or between God and himself, the "natural bent" of his argument for arguing himself is infallible. Creation, the one instance of the true "invention" and "disposition" of an argument, enjoys a closed circuit of reference predicated on the absolute affirmation of logical connection.

"WHAT DOEST THOU IN THIS WORLD?"—THE LOGICAL SUBJECT

Unfortunately, Milton's *Art of Logic* has to admit that although God is indeed perfectly logical, we are not. Defining logic as the art of reasoning, Milton adds the word "well" to distinguish "the perfection of the art" from "the imperfection of [our] natural faculty" (19). This distinction radically structures the *Art of Logic.* The same "difference in affect" that separates the absolute coupling of cause and effect from the merely fashionable consent of subject and adjunct acknowledges a shortfall from full logical perfection. For although it is a matter of formal concession that a cause may argue its effect and an effect may argue its cause "absolutely," yet "sometimes the effects, not through themselves indeed, but *as better known to us,* more plainly argue the causes than they are argued by the causes" (73; emphasis added). This admission upsets the formal hierarchy that asserts causes as "prior" and effects as "arguing less weightily" (71). Although causes are correctly to be preferred to effects because of their possession of final purpose,[17] amid the complications of practical reason this project must remain opaque to the earthbound observer. The superior legibility of effect is a concession made to fallen faculties able to intuit God's "active efficacy" only in its more immediate effects, not in its first or final cause.[18]

Milton provides an account of our more limited logical genius in his discussion of the logical "subject." A subject, for Milton, "is that which is affected toward arguing something which is joined to it in addition to that essence which it has from its causes" (79). This "something" or "addition" is called an "adjunct" and is "added to the subject over and above" his essence (85). The essence that Milton so prizes is the effect of the proximate cause wherein man is made in the image of his maker; thus, the subject "is already perfect [as] constituted by [his] causes" (79), and neither is his essence "changed by the accession or removal [of an adjunct], nor is the subject made something different" (85). The precedence and independence of the subject's original essence, to which an adjunct is only secondarily and accidentally "adjoined," are mainstays of Milton's *Art of Logic.* Howsoever an adjunct might affect the potentially beleaguered subject, his essence remains secure. It therefore follows that the relation between subject and adjunct is consentany only after a sort: "things are said to agree after a sort with the thing they prove which merely agree easily and extrinsically, that is, without touching their essence, since the subject does not give being to the adjunct as does the cause to the effect; nor does the adjunct receive its essence from the subject" (79). Thus, subject and adjunct fashionably agree; however intimately adjoined, the attributed subject yet retains full possession of his unaffected essence. "Whatever happens extrinsic to any subject, whether fortuitous or not, is an adjunct of it. The good and ills, as they are called, of the soul, the body, and the whole man, are adjuncts of the soul, the body, and the man" (85).

Such extrinsic "good and ills," however assertively they predicate the subject, touch not upon his essence, nor do all adjuncts intimate the subject with equal force. The accidental relation between subject and adjunct is therefore divided into four degrees of affection. The desirable proximity between subject and adjunct (as that which argues with the greatest strength) decreases with each succeeding mode. In the first mode, the subject sustains or is sustained by a quality; thus, the subject receives "*ingrafted* or *inherent* adjuncts" such as knowledge and virtue, ignorance and vice (81). In the second mode, the subject contains or is contained by a place. In the third mode, the subject is "collocated" by circumstance, such "adjacent" adjuncts being received only "to or about" the subject; "thus a man is the subject of riches, poverty, honour, infamy, clothing, companionship" (83). In the fourth mode, the faculties of the subject (whether sensory or virtuous) are affected by external phenomena (thus, sight is "exercised" by color and temperance by pleasure). In what follows I will concentrate on the first and most privileged mode of "ingrafted" or "inherent" adjuncts, which fit so close as to affect the soul.

Milton's definition of the subject, namely as "*that to which anything is adjoined*" (79), impacts directly on his conception of agency. Although the subject is privileged for being "prior, better known, firmer, more important" than its adjunct (101), nevertheless the two subsist only in a reciprocal relation (127): only in receiving or being receptive to adjuncts does one become a subject. Milton does not disparage this radical receptivity for its passivity; such submission entails instead the very possibility of action, for according to this account a subject is active only insofar as he "receives" action. In order to act, the primed subject must stand and wait, or sit "in order serviceable" (*On the Morning of Christ's Nativity*, 244); dramatic action, if it comes at all, comes not from within the psychological depths of an intentional subject, but extrinsically, from without. This model of passive agency invokes what Stanley Fish describes as Milton's "redefinition of action as interior," according to which Milton's "regenerate man" has to actively refrain from intentional action, to actively stand firm, to pledge allegiance, to organize that inner orientation of the soul on whose prompting faith aligns itself with Providence. Thus, for Fish, "the true form of action is not an event, but a mode of being," a "faithful performance" or constant readiness that identifies as God's the recipient subject.[19] This mutual assistance of activity and passivity characterizes logical argument equally as "that which argues as well as that which is argued" (301). Such an argument is the logical subject and Milton's model subject is the Son.

The Son has, of course, essence, which he has from his causes—he is, after all, the Son of God—but that which makes a subject of him and which subjects him to Godhead is his reception and manifestation of "inward Oracle." The Son's state of perfect receptivity to God's gifts corroborates Milton's assertion in *Christian Doctrine* that the Son is, in essence, distinct from and as such inferior to the Father (YP 6:205–98). All "attributes of divinity belong to the Father alone" (YP 6:227), and whatsoever the Son himself manifests of divine nature he receives from the Father. "The Son himself reports that he received from the Father not only the name of God and Jehovah, but also whatever else he has . . . his individuality, his life itself, his attributes, his works, and, lastly, his divine honour . . . he receives everything from the Father: everything—not only what belongs to him as mediator, but also what belongs to him as Son" (YP 6:259–60). Such "more than human gifts" (*PR* 2.137) are not external, neither physiognomical nor physical; they are, in accordance with the first adjunctive mode, internal ingrafts of divinity. The "spirit of truth" (*PR* 1.462) sent to dwell in "pious hearts" is a gift of grace and argues, as adjunct the subject, our state before God.

In *Paradise Regained,* the return to logic is presented as the privilege of quietude and stasis over style and motion. The Son, conversing only with solitude (1.191) and communing in silent walk (2.261), is goaded into speech by Satan; their encounter is a clash between logical reticence and rhetorical mobility. From the outset Satan is associated with "conversation"; he is "compos'd of lies" (1.407), of "answer[s] smooth" (1.467), "fair speech" (2.301), and "train[s] of words" (3.266). His "hollow compliments" (4.124) and "outlandish flatteries" (4.125) constitute "the persuasive rhetoric / That sleeked his tongue, and won so much on Eve" (4.4–5). Satan, aware of his own "weak arguing, and fallacious drift" (3.4–6), advances a dialectical paradigm, supposing the Son as desiring to rule "by persuasion" (4.230). The Son understands, however, that reasoning well (the "general end" of logic) is neither discourse nor disputation, but a quiet composition of the interior.

Satan's "tedious talk" (*PR* 4.307) is verbal noise that threatens to confound the Son's silent concentration. But however sleeked his solicitations and subtle his shifts, Satan's tongue is powerless to persuade him. Among the recurrent epithets of the Son's superiority, he is consistently described as being "unmoved" by Satan's rhetorical advances (2.407, 3.386, 4.109). This stasis further withstands the Son's every move, for whether "throned / In the bosom of bliss . . . or remote from heaven . . . Wandering the wilderness," the Son remains "[t]he Son of God, with godlike force endued" (4.596–602). Movement is physical, even natural, but illogical, notwithstanding (75). Wherever circumstance situates the Son, he remains inherently endued with "godlike force" from God. "Unmoved" by happenstance, the Son perfects a logical stance that is both stoic virtue and an article of faith.

Confirming the logical inclination, *Paradise Regained* reaches its high point in essential immobility. Set to stand on the temple top's highest pinnacle, Satan expects the Son either to lose balance and fall, or to cast himself down and tempt Providence. The Son instead does neither, does nothing:

"Tempt not the Lord thy God; he said and stood" (4.561). This statement both is and is not a moment of self-identification. The Son does not reply in pride to Satan's challenge by finally affecting the Godhead, but neither is God here supposed to exist without the boundaries of the confrontation. The Son has appropriated the Father's authority only insofar as he has extinguished his own; in so doing, the animate band of their axiomatic connection subsumes the Son and identifies him as his Father's instrumental cause. The programmatic inaction and expectation, abstention and silence that have characterized the Son thus far are fully repaid when what is written "as it is written" writes Jesus as Christ. The Son stands as Satan falls amazed.

Milton portrays perfect subordination to the will of God as that supreme service of standing and waiting that had been programmed in *Sonnet XVI*. This subordination is indeed the balancing act that critics have seen Jesus perform on the temple top, for "'action' and 'passivity' are relative terms" (YP 6:307). Standing "upright" is far removed from submission, and indeed requires "skill" (*PR* 4.551–52). Subsumed by the force of logical acknowledgment, the revelation of identity that discovers the proximate connection between effect and cause, adjunct and subject, the Son is then removed on the sail of angels' wings and lauded for his "victory over temptation" (*PR* 4.595), his logical confidence in "still" remaining, in spite of "place, / Habit, or state or motion," (4.600–601) "as a centre, firm" (4.534) and in "firm obedience" (1.4) "unmoved."

The question yet remains how the renunciation of individual will, of adolescent dreams of "victorious deeds" and "heroic acts" (*PR* 1.215–16) fits with the terms and tropes of Milton's *Art of Logic*. The Son's climactic experience of artificial affirmation, of the consentany relation between logical parts, is understood by Milton as but the basis of a logical praxis. Confirmed in faith, the Son then has to "publish his godlike office" (1.188). The substance of this "glorious work" (4.635) is laid out in the last two chapters of the first book of Milton's *Art of Logic*—on human and divine testimony.

"BY THINGS DEEMED WEAK"—THE FORCE OF TESTIMONY

Thus far, the bulk of Book One of the *Art of Logic* has detailed the variegations of a pure reason "quite absolute and perfect in itself." In spite of the possible "obscurity of causes" (267), the absolute relation between cause and effect was alone sufficient to "bring forth knowledge" (89). It had to be conceded, however, that the profession of artificial logic was inadequate to such arguments as had fallen from the perfection of privileged consent. Howsoever perfect in essence, the logical subject lacked the primitive "use and dignity" that existed between cause and effect in the nuptial bliss of their knowledgeable conjunction. The impaired relation of subject and adjunct suffered "for the most part" merely "to bring forth conjecture" (89). The difference in affect between knowledge and conjecture redraws the distinction between perfection and imperfection, absolute and fashionable consent, pure and practical reason. It further distinguishes artificial from inartificial reason.

Inartificial argument is imperfect; with no "share in . . . art and in the faculty of arguing something," artless argument is adequate only to the concession of conjecture. As such, it has *"little force for proof"* (281). Lacking art to "touch the nature of the thing" (279), inartificial argument serves but as "mere attestation by someone concerning something" (281): *"In one word, this is called testimony"* (279). Neither incontrovertible nor apodictic, testimony lacks the constitutive power of artificial reason, for that which a witness affirms does not therefore come to be in the same way that the consentany cause *"gives being to a thing"* (29). Without this artificial determination, "things [neither] exist because of affirmation nor are they without existence because of denial; therefore testimony from itself and its nature does not prove anything" (281). Lacking proof, testimony is subjective, but as a product of the fallen subject, testimony, for all its imperfection, can yet accomplish great things (*PL* 12.567). By the absolute standard of art, subject and testimony are alike deemed weak, but inasmuch as, "By humiliation and strong sufferance," weakness can "o'ercome" even "Satanic strength" (*PR* 1.161), subject and testimony admit of great expectations. In particular, Milton conceives the work of testimony as setting about the partial redemption of the subject's fallen imperfection.

Testimony stakes its every claim on the credible charisma of its author. For this reason, the force of testimony is "especially to be discerned in the effects of the one bearing witness and in adjuncts" (281). Credible effects derive of free causation, for testimony extracted under duress bears little power of convincement. Recall that a *"cause works of itself which works by its own power,* that is, which produces an effect from an internal principle" (39). Sincere testimony comes freely from conviction, the internal principle that motivates the effects of speech and confers their "especial credit."

Between subject and testimony there exists in the world of *"human affairs"* a reciprocal relation: testimony *"gains especial credit from the character of the man arguing, if he is a person of prudence, probity, and benevolence"* (281), and the character of the subject gains "especial credit" both by the fact that he so testifies and from the truth to which he testifies: "For as testimony does not by its own force argue what is testified to, but rather the authority of the witness does so, so in turn the thing testified to does not argue the testimony itself, but the authority of the witness" (293). This mutual assistance admits a circular relation similar to that administered by the axiomatic band (whereby cause proves effect and effect proves cause); in this inartificial variant, the credibility of the witness assures and is in turn assured by the credibility of the testimony. In *Paradise Regained,* the publication of godlike office is described in terms no less reciprocal; thus, the Son testifies of heaven as surely as he "receive[s] / The testimony of heaven" (*PR* 1.77–78). The subject affirms his faith and is confirmed by faith in a closed economy that both proves and improves the witnessing subject.

The Son in *Paradise Regained* is Milton's model witness, who as God's "living Oracle" speaks not his own but his father's glory. "I seek not mine, but his / Who sent me, and thereby witness whence I am" (3.106–7). The Son's testament of "truth requisite for men to know" is the simple acknowledgment of Creation, the assured conjecture of "whence" we are. The Son, as first effect of Creation, is supremely placed to argue "whence I am," completing in so doing the consentany circuit of God's monist disposition. Since God's self-disclosure is made "more plainly" known to us in his every effect (73), it follows that we should learn both in the Son (as divine first effect) and from the Son (as Oracle) how God argued Creation "to show forth his goodness, and impart / His good communicable to every soul" (*PR* 3.122–26). The divine deixis of Creation bespeaks God's "beneficence" (*PR* 3.133); such beneficence requires in return "benediction, that is, thanks, / The slightest, easiest, readiest recompense" (3.127–28).

Creation demands that we speak well of it, but such slightly required recompense raises the question of whether, as the *Art of Logic* gives us to suppose, speech, as implicated in the failings of rhetoric and dialectic, is wholly to be disparaged. If by speech we mean the concatenation of words, then there can be no doubt—"An argument in the proper sense of the word is not a word or a thing, but a certain fitness of something for arguing" (25). Fitness, the soul of logic's proximate art, is primitively preverbal, and what is termed logical disposition "is entirely a matter of the reason as well conceived in the mind as uttered by the voice" (301). Milton repeatedly advances the basic distinction between "external speech" (*orationis exterioris*) and "internal reason" (*rationis interioris*) (300): "we distinguish between exterior speech, which is uttered with the mouth, and internal, which is conceived in the mind alone" (301).[20] Because "there can be much use of reason without speech, but no use of speech without reason" (17), logic is held to be superior to dialectic and therefore prior to discourse. The living Word, rooted in the pious heart, is a formal understanding of the interior and neither a gambit of common parlance nor ever to be confused with rhetoric's "resistless eloquence" (*PR* 4.268).

Milton's *Art of Logic* admits a distinct aversion to verbalism and to public discourse. It seems to contemn these as the betrayal of thoughts from their only adequate security—the unuttered privacy of the mind. The work distrusts the clothing of "axioms mentally conceived" with such ambiguous "symbols and signs of simple notions" as are "words" (301). With words held suspect, the *Art of Logic* credits them only as optional and, if not always pernicious, at least inessential. When Milton then concedes a "very necessity for speaking" (25), he seems to gesture beyond the mere word to an almost psychological (and perforce inscrutable) urge to disclosure shared by God and humankind, as well as to a debt of gratitude shared alike by all of God's animate subjects.

Such "very necessity" might seem to represent a constraint on the freedom of the logical subject, for by necessity is understood the impulsion of an external force opposed to the internal principle whereupon, "by the guidance of thought" (43), we freely act. But Milton makes clear that such infringement is neither coercive upon nor extrinsic to our freedom; the imposition of benediction is, rather, constitutive of our liberty as it is defined by the *Art of Logic*. It is not that speech renders us unfree by its "necessity," but that, for Milton, we are only ever free "on the hypothesis of the divine will, which in the beginning gave [us] the power of acting freely" (43). As a gift of God, our freedom necessarily bespeaks our createdness. Human freedom acknowledges the essential perfection that we have of our causes, the knowledge of "whence" we are. It is thus to our artificial dependency we speak when we freely testify. Freedom of speech is "very necessity for speaking" and witnesses our logical subjection to the first cause. "Necessity for speaking" is not so much a verbal as it is an existential imperative, the self-confirming performance of our obedient alignment with the principle of our being. The fit service of the logical subject is the constant benediction of our own being, and because our being is perforce rational, such gratitude is nothing less than "reason" (*PR* 3.121), the thanks we owe "who could return him nothing else" (3.129). Thanks, of course, lacks art and "proves" nothing; it does but attest.

Poetry likewise acts as testimony and from the "necessity of speaking." Poetry is not, as Ramus thought it, the capacity merely to amplify and dissemble arguments in words. Milton is quick to dissociate the art from Ramus's disregard and to make poetry more than the sum of its words. He adds, as a codicil to his very last chapter (on method), that "to orators and poets should be left their own account of method" (485). Poetry, as a "special" art, is granted this methodological dispensation for the simple reason that the *Art of Logic* distrusts its words, excepting that they be "distinct and certainly not ambiguous and not inappropriate" (25). Poetry subserves logic, which, as "reason," remains "first of all the arts" (7); the relation is structured on the same difference that obtains between inartificial and artificial argument. Poetry serves as testimony and derives its "especial credit," not from the content its words convey but from the discernible fitness of their author. Poetry operates as an extension of its author's person, its value to be perceived in the character of the author, the adjuncts of the one bearing witness.

Testimony's force of conviction evidences the free choice (*ex hypothesi*) of the witness in "doing or not doing this or that" (43), a choice that directly impacts on the soul. The Holy Spirit "doest prefer / Before all temples the upright heart and pure" (*PL* 1.17–18) where adjuncts inhere to confirm and inspire the testimonial inflection of the loyal subject. In *Paradise Lost* God praises Abdiel, who "for the testimony of Truth hast borne / Universal reproach" (6.33–34), a stance later adopted by Noah, when in response to the "civil Broils" of his people, he "of their doings great dislike declared, / And testified against their ways" (1.718, 720–21). In each of these instances, a voice testifies to its sustenance, its sponsorship by another. Even Comus is not oblivious of the process. He discerns an ingraft in the Lady's "mortal mixture," "something holy" lodged in her breast that testifies to its "hidd'n residence" ("Comus," 246–48). Just as the witness aligns herself with deity, so, too, is she subject to that which resides in her.

In *Paradise Lost,* Milton describes his task as that of *asserting* "the eternal providence" and of justifying "the ways of God to men."[21] It should be clear from the context of these lines at the end of the first invocation that Milton is not himself making the "great argument."[22] Milton asks for "illumination" and "support" that "to the height of this great argument," which is nothing less than the full artificial disposition of redemptive history, he may *assert* Providence. Providence is the final cause of that solitary first cause that brought Creation into being and as such is of none but God's making. Milton's *Art of Logic* confirms that a final cause "is the cause for the sake of which a thing is . . . [and] is not other than some good" (63). It would be idolatrous to suppose even Milton's logical faculties adequate to reproducing God's third act of Creation. Milton is not arrogating omniscience; were he to deny Providence, Providence would not therefore be "without existence." This attestation of Providence is an act, not of artificial disposition, but of testimonial deposition.

Milton's invocations ask aid to trespass on the scenes of crime so that, as "earthly guest" (*PL* 7.390), Milton may witness God's artificial narrative. What Milton cannot see himself he gathers from credible sources, as, for example, from the Holy Spirit that "from the first / Wast present" (1.19) and from the "holy light, offspring of heaven first-born" (3.1). Milton takes the reliability of these testimonials on faith, for what applies to human testimony applies equally to divine; "divine testimony affirms or denies that a thing is so and brings about that I believe; it does not prove, it does not teach, it does not cause me to know or understand why things are so" (383). *Paradise Lost* thus calls multiple witnesses to the stand whereon it, too, attests to what it can of eternal Providence. Testimony, whether divine or human, "gets all its force from [its] author, and has none in itself" (283). Milton's ambitious song is crucially determined by the inherence of first order adjuncts (such as knowledge and virtue) that alone condition its author's integrity and thus its force as testimony. The authority of the poet—who ought himself "to be a true poem, that is, a composition, and patterne of the best and honourablest things" (YP 1:891)—is testimony's full support and special credit.

Conclusion: "Sir, what ill chance hath brought thee to this place"

When in 1673 Marvell defended Milton against the charge made in Samuel Parker's *Reproof* that Marvell's *The Rehearsal Transpos'd* afforded as "good Precedents for Rebellion and King-killing as any we meet with in the writings of *J. M.*," Marvell answered the slander with a potted life of "J. M." It was Milton's "misfortune," Marvell attested, "living in a tumultuous time, to be toss'd on the wrong side." Marvell describes how Milton, on taking advantage of the Restoration's "Regal Clemency," "has ever since expiated himself in a retired silence."[23] This account must be read against Milton's own invocation to Book Seven of *Paradise Lost*, which describes his mortal voice as "though fallen on evil days," "unchanged / To hoarse or mute" (1.25). For Milton, if not for Marvell, there is action in "constant perseverance" (*PR* 1.148), in holding one's firm conviction "secure . . . Against whate'er may tempt, whate'er seduce, / Allure, or terrify, or undermine" (1.176–79). This stability, exercised "[b]y humiliation and strong sufferance" (*PR* 1.160), is as much an active logical station as a passive Stoic stance.

Marvell's allegation of "retired silence" cannot, however, be dismissed entirely, when one remembers how Milton's *Logics* of 1672 and 1673 privilege retirement and silence as contributing precisely to that wordless proximity that defines logic as reason. Logic holds at bay the elenctic and sophistic complications of words so that it may erect in their stead the formal primacy of fitness as manifested by artificial disposition and artless deposition. As we have seen, Milton places special emphasis on testimony and on the conviction that inartificial argument is less a singular performance than it is the continual action of keeping in tune and tending essence, of witnessing "whence" we are.

Insofar as testimony is a configuration of "the inner man" (*PR* 2.477), its temporal virtue is constancy. Constancy is the power to remain "unmoved" if tossed amiss; it is inimical to the motive persuasion of rhetoric and inimical to the doctrine of place. Unhoused at the Restoration, Milton must regard his national home as no longer a topical place but a qualitative locative: for Milton, as pointedly as for Cicero before him, one's *patria* becomes "wherever it is well with him."[24] In reducing the territorial limits of place to an internal quality of the subject, Milton returns us to the "highest pinnacle" of the temple in Jerusalem.[25] Milton's England becomes the uneasy balance whereon the loyal subject awaits the occasion, the location from where all "movement," save on the sail of angels' wings, is unthinkable. "There stand, if thou wilt stand; to stand upright / Will ask thee skill" (*PR* 4.551–52). There is skill indeed in standing and withstanding, but such "uneasy station" (4.584) is rewarded with intimations of Godhead and the hoped-for overthrow of mortal foe. To advocate the better fortitude of "stand and wait" is not, however, to cast Milton's logical turn as a quietist gesture; his testament for fit though few admits instead a possible political strain that it derives from the epistemological configuration of God's artificial logic.

Miltonic knowledge is apodictic for the simple reason that to be true, it must be sufficient in and of itself by the "innate and peculiar force" of its a priori artifice. "Thus logic uses reason, yet does not teach the nature of reason but the art of reasoning"—we take logic on faith precisely because what it teaches is immanently self-evident. The conviction that logic confirms provides "the touchstone of itself and of the wrong[;] the doctrine of truth itself when rightly presented indicates through itself and also refutes every error" (373–75). Truth is self-sufficient and declines augmentation; its "contracted form [is naturally] more explicate than [any] explicated form" (399). Truth, being more a condition of exact definition than a property of elaborate description, is fully adequate to the contract frame of its essence, its formal fist eschewing the "ornate" manipulations of rhetorically inflected dialectic. The dubitable inflections of dianoetic deduction do not reveal truth "manifest through itself" (365); rather, they betray the "weakness of the human intellect" (367). Knowledge waits instead to confirm the mind that perfectly conceives its logical truth. Such truth appears intuitive, but only when the receiving mind is properly conditioned to the claims made on right reason by the divine deictic of Creation. Knowledge is but the adequate comprehension of the absolute consentany affirmation of cause and effect; as such, all knowledge reveals God's causal agency and contains his providential purpose.

Logic underwrites knowledge and in its final cause "conserves" Providence. Logic and Providence endow each other; both, according to their artificial predisposition, argue to their given conclusion. This axiomatic epistemological inflection confers upon the logician something of a prophetic strain. To testify God's ways to men is to assert Providence and predict, if not in omniscience at least in faith, the course of human history. When Milton cries with the voice of the Prophet "*O earth, earth, earth!*" and tells "the very soil itself what her perverse inhabitants are deaf to" (YP 7:388, 462), he bears witness according to his model of inartificial argument. This famous assumption of the prophetic mantle occurs in the two editions of *The Readie and Easie Way to Establish a free Commonwealth* of 1660. In the second edition, the phrase is immediately associated with "the language of that which is not call'd amiss *the good Old Cause.*"

The Restoration furnished Milton with ample opportunity to meditate on the primitive logic of cause, and however much he might protest against the introduction of content-ridden canons into the formal compass of logic, I wonder to what extent he allows his understanding of logical cause to inflect his commitment to the "good Old Cause." For the *Art of Logic,* the procreation of effect from cause is a matter of formal logical concession and the effect's consequence—if the cause be "not called amiss"—a matter of theological necessity. In the experience of defeat, Milton seems to sanction a coincidence between the logical and political registers of cause, which expresses the hope that the commonweal, as consentany effect of consenting common cause, might not yet pass without effect.

The *Art of Logic*, which sustains both artificial and inartificial argument, is root and branch of Milton's pure and practical reason. The conviction that thought need not commit itself to a trial of public persuasion, but rather that it rest assured in the inviolable self-sufficiency of its claim on truth, is born both of logical method and of "evil days" (*PL* 7.27). The conjunction is not accidental. The *Art of Logic* articulates a method dictated both by political exigency and epistemological necessity. But howsoever the encompassing dangers of the Restoration assail the subject, logic is their match. Logic guarantees that external forces impinge not on that essence that, born of the logic of cause and further strengthened by the inherence of adjunct, confirms in the confident subject's mortal mixture the "hidden residence" of "something holy." Of the four modes of adjunct that attend subjectivity, two argue in their remit place and circumstance, but neither place nor circumstance argues the subject with the fitness and proximate strength reserved for those inherent and ingrafted adjuncts of character that most nearly attend the individual's incorruptible essence. Compared with adjuncts of the first order, circumstance is but happenstance and place but an "external affection" of the "thing located" (83).

The interior is the site of Milton's logical retirement from the experience of defeat, the subjective station where first order adjuncts ingraft and inhere, the site of that proximate connection between God and man which is logic, grace, and faith. The essential complexion of "man's nobler part" is that "internal reason" which, distinguished from "exterior speech," is "conceived in the mind alone" (300). Secure in the mind and upright heart, reason draws from the loyal subject the "high attest" and "higher argument" of logic's art. "God attributes to place / No sanctity" (*PL* 11.641), but in the active interiority of a logical station resides the "home-felt" hope of a happier restoration to blissful seat and happy state.

University of Pennsylvania

NOTES

1. Most notably, Walter J. Ong, S.J., "Logic and the Epic Muse: Reflections on Noetic Structures in Milton's Milieu," in *Achievements of the Left Hand: Essays on the Prose of John Milton,* edited by Michael Lieb and John T. Shawcross, 239–68 (Amherst, MA, 1974). Ong's first footnote lists previous interpretations of the *Art of Logic.*

2. Various dates are suggested for the composition of the *Art of Logic*: (1) Milton's postgraduate years at Cambridge, 1629–1632; (2) the years 1640–1647, when Milton was teaching his nephews, Edward and John Phillips, as well as later some other pupils; (3) the spring and summer of 1648; and (4) the period after the Restoration, at least for revising the work for publication. I concede that the work was most probably written some time in the 1640s for the pedagogical purposes outlined in *Of Education,* but I would argue that it underwent close revision in the 1670s, gaining perhaps its preface as well as some of the examples and asides that elaborate upon the precepts. Walter Ong's introduction to the *Art of Logic* agrees that "the 1641–7 date would of course not preclude Milton's touching up the manuscript much later, before he gave it to Spencer Hickman for publication in 1672." Ong's introduction is from *Complete Prose Works of John Milton,* 8 vols., ed. Don M. Wolfe et al. (New Haven, 1953–82), 8:146. All quotations from Milton's prose, except those of the *Art of Logic* itself, are taken from this edition, hereafter designated YP and cited parenthetically by volume and page number. Milton's one anti-Trinitarian reference (book 1, chapter 7), out of place in a work that specifically eschews theological controversy as illogical, would seem especially to accord with a later revision date and an author who had recently argued his position in *De Doctrina Christiana.* In this instance, and throughout this essay, I presume Milton's authorship of the *Christian Doctrine.* On the fallibility of my presumption, compare Michael Lieb, "*De Doctrina Christiana* and the Question of Authorship," in *Milton Studies* 41, ed. Albert C. Labriola (Pittsburgh, 2002), 172–230.

3. William Riley Parker, *Milton: A Biography,* 2nd rev. ed., 2 vols., ed. Gordon Campbell (Oxford, 1996), 1:325, 621.

4. Stanley Fish, "Reasons That Imply Themselves: Imagery, Argument, and the Reader in Milton's *Reason of Church Government,*" in *Seventeenth-Century Imagery,* ed. Earl Miner (Berkeley and Los Angeles, 1971), 83.

5. All citations of the *Artis Logicae Plenior Institutio ad Petri Rami Methodum concinnata* are from the Columbia bilingual edition of the *Works of John Milton,* vol. 9, ed. and trans. Allan H. Gilbert (New York, 1935). Page references are hereafter cited parenthetically. The two books of the *Art of Logic* (inherited from the later Ramist division of dialectic) come with an "analytic praxis and a life of *Peter Ramus*" appended. The *"praxis analytica"* is culled from George Downham, *Commentarii in P. Rami . . .* (1601), and the *Life* is redacted from Freige, *Petri Rami vita* (1575). The inclusion of the truncated *Life* suggests that Milton was not entirely insensible to the implications of his predecessor's biography. At the end of a successful if stormy career at

the University of Paris, Ramus was defenestrated in the St. Bartholomew's Day massacre. He was adopted by many as a Protestant martyr. According to Barbara Lewalski, *The Life of John Milton: A Critical Biography* (Oxford, 2000), "the analogies in this story with Milton himself are left unstated, but the fit reader might recognize them" (498).

6. See P. Albert Duhamel, "Milton's Alleged Ramism," *PMLA* 67 (1952): 1035–53; but compare also Wilbur S. Howell, *Logic and Rhetoric in England, 1500–1700* (Princeton, 1956), 216.

7. According to Norman E. Nelson, "Peter Ramus and the Confusion of Logic, Rhetoric and Poetry," *University of Michigan Contributions in Modern Philology*, no. 2 (Ann Arbor, 1947), Ramus did not, in fact, write "a logic, that is, an *organon* or instrument of inquiry, but a rhetoric or method of ordering arguments persuasively. Thus logic and rhetoric, the connections and distinctions between which Aristotle had carefully set forth, were hopelessly confused" (4–5). Kees Meerhoff, " 'Beauty and the Beast': Nature Logic and Literature in Ramus," in *The Influence of Petrus Ramus: Studies in Sixteenth and Seventeenth Century Philosophy and Sciences,* edited by Mordechai Feingold, Joseph S. Freedman, and Wolfgang Rother, 200–215 (Basel, 2001), rejects this argument. For Meerhoff, given that Ramus "never ceased to proclaim the marriage of logic with literature," we are wrong to hold him up to "the sole spotlight of the evolution of logic" (under which success is defined as the excoriation of language from logic) without respecting his professed intention of uniting the two. It has further been suggested that Aristotle was confused as to the exact nature of the relationship between rhetoric and dialectic; see Lawrence D. Green, "Aristotelian Rhetoric, Dialectic and the Traditions of Antistrophos," *Rhetorica* 8 (1980): 26.

8. Milton explains his choice of the term thus: "I have thought it proper to use the word *logic* rather than, with Peter Ramus, *dialectic,* because by logic the whole art of reasoning is aptly signified; while dialectic, derived from the Greek διαλέγεσθαι, indicates rather the art of questioning and answering, that is debating" (19–21). Walter Ong acknowledges in the switch "a whole history here of the detachment of thought from discourse and of the individual from society: Earlier ages tended to associate thought with discourse, later ages to dissociate the two" (YP 8:218). Milton is not the first Englishman to advance this definition; Abraham Fraunce, *The Lawiers Logike* (1588), contends that "Logike is an art of reasoning" and further adds, much in line with Milton, that "the whole force and virtue of Logike consisteth in reasoning, not in talking: and because reasoning may be without talking, as in solitary meditations and deliberations with a mans selfe" (book 1, chap. 1, 2–4). Donald Clark, *John Milton at St. Paul's School* (New York, 1948), suspects in Milton's choice of term the formative influence of his schoolmaster at St. Paul's, Alexander Gil. While he was teaching Milton, Gil was apparently preparing an "Art of Logic" to complement his *Logonomia Anglica* (1621). Although the text is now lost, Clark "like[s] to think that it was because of what Gil taught him in school" (77) that Milton came to prefer logic to dialectic.

9. Compare Walter J. Ong, S.J., *Ramus, Method and the Decay of Dialogue,* (Cambridge, MA, 1958), 44. Milton shares Aristotle's desire to increase the remit of reason rather than Ramus's wish to restrict logic to dialectic. As Ong observes in a footnote to his edition of the tract, "Milton's preference for *logica* . . . follows the general drift in the sixteenth, seventeenth and eighteenth centuries away from a social treatment and toward a solipsistic treatment of thought" (YP 8:217).

10. Milton's aversion to logicians who "commonly confound physics, ethics and theology with logic" (3) stems from his understanding of logic as prescriptive of method rather than as descriptive of content. Milton defines logic by its end as *"the art of thinking well,"* whereas he defines "physics" by its object as *"the knowledge of natural things"* (269); as for those "theologians [who] fetch out as though from the heart of logic canons about God and about divine

hypostases and sacraments," Milton affirms that "nothing is more alien from logic or in fact from reason itself" (7).

11. Cited in Ong, *Ramus, Method and the Decay of Dialogue*, 60–61. Milton, of course, refers to *loci* but, following Ramus, he prefers to call his topics "arguments" and his treatment "summary" (23).

12. Rudolph Agricola, *De inventione dialectica libri tres* (Amsterdam, 1539), ed. Lothar Mundt (Tübingen, 1992), 210–12.

13. Ibid., 230. Compare Milton's treatment of question in logic (23–25). Although he grants the relevance of the question (arguments are "affected to that of which there is question"), Milton prefers to bypass query (sidestepping Aristotle, Boethius, and Agricola) to arrive at indubitable proof.

14. Absolute perfection is "knowledge" or "the completed circuit of erudition, quite perfect in itself, or philosophy" (9). Absolute perfection is God's alone; he is "the primal mover of every art" and "author of all wisdom" (11).

15. For Milton, the orthodox account of the Trinity fails to observe that unity of essence (one God) predicates unity of number (one person) and unity of causation (sole cause). If the Father and the Son differ in causation, they must differ also in number and essence. Equality can exist only between a plurality of essences, and if the orthodox account asserts the equality of Father and Son, both Father and Son must then be different essences. Running the heretical gauntlet, Milton's anti-Trinitarian theology of the Creation avoids Sabellianism by holding the Son and the Holy Spirit to be separate persons rather than modes or manifestations of the one God; it avoids Arianism by holding that God created the Son out of his own substance rather than out of nothing; and it avoids Socinianism by holding the Holy Spirit to be a person and not just a power of the Father.

16. That God created *ex nihilo* is, "as logicians say, arguing from an unproved premise" (YP 6:306).

17. Every cause sustains a providential or "final" purpose, for "the end is the cause for the sake of which a thing is . . . [and] is not other than some good" (63).

18. Compare "*as the special nature of things is, so will be the explanation if it can be found* . . . the cause which especially constitutes the essence, if it is noted, above all brings knowledge. But to know the internal form of anything, because it is usually very remote from the senses, is especially difficult" (61–63). "Internal form" or formal cause confers "essential distinction," for "form is the source of difference" (61) and "difference is the fruit of form" (265).

19. Stanley Fish, "The Temptation to Action in Milton's Poetry," *ELH* 48 (1981): 527–29.

20. If Milton here seems to equate "internal reason" with an interior "speech," it is not so much that he imagines a pure rhetoric, freed of the contingencies of *ad placitum* discourse, but that he recalls the medieval preoccupation with the question of propositional mental language. The key work was Gregory of Rimini's *Sentence Commentary*, which elaborated upon Boethius's readings of Aristotle's *De interpretatione*. Mental language is a form not of rhetoric but of preverbal logic; Milton, while he admits "the very necessity of speaking" (25), is consistent in privileging reason—not speech—with the task of "thinking well."

21. The *OED* glosses "to justify" in the context of Milton's professed intention as (6) seeking "to show or maintain the justice or reasonableness of (an action, claim, etc.); to adduce adequate grounds for; to defend as right or proper." When Milton asks "what cause . . . ?" (*PL* 1.28), it is not at all obvious that he can easily adduce "adequate grounds" for humanity's, and more subtly, for Satan's acts of rebellion, or for the providential purposes contained therein. The dictionary notes, however, that this definition (6) has come to color and obscure the one that precedes it (5), which allows that to justify is "to affirm or support" an argument "by attestation of evidence."

22. I disagree with Leon Howard, "The Invention of Milton's Great Argument: A Study of

the Logic of God's Ways to Men," *Huntington Library Quarterly* 9 (1945–1946): 152–53, that Milton's theodicy is intended as an artificial argument and suggest instead that *Paradise Lost* can be read as an act of *inartificial* logic, as testimony or as witness-statement to the self-evident truth it attests.

23. Andrew Marvell, *The Rehearsal Transpos'd* and *The Rehearsal Transpos'd—The Second Part*, ed. D. Smith (Oxford, 1971), 312.

24. Letter 41 to Peter Heimbach, 15 August 1666, in YP 8:2–4; Milton invokes *Tusculan Disputations* 5:108—"Itaque ad omnem rationem Teucri vox accomodari potest, 'Patria est, ubicumque est bene.'"

25. Milton's *Art of Logic* observes how, in special circumstances, "position may be a sort of passion of a thing located and thus pertain to the prior mode" (93); thus, place, a second order and extrinsic adjunct, may become, like virtue, a first order adjunct, passionate and inherent.